【英汉对照】

当代国际商务文化阅读丛书
Readings for Modern International Business Culture

多米诺骨牌效应
——『商务知识』篇

The Domino Effects
Business Knowledge

吴斐 编著

武汉大学出版社
WUHAN UNIVERSITY PRESS

图书在版编目(CIP)数据

多米诺骨牌效应:"商务知识"篇:英汉对照/吴斐编著.—武汉:武汉大学出版社,2016.5

当代国际商务文化阅读丛书

书名原文:The Domino Effects:Business Knowledge

ISBN 978-7-307-13994-7

Ⅰ.多⋯ Ⅱ.吴⋯ Ⅲ.商务—基本知识—英、汉 Ⅳ.F7

中国版本图书馆 CIP 数据核字(2014)第 181965 号

封面图片为上海富昱特授权使用(ⓒ IMAGEMORE Co. , Ltd.)

责任编辑:郭园园 金 军   责任校对:鄢春梅   版式设计:韩闻锦

出版发行:**武汉大学出版社** (430072 武昌 珞珈山)
        (电子邮件:cbs22@whu.edu.cn 网址:www.wdp.com.cn)

印刷:武汉中远印务有限公司

开本:880×1230 1/32 印张:10.625 字数:232 千字

版次:2016 年 5 月第 1 版   2016 年 5 月第 1 次印刷

ISBN 978-7-307-13994-7   定价:28.00 元

前　言

　　人类社会进入 21 世纪后，国家间的商务往来更加频繁，商务交际手段随着互联网的诞生和电子信息的进步日新月异，国际化企业的文化和理念千差万别，商务话题的表达和沟通能力无疑是人们所遇到的最大障碍。在我们熟知的生活英语、学术英语之外，商务英语不仅是我国目前从事或即将从事涉外商务人员英语实际应用能力不可多得的辅助工具，更是商务工作人员在这个国际化的高科技时代商务竞争能力、外贸业务素质和英语水平的重要体现。《当代国际商务文化阅读》（英汉对照）丛书以从事国际商务活动所必需的语言技能为经、以各种商务活动的具体情景作纬，将商务精神和商务元素巧妙融合，展示时尚而又经典的商务文化世界流行风，为广大读者提供一套语言规范、内容新颖、涉及面广、趣味性强、具有实用价值、富于时代精神的读物，既注意解决人们在国际商务环境中因遇到不熟悉的专业词汇而无法与外国合作者就工作问题交流沟通的难题，又着力解决人们学外语单纯地学语言而缺乏商务专业知识的弊端。

　　《当代国际商务文化阅读》（英汉对照）丛书由 10 个单行本组成：《拥抱新欢亚马逊（Embracing Amazon Service）—电子商务篇

（E-Commerce）》、《华尔街梦魇（Nightmare on Wall Street）—商界风云篇（The Business Circles）》、《路易斯·波森的朋克摇滚（The Punk Rock of Louis Posen）—商界精英篇（Business Elites）》、《希波克拉底誓言（Hippocratic Oath）—商务交际篇（Business Communication）》、《强烈的第一印象（A Powerful First Impression）—商务礼仪篇（Business Etiquette）》、《企业帝国继承权之争（Corporate Empires Grappling with Succession）—商务文化篇（Business Culture）》、《紫色血液（The Purple Blood）—商务心理篇（Business Psychology）》、《多米诺骨牌效应（The Domino Effects）—商务知识篇（Business Knowledge）》、《公开的赌注（Public Stakes）—商务演讲篇（Business Speeches）》、《伊斯特林悖论（The Easterlin Paradox）—感悟财富篇（Comprehension of Wealth）》。 这套丛书的编写旨在帮助读者在国际商务环境下，能够读懂英文的商务信息和商务新闻，并能对某一商务话题的知识有全面透彻的了解，领悟当代时尚商务文化成长的环境和思维方式，提高在全球化高科技时代的商务竞争能力、外贸业务素质和英语交际水平。 丛书中的阅读材料力求做到题材广泛，内容精辟，语言规范，遵循趣味性、知识性和时效性原则，培养读者在商务环境下的英语竞争能力和综合应用能力。 丛书融时代性与经典性为一体，内容经得起时间考验，文字经得起反复咀嚼，保证其可读性。 读者在阅读过程中接收大量的语言输入，为合理组织和娴熟运用英语语言表达自己的思想打下牢固的基础。 丛书的单行本包括以一个主题为中心的 30 篇文章，每篇文章包括题记、英语原文、汉语译文、生词脚注和知识链接。"题记"用丰富生动的语言点评文章的精髓，对文章的内容起

到提炼和画龙点睛的作用。"英语原文"主要摘自当代国际主流报纸杂志，具有语言规范、内容新颖、涉及面广、趣味性和时代感等特点。"汉语译文"力求准确流畅，既关注译文的文化语境及其内涵，也重视译文的外延和现当代标志性语言符号。"生词脚注"的难度把握在大学英语六级和研究生英语词汇程度，以帮助读者及时扫清阅读障碍。"知识链接"根据文章内容，或精解一个专业术语、或阐释一种新的商务理念、或介绍叱咤商界的企业或公司，以帮助读者培养游弋商海、运筹帷幄的能力，具备洞悉中西文化的国际视野。

《多米诺骨牌效应》（ The Domino Effects ）—商务知识篇（ Business Knowledge ）给读者展示了商务知识作为企业最重要的资源之一，在提高企业竞争力方面所起的关键作用。 金融危机知识对企业的影响犹如警世之钟。 在全球股市一个接一个地轰然倒塌之时，多米诺骨牌效应的魔咒搅得整个市场动荡不宁。 贝尔斯登危机令人唏嘘之处并不在于一家主要的投资银行被自己的客户和债权人抛弃，而是它在这场危机中没有抢先爆发。 不在沉默中爆发，就在沉默中灭亡。 商务经营战略与策略知识强调了人的重要性。 无论是投资组合的多元化，还是首席执行官的黄金销售原则；无论是低成本竞争战略，还是首次公开募股中的投资人，他们都会不择手段：当市场疯狂时，多数人都是舞会中的灰姑娘，明知在舞池中多待一会，现出原形的几率就越高，但多数人还是舍不得错过这场盛大舞会的高潮部分。 多元化经营知识使企业收获了巨大的机遇与发展。哈利·波特的旅行故事创造了一个多元化经营的财富童话：随着《哈利·波特》系列图书的问世，与之相关的电影、DVD、电视、游戏、服装、文具、主题公园、主题旅游已经渗透到现代人的生活之

中，形成了一个庞大的产业链，创造出上千亿的商业价值和文化价值。 新兴市场经济知识指明了实现经济社会全面协调可持续发展的路径。 金融危机让西方发达国家的经济陷入泥潭，而一度前途未卜的欧债危机又为世界经济的前路蒙上阴影，但作为新兴经济体的典型代表——俄罗斯、印度、巴西和中国却用经济增长的强劲表现推动着世界经济走出阴霾，他们在塑造责任感的同时，引导新兴市场经济从封闭市场转向开放市场，并给那些敢于增加投资组合风险的投资者提供了发展机会。 货币战争与欧债危机轮番上演，他们将爱琴海文明造就的西方近代的战略文化、以"生存竞争"、"弱肉强食"作为人之本性和认知世界的基本范式、以社会达尔文主义演绎的竞争和冲突作为生存的基本法则淋漓尽致地呈现给世界。 商务知识将企业经营的显性知识和人类储存的隐性知识推向了全球化的大舞台。

本书的主要阅读文章包括：金融危机对世界经济的影响，商务经营战略与策略，多元化经营的优势，新兴市场经济，货币金融战争，欧债危机，公司资源管理，国际贸易知识，精彩纷呈的商标设计，电子商务的技术路线图等商务知识。

最大限度地掌握和利用商务知识无疑可以提高企业的应变和创新能力，助经济的增长和腾飞一臂之力。 让我们跟随时代潮流，追赶知识经济发展的步伐，享受世界流行文化创造的快乐、荣誉、价值和成就感！

作 者

2016 年 1 月

目 录

目 录

目 录

题 记

　　公司救助计划在众议院未获通过之后，美国股市大幅下跌。尽管政府竭尽全力，企图通过一揽子交易政策力挽狂澜，拯救股票市场持续下跌的态势，但仍然力不从心，难以收拾残局。美联银行的股票价值一夜之间闪电下跌90%，摩根士丹利下跌11%，高盛下跌8%，伦敦和巴黎的股票下跌超过5%，法兰克福下跌约4%，香港基准指数一夜间骤然下跌4.3%；东京的日经225指数下跌1.2%，总部设在布鲁塞尔的德夏银行的股票下跌22.7%，标准普尔/澳洲证交所200指数周一轻微上升后收盘下跌2%，桑坦德银行的股票下跌2.8%，瑞银的股票下跌7.7%，中国台湾股市在台风蔷薇登陆台北的情况下被迫关闭，中国内地上海和深圳的股市因国庆节而停市。信任危机已经形成了多米诺骨牌效应，全球股市一个接一个地轰然倒塌。

The Domino Effect

U.S. stocks dropped dramatically Monday after the bailout plan being voted on by the House of Representatives failed to pass. The Dow Jones industrial average fell nearly 778 points, or 7 percent, while the Standard and Poor's 500-stock index lost 106. 59 points, or 8. 79 percent. Lawmakers scrambled①, but failed, to round up votes to pass the package on Monday, with the House defeating the bill by a vote of 228-205; a second attempt to pass the bill was planned.

The drop in stocks reinforced the fear coursing through Wall Street as investors wondered whether the bailout plan would eventually pass Congress. Before the vote, supporters of the bill said they thought the legislation would squeak② through with a slim majority. But as the initial period of voting ended, the bill appeared to be in danger of not passing the House. Shares had fallen earlier in the day despite what lawmakers had described as an agreement on the bailout plan. Citigroup also snatched up the core business of Wachovia, the ailing banking giant, which had been in danger of collapse. The Wachovia move, which was spearheaded by

---

① scramble ['skræmbl] *vi.*争取
② squeak [skwi:k] *vi.* 以尖厉的声音说话

多米诺骨牌效应

公司救助计划在众议院未获通过之后，美国股市在周一大幅下跌。 道琼斯工业平均指数下跌近 778 点，跌幅 7%，同时，标准普尔 500 股票指数下跌 106.59 点，跌幅 8.79 %。 尽管立法者竭尽全力，以期在周一通过一揽子交易政策，但仍然难以挽回残局。 众议院以 228 对 205 的票数否决了该法案。 国会议员们将计划再做一次尝试，推动该法案的通过。

股市下跌加剧了笼罩在华尔街的恐惧，投资者胆战心惊，想知道救助计划是否最终会得到国会通过。 表决前，法案的支持者说，他们认为这项法案将以微弱的优势勉强通过。 但是最初的投票结束后，该法案似乎出现了在众议院难以通过的危险迹象。 尽管议员们介绍了救助计划协议，但当天早些时候股价已经下跌。 花旗银行还突击并购了美联银行的核心业务，尽管这家境况不佳的银行业巨头已濒临亏损的崩溃边缘。 美联银行此举被视为联邦监管机构调整的第一步，可以看做是政府急于恢复金融体系稳定性的信号。 但是，美联银行是全美第四大银行，它的濒临崩溃可能会加剧投资者不安的感觉，即任何银行在目前都很容易陷入危机。 全球信贷市场也依

federal regulators, could have been taken as a sign that the government was eager to restore stability to the financial system. But the near-collapse of Wachovia, which was the nation's fourth-largest bank, may have underscored the troubling sense among investors that any bank is vulnerable in the current crisis. The world's credit markets also remained under pressure. Yields on Treasuries dropped and lending rates stayed high, signs that investors remained deeply ill at ease about the health of the financial system.

The past few months have seen one trust after another collapse in a domino effect. Responding to the strain, the Federal Reserve moved to vastly increase the amount of liquidity it makes available to major players in the world financial system. The Fed will triple the size of its regular auctions for banks and work with nine other central banks to increase the flow of credit.

The Fed is hoping to combat a hoarding mentality that has arisen among banks, whose reluctance to lend — even to healthy institutions — has jammed up critical financial arteries① that many small businesses depend on. On Monday, the cost of borrowing Euros for a three-month period rose to the highest price on record. Banks are charging enormous premiums for short-term financing. And money continued to flow into the safe space of Treasury bills and traditional hedges like gold, the price of which rose 2.2 percent. Shares of Wachovia lost 90 percent of their value in electronic overnight, but the stock never opened on Monday morning as officials halted trading before the opening bell. Citigroup shares fell,

---

① artery [ˈɑːtəri] *n.* 动脉

然受到压力。 国库券收益率下降，贷款利率持续居高不下，有迹象表明，投资者仍然对金融体系的健康状况焦虑不安。

在过去的几个月中，信任危机已经一个接一个地出现，形成了多米诺骨牌效应。 迫于压力，美联储开始大大增加资金的流动性，世界金融体系的主要参与者都可受益。 美联储将使其定期的银行拍卖规模扩大两倍，并与其他九个中央银行联手以增加贷款的流动性。

美联储希望打击银行之间出现的囤积心态，他们甚至不愿意贷款给运营健康的机构，因为这将堵塞许多小企业赖以生存的重要财政动脉。 周一，为期三个月的欧元借贷成本上升到历史最高价纪录。 银行趁机赚取巨大的短期融资费用。 资金继续流入国库券的安全空间和传统的对冲黄金，使其价格上涨 2.2% 。 美联银行的股票价值一夜之间闪电下跌 90% ，但官方在周一上午股票开盘前就停止了交易。 花旗集团的股价下跌，金融类股票交易下跌。 摩根士丹利下跌 11% ，高盛下跌 8% 。 纽约一开市，欧洲股市也开始大幅下跌，比华尔街的股票跌得更惨。 伦敦和巴黎的股票下跌超过 5% ，法兰克福下跌约 4% 。 在亚洲，香港基准指数一夜间骤然下跌 4.3% ；东京的日经 225 指数下跌 1.2% 。 布什总统周一上午 7:30 开市之前出现在白宫外，签署了最终于周末商定的救助法案。 总统发表了一份简短声明："投票支持该法案是保护你和你的国家免受经济损失。 随着时间的推移，信贷危机和房市的修正将继续影响我们的金融体系和我们经济的发展。 但我相信，从长远来看，美国将会克服这些挑战。"

and shares of financial stocks traded lower. Morgan Stanley fell 11 percent and Goldman Sachs was off 8 percent. European stocks, already sharply down at the New York open, fell further after the declines on Wall Street. Stocks in London and Paris were down more than 5 percent, and Frankfurt was down about 4 percent. In Asia, the benchmark Hong Kong index plummeted① 4. 3 percent overnight; Tokyo's Nikkei 225 lost 1. 2 percent. President Bush appeared outside the White House at 7:30 a.m. on Monday, before the markets opened, to endorse the bailout legislation that was agreed upon over the weekend. "A vote for this bill is a vote to prevent economic damage to you and your community, " the president said in a brief statement. "The impact of the credit crisis and housing correction will continue to affect our financial system and growth of our economy over time. But I am confident that in the long run, America will overcome these challenges."

The problems in Europe came after government bailouts of several banks, including the British lender Bradford & Bingley and the Belgian-Dutch financial group, Fortis. If anything, the moves created uncertainty about which institution would be next, said Jean Bruneau, a trader at Société Générale in Paris. Shares of the Brussels-based lender Dexia fell 22. 7 percent as investors worried that it might be the next bank to need government help. The company may soon announce a plan to raise capital, the French newspaper Le Figaro said, without citing a source. The agreement on Capitol Hill on the terms of the bailout package failed to lift the mood in Europe. "The U.S. bailout doesn't change some negative short-

---

① plummet ['plʌmit] *vi.* 骤然跌落

政府救助了包括英国的布拉德福德宾利银行和比利时-荷兰金融集团富通在内的几家银行之后，问题就在欧洲出现了。 法国巴黎兴业银行的一名商人简·布鲁诺认为，如果有什么区别的话，那就是此举让下一个被救助的对象变得不确定了。 总部设在布鲁塞尔的德夏银行的股票下跌22.7%，投资者担心，它可能成为下一个需要政府帮助的银行。 法国费加罗报指出，该公司可能很快就会宣布一项筹集资金的计划，但它没有任何引用的来源。 美国国会关于救助困难企业的一揽子交易条款并没有提高欧洲人的情绪。 慕尼黑信贷市场和投资银行战略家塔莫·格雷特菲德认为，"美国援助并不能改变一些负面的短期因素，包括经济前景疲软和盈利前景薄弱。 关键问题是援助计划能否调动投资者的乐观情绪，使他们关注中期改善，忽略短期弱点。 我们还没有看到好处，一切都还任重道远"。

美元兑欧元和英镑一路走高，兑日元则保持相对稳定。 亚洲股票市场担心全球信贷紧缩而再度下跌，国会在周末通过协议后，指数稍有回升。 标准普尔/澳洲证交所200指数周一轻微上升后收盘下跌2%。 在汉城，韩国股价综合指数激增1.2%后下跌1.3%。 英国布拉德福德宾利银行在信用危机关闭融资渠道和竞争对手拒绝购买客户难以偿还的按揭贷款后被政府接管。 财政部声称，西班牙桑坦德银行将支付11亿美元收购布拉德福德宾利银行的分支机构和存款。 桑坦德银行的股票下跌2.8%，至10.61欧元。 瑞银的股票下跌7.7%。 中国台湾股市在周一台风蔷薇登陆台北的情况下被迫关闭。 中国大陆上海和深圳的股市因国庆节而在这个星期停市。

term factors — that the economic outlook is weak and that the earnings outlook is weak," said Tammo Greetfeld, a strategist at UniCredit Markets & Investment Banking in Munich. "The key question is can the bailout create enough optimism among investors that they focus on the medium-term improvement and ignore short-term weakness. We're not there yet, the benefits look to be too far down the road."

The dollar gained against the euro and the pound, and was stable against the yen. Stock markets in Asia fell on renewed fears of a global credit crunch①, erasing earlier gains that came after the weekend agreement on Capitol Hill. The Standard and Poor's/Australian Stock Exchange 200 Index fell 2 percent after rising slightly on Monday morning. The Kospi Index was down 1. 3 percent after an early 1. 2 percent surge in Seoul. Bradford & Bingley, the British lender, was seized by the government after the credit crisis shut off financing and competitors refused to buy mortgage loans that customers were struggling to repay. Banco Santander, the Spanish lender, will pay $ 1. 1 billion to buy Bradford & Bingley branches and deposits, the Treasury said. Santander shares declined 2. 8 percent, to 10. 61 euros. Shares in UBS, the Swiss bank, fell 7. 7 percent. The stock market in Taiwan was closed on Monday as Typhoon Jangmi passed directly over Taipei. Mainland China's stock markets in Shanghai and Shenzhen are closed this week as part of a national holiday.

(963 words)

---

① crunch [krʌntʃ] *n.* 困难时刻

知识链接 🔍

Morgan Stanley 摩根士丹利。财经界俗称摩根士丹利为"大摩"，它是一家成立于美国纽约的国际金融服务公司，提供包括证券、资产管理、企业合并重组和信用卡在内的多种金融服务。摩根士丹利总公司下设 9 个部门，包括：股票研究部、投资银行部、私人财富管理部、外汇/债券部、商品交易部、固定收益研究部、投资管理部、直接投资部和机构股票部。涉足的金融领域包括股票、债券、外汇、基金、期货、投资银行、证券包销、企业金融咨询、机构性企业营销、房地产、私人财富管理、直接投资、机构投资管理等。摩根士丹利目前在全球 27 个国家的 600 多个城市设有代表处，雇员总数达 5 万多人。

题　记

　　避险型的机构投资者往往对进入高风险的金融市场踌躇不定，要么担心金融工具种类、特别是避险工具的种类相对缺失，要么害怕被严重套牢或损失惨重。投资组合作为保本基金的投资策略，既能锁定资产组合下跌的风险，又保有向上获利的机会。在严重衰退的金融市场，随着风险资产投资比例的不断下降，投资组合能够最终保持在最低价值的基础之上。为了保护客户的投资组合，基金管理者们大量使用复杂的对冲工具，为的是补偿核心股票持有带来的风险。指数的多元化和交易的便利性极大地方便了机构投资者根据策略变化灵活地配置各种风格特征的资产，风险最小化的唯一方法就是投资组合的极端多样化，增加更多的资产类别，彼此以不同的方式运转。正如俗话所说："不要把所有鸡蛋都放在一个篮子里。"

Once Burned, Twice Shy

Once burned, twice shy. Even though the major stock indexes are trading at record highs and concerns about a possible credit crunch-led recession have abated slightly, many of today's investors have vivid memories of the market meltdown of 20 years ago. No surprise, then, that one feature distinguishing the current stock market from the one that crashed previously, is evidence of more caution among investors. It wasn't that way back when Gordon Gekko of Wall Street was telling investors that "Greed is good." Twenty years ago, traders in thrall① to the possibilities of making money by exploiting the differentials between stock index futures and the underlying stock indexes were buying and selling without covering themselves with an opposing transaction, a strategy that would have afforded them some protection when their bets went sour. Today, they're much more likely to put safeguards in place to hedge against downside risks. Since then, the average daily trading volume of options has more than tripled, with index options in particular seeing growth in volume.

---

① thrall [θrɔːl] *n.* 束缚

一朝被蛇咬，十年怕井绳

一朝被蛇咬，十年怕井绳。 虽然主要股指创出了历史新高，合理的信贷紧缩导致的衰退焦虑略有减缓，但是，大部分投资者至今依然对 20 年前的股市崩溃记忆犹新。 那么，毫不奇怪，区分当前股市和以前股市崩盘的一个特征是投资者更为谨慎。 这并不意味着戈登·杰克在电影"华尔街"中告诉投资者"贪婪是好事"的年代又回来了。 20 年前，这些被绑架的交易者利用股指期货之间的利率差赚钱，底层股指买卖无法获得相反交易的覆盖，即赌博失败时可以提供一定保护的策略。 今天，他们更加趋向于对冲下行风险来提供防护措施。 自那时以来，平均每天的期权交易量增长了两倍多，特别是指数期权交易量获得了增长。

更多的交易人，更多的保护工具

专门从事指数期货交易的芝加哥商品交易所产品资本部门的常务董事斯科特·沃伦指出，今天的指数期货市场和 20 年前的股市之间最大的不同点在于，现在有更多的参与者，包括对冲基金，由此

More Players, More Protective Tools

The primary difference between today's index futures market and that of 20 years ago is that there's now a much larger pool of participants, including hedge funds, creating a more diverse and liquid market, says Scott Warren, managing director of equity products at the Chicago Mercantile Exchange, which specializes in index futures. Circuit breakers in the futures, cash, and options markets that temporarily halt trading after a drop of a certain percentage also limit the magnitude of bearish events, he says. "In addition to the market's much greater ability to absorb large buy and sell orders of stocks and options, there's also a much better understanding of the strengths and limitations of protection strategies." says Jim Bitman, senior instructor at the Chicago Board of Options Exchange's Options Institute. "People still remember 2001 and 2002 a little bit, so they're probably trying to take some protective measures, and leaving more money on the sidelines." says Jody Team, president of Team Financial Strategies in Lewisville, Tex. To protect clients' portfolios, money managers are using a host of sophisticated hedging tools intended to offset① risk to their core stock holdings. One such tool: inverse index funds. These so-called bear funds② are designed to move in the opposite direction of the index to which they are benchmarked, such as the Standard & Poor's 500-stock index.

---

① offset ['ɔfset] *vt.* 抵消
② bear funds 熊市基金

创造了更加多元化和更具流动性的市场。 他认为，期货市场、现金市场和期权市场在一定百分比的跌幅之后暂停交易的跌停板制度同时限制了利空事件的幅度。 芝加哥期权交易所董事会下属期权研究所的高级指导师吉姆·彼特曼认为，"市场除了具备更强大的消化能力、可以大量购买和出售股票和期权订单之外，还必须更好地理解保护策略的能量和限度。" 德州路易斯维尔财政策略小组主席乔迪·提姆也谈道："股民们仍然依稀记得 2001 年和 2002 年的股市，所以他们会试图采取一些保护措施，将更多的钱留在股市之外。" 为了保护客户的投资组合，基金管理者们大量使用复杂的对冲工具，为的是补偿核心股票持有带来的风险。 其中一种工具是逆指数基金。这些所谓的熊市市场基金旨在与基准指数（如标准普尔 500 指数）逆向变动。

逆向投资指数基金

瑞德克斯基金的逆指数共同基金没有做空自己的指数。 瑞德克斯基金投资组合管理委员会的董事吉姆·金指出，他们利用指数期货类的衍生工具，相比做空自己的股票，这些衍生工具可以以更低廉的价格被交易和转存，从而进入后期市场。 他们依然存在贬值的风险，但损失不会超过投资基金的数额。 投资者做的是长期基金，而基金做的是空头头寸，但是两者的回报相同，好似客户做空指数一样。 他说："我们的责任是保护现有基金，以免损失

15

Inverse Index Investing

The inverse index mutual funds at Rydex Investments don't short the indexes themselves. Instead, they use derivatives① such as index futures, which can be traded and rolled over into later periods more cheaply than shorting the stocks themselves, says Jim King, director of portfolio management at Rydex. They're still at risk of losing money, but they can't lose any more than they put into the fund. Investors are "long" the fund, while the fund takes the short positions, but the returns are the same as if clients were actually short the index. "It's up to us to keep the fund from losing more money than it has, " he says. Inverse funds can be especially useful in retirement accounts, where investors don't otherwise have options to short the market. Among the 11 inverse funds that Rydex manages are a few that give shareholders twice the leverage to the underlying index. The Inverse S&P 500 2x Strategy, for instance, gives investors twice as much return for each percentage move down in the S&P 500, but it also generates double the loss for any uptick in the index.

A Little Leverage Goes a Long Way

One reason for the popularity of these extra-leveraged bets, also known as ultra funds, is that they give investors the same amount of exposure as the regular fund, with a commitment of only half the money. But because they're twice as risky, Rydex tries to make sure customers understand the implications and prefers they work with financial advisers instead of buying directly from Rydex. Of course, leverage has to be used

---

① derivative [di'rivətiv] *adj.* 衍生的

更多的钱。"逆向基金对退休账户特别有用，因为这些投资者没有别的期权做空市场。瑞德克斯基金管理的 11 种逆指数基金中，很少返回给投资者两倍于基本指数变动的收益。相反，标准普尔 500 的逆指数基金在基金指数下降每一百分点时，大多能给出两倍的回报，但指数上升时它亦带来双倍的损失。

小杠杆，大跨步

额外杠杆押注也被称为超基金，他们流行的一个原因就是给予投资者同等数量的定期基金，并承诺只需要支付一半的资金。但由于它存在双倍的风险，瑞德克斯基金正在设法让客户了解这种投资的含义，并希望他们与财政顾问合作，而不是直接在瑞德克斯购买。当然，这种杠杆基金必须合理使用。当金融崩盘时，使用股票指数期货就会加速抛售压力，但这主要是使用这种方式的结果，与这种工具本身的根本性缺陷截然相反。金认为，"所有这一切都归结到杠杆的程度。我们的基金杠杆率最多可达 2 比 1，使用指数期货的人只要愿意便可以达到接近 10 比 1 的杠杆效率。这又使人们陷入困境。他们使用了许许多多的杠杆手段，即使是市场上的微小变动也可能彻底摧毁他们的地位。"这种投资赚钱的诀窍就在于利用股票价格下跌时买进。

健康的利润率

约瑟夫·比尔多曾坚信保护投资组合是件轻而易举的事，结果

17

wisely. The use of stock index futures accelerated selling pressure in the crash, but that was primarily a result of the way they were used, as opposed to a fundamental flaw in the instruments themselves. "It all comes down to the degree of leverage," King says. "Our funds are leveraged at most 2 to 1. A person using index futures could get leverage approaching 10 to 1 if he wanted to. That's where folks get into trouble. They take on a lot of leverage, where even a small move in the market can wipe out their position." The trick to making money from inverse funds is to invest in them before stock prices start to fall.

A Healthy Margin

Having been caught in the downdraft, losing a lot of his clients' money, Joseph Biondo Sr. believes in keeping portfolio protection simple. Since the large amount of money borrowed on margin to boost positions was a key contributor to both the 1929 and 1987 crashes, "we limit the amount of margin we'll have a client use to 20% instead of the 50% cap that regulations allow," says Biondo, the founder and senior portfolio manager of Biondo Investment Advisors in Milford, Pa. For a client who has put up $ 100,000 to buy $ 200,000 in stock, it takes just a 50% drop in the market to wipe out the initial investment and force the investor to use the remaining $ 100,000 to pay back the loan. "We'll only borrow 20% to buy stock, so essentially stocks have to go down 80% for a client to be bankrupt instead of 50%, and that's never happened," he says.

Hedging with Exposure to All Asset Classes

There seems to be an unspoken belief in the financial industry that history repeats itself, but Bill Neubauer, an independent financial

在股市崩盘时被套，导致客户的大部分资金付之一炬。 宾夕法尼亚州米尔福德的比尔多投资顾问公司的创立者兼高级投资顾问比尔多认为，由于大量的资金是以保证金的形式借来的，因而抬高了价位，这就是 1929 年和 1987 年金融危机的主要因素。"我们限制了保证金的数量，允许客户使用 20% 的保证金，而不是常规认可的 50% 上限。"任何一位投资 10 万美元、购买 20 万美元股票的客户，只需要将 50% 的资金投入市场，即可抵消原始投资，并迫使投资者使用剩下的 10 万美元偿还贷款。 他说："我们只借其中的 20% 来购买股票，所以实质上，股价下跌 80% 、而不是 50% 时，客户才濒临破产的边缘，但这种事从来就没有发生过。"

将所有资产类别纳入对冲风险敞口

金融界似乎有一个心照不宣的信念，那就是历史将会反复重演，但是迈阿密的私人财务规划师比尔·纽鲍尔说，他试图在危机尚未出现前给客户定位。 对纽鲍尔来说，风险最小化的唯一方法就是投资组合的极端多样化，增加更多的资产类别，彼此以不同的方式运转。 四年前，他开始将房地产投资加入到客户的投资组合之中。 然后，他开始转而更大量地投资国际性的所有资产类别，从股票扩展到包括证券、货币和房地产在内的资产。 国际资产目前占客户投资组合的 70% ，总数约达3 000万美元。 他表示，"为了使它们具有对冲功能，它们必须具备相当意义的数量"，至少是总投资组合

planner in Miami, says he tries to position his clients for crises that haven't been seen before. For Neubauer, the only way to really minimize risk is through extreme diversification, by adding more asset classes that behave differently from one another. Four years ago, he began adding real estate to clients' portfolios. Then he began to shift toward greater international exposure in all asset classes, expanding from stocks to include bonds, currencies, and real estate. International assets now account for 70% of his clients' portfolios, which total roughly $ 30 million. "For them to have a hedging function, they have to be in fairly meaningful quantities," at least 5% of the total portfolio, he says. "The thing people really worry about is correlations and negative correlations being tossed out the window when everything goes down at once." Dispersing his clients' portfolios among five or six major asset classes and 18 subclasses has produced a much smoother ride, he says.

(1,120 words)

的 5% 。"人们真正关心的是，当所有股票一次性下跌时，这些投资组合的相关性和负相关性。"他认为，将客户的投资组合分散到 5 至 6 个主要的资产类别、甚至 18 个子类别会有更加平稳的收益。

知识链接 🔍

Gordon Gekko　戈登·杰克是 1987 年著名的电影《华尔街》里的男主角，他曾做过"贪婪是好事"的演讲。

题　记

　　贝尔斯登公司曾是美国华尔街第五大投资银行，2008年美国出现次贷危机之时被竞争对手美国摩根大通公司收购，成为第一家葬送于次贷市场的著名投行。为了协助摩根大通收购贝尔斯登，美联储给摩根大通提供了300亿美元的财政支持，以抵减贝尔斯登风险投资组合的漏洞。这次收购再次验证了金融界广为接受的不成文规则，即"大到不能倒"定律。贝尔斯登虽不是华尔街上最大的银行巨头，但它却是主要的股票交易清算中心，掌控着几千亿美元的借贷交易，贝尔斯登的崩溃会轻而易举地搅得整个市场动荡不安。当处于次级市场崩溃风暴中心的银行也同样处在衍生品泡沫危机的中心时，贝尔斯登危机令人唏嘘之处并不在于一家主要的投资银行被自己的客户和债权人抛弃，而是它在这场危机中没有抢先爆发。不在沉默中爆发，就在沉默中灭亡。

The Bear Stearns Crisis:
Too Dumb To Fail

In 1984, Continental Illinois, then one of the country's largest banks, found itself on the verge of collapse, after billions of dollars' worth of its loans went bad. To avert① a crisis, the government stepped in, purchasing $3.5 billion of the soured loans and effectively taking over the bank. Later that year, at a congressional subcommittee hearing, Representative Stewart McKinney summed up the lesson of the rescue effort: "Let us not bandy words. We have a new kind of bank. It is called too big to fail. T.B.T.F., and it is a wonderful bank."

Since then, T.B.T.F. has become a generally accepted, if unwritten, rule in the financial world. Two weeks ago, though, it was given a new twist when the Federal Reserve acted to save the investment bank Bear Stearns, orchestrating② the company's sale to J. P. Morgan Chase by providing Morgan with up to thirty billion dollars in financing to cover Bear Stearns's portfolio of risky assets. Previously, the government had intervened to protect only commercial banks — which take deposits and

---

① avert [ə'vəːt] vt. 避免
② orchestrate ['ɔːkistreit] vt. 配合

贝尔斯登危机:不在沉默中爆发，就在沉默中灭亡

1984 年，作为当时最大银行之一的伊利诺伊斯州大陆国民银行，由于几十亿贷款坏账的出现，发现自己突然濒临破产的边缘。为避免危机的发生，政府决定介入，买入该银行 35 亿美元的坏账，有效掌管了银行的运作。 当年的晚些时候，在一次国会附属委员会的听证会上，众议员司徒亚特·麦金莱总结了此次救助行动带来的启示："我们不必浪费口舌。 我们国家将出现一种新型银行。 它将被称之为'大到不能倒'的银行，简称 T.B.T.F.。 这是一种极好的银行模式。"

从那以后，"大到不能倒"定律成为金融界广为接受的不成文规则。 然而，当美联储两周前对投资银行贝尔斯登启动救援措施之时，又出现了意想不到的新进展。 美联储给摩根大通提供了 300 亿美元的财政支持，以抵减贝尔斯登风险投资组合的漏洞，协助摩根大通收购贝尔斯登。 此前，政府插手保护的救援对象仅限于商业银行，因为商业银行吸收存款和发放传统型贷款，并受到严格的监管。 而美联储此次又开创了先河：允许投资银行向其贷款。 但贝尔斯登交易表明，"大到不能倒"定律如今也适用于投资银行。 与

issue traditional loans, and which are heavily regulated. Another first: the Fed is now allowing investment banks to borrow from it directly. The Bear Stearns deal means that the T.B.T.F. rule now applies to investment banks as well. Suddenly, the federal government is committed to saving a whole lot more companies than it was a couple of weeks ago.

Rescuing failing companies obviously runs the risk of creating moral hazard — if we insulate people from the consequences of their irresponsibility, they're more likely to be irresponsible in the future. But the Fed did a good job of lessening that risk, making sure that Bear suffered a heavy toll. The sale punished Bear shareholders severely, valuing Bear at just two dollars a share, down from sixty dollars a few days before, while thousands of Bear employees are likely to lose their jobs. That's about as harsh as a bailout gets. More to the point, the threat of moral hazard in this case was simply less dire① than the threat of financial contagion. The Fed could have done what it did in February, 1933, when it stood quietly by while Detroit Bankers Corp. and the Guardian Detroit Union Group, Detroit's two largest banks, foundered after a series of bad loans. But the failure of those two banks quickly led to bank runs in neighboring states — Cleveland's two biggest banks failed soon after — and eventually to a national banking panic. Bear Stearns's collapse, similarly, could easily have provoked market chaos. Bear wasn't among the largest Wall Street banks, but it was a major clearinghouse for stock trades and played a central role in hundreds of billions of dollars of credit deals. If not too big, it was too important to fail.

The Bear deal does mark a major policy shift, since the Fed has now

---

① dire [ˈdaiə] *adj.* 可怕的

几周前相比,联邦政府忽然之间将致力于拯救一大堆更多的公司。

　　拯救濒临倒闭的公司显然有可能引发道德风险。 如果我们一再为企业不负责的行为买单,那么它们在将来的日子里就更有可能玩忽职守。 但是美联储却很好地降低了道德风险,确实让贝尔斯登付出了沉重的代价。 收购严重地打击了贝尔斯登的持股人,将贝尔斯登股票的账面价格由几天前的 60 美元/股压缩到仅 2 美元/股。 收购还将导致贝尔斯登的大量员工下岗。 这是极尽苛刻的救助条件。更应该指出的是,在此个案中比道德风险更加可怕的是金融危机的蔓延。 在 1933 年 2 月的经济大萧条时期,底特律两家最大的银行——底特律银行家公司和卫报底特律联盟组织——在一系列坏账的困扰折磨中痛苦地倒闭,美联储原本可以实施经济救援,但它却袖手旁观,无动于衷。 正是这两家银行的倒闭,迅速引起了邻州的银行挤兑,克利夫兰市两家最大的银行破产,最终导致全美银行业的恐慌。 与此类似,贝尔斯登的崩溃会轻而易举地搅得整个市场动荡不安。 贝尔斯登虽不是华尔街上最大的银行巨头,但它却是主要的股票交易清算中心,掌控着几千亿美元的借贷交易。 即使不是太大的银行,却也是因为太重要了而不能倒闭。

　　贝尔斯登交易的确标志着主要政策的转变,因为美联储目前已经默认,投资银行倒闭之时它们将施加援助。 但是,这种转变实际上只不过承认了某种必然性,设定了当今世界借贷的本质。 目前,大部分借来的钱不再出自商业银行,商业银行提供的贷款仅占不到总借贷资产的30%。 取而代之的是各种各样的形式,贷款被打包,并作为抵押品出售。 自投资银行大量买卖这些有价证券以来,他们在金融市场发挥的作用比以往任何时候都要大。 20 年前,美联储可

27

implicitly admitted that it will catch investment banks when they fall. But that shift really just ratifies① the inevitable, given the nature of credit in today's world. Most money that's borrowed these days no longer comes from commercial banks, which are responsible for less than thirty per cent of all lending. Instead, in one form or another, the loans are packaged and sold as securities. And since investment banks do much of the selling and buying of those securities, they play an ever bigger role in financial markets. Two decades ago, the Fed could afford to let a firm like Drexel Burnham Lambert, which, admittedly, was dealing with criminal charges in addition to its economic woes, go under without worrying too much about the ripple effects. It would demand very steady nerves to do the same thing today.

You might, then, see the Fed's willingness to help investment banks as evidence of their indispensability. But what it really underscores is how badly Wall Street has managed its business in recent years. Because investment banks' trades and investments are typically very highly leveraged — Bear Stearns, for instance, had borrowed thirty dollars for every dollar of its own — the banks need to be exceptionally good at managing risk, and they need to insure that people trust them enough to lend them huge sums of money against very little collateral②. You'd expect, then, that Wall Street firms would be especially rigorous about balancing risk against reward, and about earning and keeping the trust of customers, clients, and lenders. Instead, most of these firms have taken on spectacular amounts of risk without acknowledging the scale of their

---

① ratify [ˈrætifai] vt. 认可
② collateral [kɔˈlætərəl] n. 担保品

以放心大胆地对德崇证券之类的公司听之任之,不必太过担心连锁效应。无可否认,德崇证券当时除了深陷经济困境之外,还面临着刑事指控。然而,如今对于同样的状况,我们却得万分谨慎小心。

此外,你或许会认为,美联储此番心甘情愿地帮助投资银行的行为是为了证明其不可或缺的地位。但实际上,我们更应该关注华尔街近年来业务上的失利。因为投资银行的交易和投资具有典型的强势杠杆效应,举例来说,贝尔斯登以自有的每一份资产借入了高于其 30 倍的资产,所以银行需要格外精明地管理风险,它们需要确保人们对它们足以信任,将巨额资金借给它们,而不是极少量的抵押品。那么,你也许会认为,华尔街的公司对平衡风险和收益的管理特别严谨,且既会赚钱,又能始终保持消费者、客户和债权人的信任。然而,相反的是,这些公司中的大多数已经呈现出惊人的大量风险,根本就没有让外界了解他们赌注的规模,现在看来,甚至它们自己也被蒙在鼓里。这就是为什么自房产泡沫破裂以来,我们已经惊恐地目睹借贷市场上几百亿美元的资产贬值,甚至完全坏死。当你认为处于次级市场崩溃风暴中心的银行也同样处在衍生品泡沫危机的中心时,贝尔斯登危机令人唏嘘之处并不在于一家主要的投资银行被自己的客户和债权人抛弃,而是它在这场危机中没有抢先爆发。

既然美联储已经插手此事,相信一切都会慢慢步入正轨。但也希望千万别矫枉过正:在过去的十年里,金融市场存在的最大问题之一就是,债权人、客户、甚至是普通的小型投资者对华尔街上的公司具有的神奇魔力都迷信不已,从未合理地审视他们的承诺和表现。市场以信任为基点顺利运行,当信任缺失时,人们无异于在钢

bets to the outside world, or even, it now seems, to themselves. That's why, since the bursting of the housing bubble, we have seen tens of billions of dollars in surprise write-downs and complete paralysis in the credit markets. When you consider that the banks at the center of the subprime debacle① were also at the center of the tech-stock bubble, the surprising thing about the Bear Stearns crisis isn't that a major investment bank was abandoned by its customers and lenders but, rather, that it didn't happen sooner.

Now that the Fed has stepped in, it's possible that things will go back to normal. But let's hope they don't get too normal: one of the biggest problems in the market in the past decade has been that lenders, clients, and even ordinary small investors have put far too much faith in the magical abilities of Wall Street firms, and have failed to give their promises and performance proper scrutiny. Markets require trust to work well, but when trust is blind they are almost guaranteed to go haywire②. We don't want the paralytic level of skepticism that has reigned in the marketplace in recent months to continue, but we don't want a return to the way things were, either. It's a good thing that Bear Stearns was saved. But it's also a good thing that it nearly died.

(976 words)

---

① debacle [dei'bɑ:kl] *n.* 崩溃
② haywire ['heiwaiə] *adj.* 混乱的

丝上行走。 我们不希望看到近几个月来持续支配市场的怀疑论处于瘫痪的程度,也不想再重蹈覆辙。 救助贝尔斯登是一件好事。 但它的行将灭亡同样也会警醒世人。

知识链接 🔍

Bear Stearns Cos. 贝尔斯登公司。贝尔斯登成立于 1923 年,总部位于纽约,是美国华尔街第五大投资银行。公司主要业务涵盖机构股票和债券、固定收益、投资银行业务、全球清算服务、资产管理以及个人银行服务。2008年美国出现次贷危机,房地产泡沫破裂,美国摩根大通公司收购了对手贝尔斯登公司,使其成为第一家葬送于次贷市场的著名投行。

题 记

　　无管制的金融市场产生的资产泡沫就像墨西哥湾的飓风，在宽松的信贷条件下造成"看不见的手"在多个经济领域无法发挥作用，然后竭尽全力搅动起强劲旋转的投资气流，从金融中心向市场周围翻腾和辐射。深深植入全球化经济链条每一个经济体中的恐慌，在危机爆发的那一刻迅速蔓延。如同竞技体育运动一样，短跑运动员获得的奖励并非取决于他在绝对条件下跑得有多快，而是与其他人相比他用时有多少。投资基金的成功与否不一定取决于其绝对的回报率，而是取决于与那些竞争对手相比较的利率。如果短跑选手服用合成代谢类固醇可以获胜，哪怕是为健康问题承担少许风险，权衡得失的结果也会使许多竞争者铤而走险；如果一种基金拥有比其他基金更高的收入，资金会立即流入这种基金。证券对投资者的诱惑是永远的边缘追求。

Pursuit of an Edge,
in Steroids① or Stocks

Asset bubbles like the one that caused the current economic crisis have long plagued financial markets. But like hurricanes in the Gulf of Mexico, these disasters have been occurring with increasing frequency. If we want to prevent them, we must first understand their cause.

It isn't simply "Wall Street greed," which Senator John McCain has blamed for the crisis. Coming from Mr. McCain, a longtime champion of financial industry deregulation, it was a puzzling attribution, squarely② at odds with the cherished belief of free-market enthusiasts everywhere that unbridled③ pursuit of self-interest promotes the common good. As Adam Smith wrote in "The Wealth of Nations," "It is not from the benevolence of the butcher, the brewer, or the baker that we expect our dinner, but from their regard to their own interest." Greed underlies every market outcome, good or bad. When important conditions are met, greed not only poses no threat to Smith's "invisible hand" of

---

① steroid ['stiərɔid] *n.* 类固醇
② squarely ['skwɛəli] *adv.* 完全地
③ unbridle ['ʌn'bridl] *vt.* 对……不加约束

边缘追求——类固醇还是股票

貌似造成目前经济危机的资产泡沫已经长期地困扰着金融市场。 但是，就像墨西哥湾的飓风，这些灾害的发生越来越频繁。如果我们想阻止它们，就必须先了解引发危机的原因。

参议员约翰·麦凯恩指责此次金融危机时声称，造成危机的原因并不仅仅是"华尔街的贪婪"。 这种观点来自金融业放松管制的长期倡导者麦凯恩先生，这真是一个令人费解的现象，它完全不符合热衷自由市场的人所珍视的信仰，即为了促进共同利益而不加约束地追逐自身的利益。 亚当·斯密在《国富论》中这样写道："贪婪不是来自屠夫、酿酒商或面包师对我们期盼晚餐而表露的慈善，而是来自他们对自身利益的追求。"不管是好还是坏，贪婪是形成每一个市场结果的潜在原因。 当重要的条件得到满足时，贪婪不仅对史密斯"看不见的手"的竞争不构成威胁，反而是它的一个重要组成部分。

造成目前危机的力量实际上反映了一种强大的动力，这种动力影响着各种竞争性的努力。 在体育界也许可以清楚地观察这种竞争。 考虑一下短跑选手是否服用合成代谢类固醇的决定。 短跑运动员获得的奖励并非取决于他在绝对条件下跑得有多快，而是与其

competition, but is an essential part of it.

The forces that produced the current crisis actually reflect a powerful dynamic that afflicts all kinds of competitive endeavors. This may be seen clearly in the world of sports. Consider a sprinter's① decision about whether to take anabolic steroids. The sprinter's reward depends not on how fast he runs in absolute terms, but on how his times compare with those of others. Imagine a new drug that enhances performance by three-tenths of a second in the 100-meter dash. Almost impossible to detect, it also entails a small risk of serious health problems. The sums at stake ensure that many competitors will take the drug, making it all but impossible for a drug-free competitor to win. The net effect has increased health risks for all athletes, with no real gain for society.

This particular type of market failure occurs when two conditions are met. First, people confront a gamble that offers a highly probable small gain with only a very small chance of a significant loss. Second, the rewards received by market participants depend strongly on relative performance. These conditions have caused the invisible hand to break down in multiple domains. In unregulated housing markets, for example, there are invariably too many dwellings built on flood plains and in earthquake zones. Similarly, in unregulated labor markets, workers typically face greater health and safety risks.

It is no different in unregulated financial markets, where easy credit terms almost always produce an asset bubble. The problem occurs because, just as in sports, an investment fund's success depends less on

① sprinter ['sprintə] n. 赛跑选手

他人相比他用时有多少。 试想有一种新药物，它能使运动员在 100
米短跑中加快 0.3 秒。 即使它几乎是不可能被察觉到的，但它也要
为造成严重影响健康的问题承担少许风险。 权衡得失的结果使许多
竞争者服用药物，而没有服用药物的选手根本无法获胜。 这种有效
效应增加了所有运动员的健康风险，而社会却没有真正获益。

当两个条件都得到满足时，这种特殊类型的市场就会失灵。 首
先，人们面对这样一场赌博：极有可能获利甚微，但出现重大亏损
的几率也可忽略不计。 其次，市场参与者所获得的奖励主要取决于
相对表现。 这些情况已经造成"看不见的手"在多个领域无法发挥
作用。 例如，在无管制的住房市场，总是会有太多的住房建立在洪
泛区和地震带。 同样，在无管制的劳动力市场，工人通常会面临更
大的健康和安全风险。

无管制的金融市场也同样如此，在宽松的信贷条件下，几乎总
是产生资产泡沫。 之所以出现此类问题，是因为就像在体育运动中
一样，投资基金的成功与否不一定取决于其绝对的回报率，而是取
决于与那些竞争对手相比较的利率。 如果一种基金拥有比其他基金
更高的收入，资金立即流入这种基金。 而且由于管理人员的薪酬主
要取决于基金监管的资金数额，所以管理人员希望迅速得到相对较
高的回报。 增强基金回报的一种途径是投资略有风险的资产。 这
种投资通常会有更高的回报，因为规避风险的投资者不再愿意持有
这些资产。 在当前的危机之前，一旦有些基金经理开始提供收入更
高的抵押贷款支持证券，其他基金经理就会在持续增长的压力下跟
进，以免客户抛弃他们。

沃伦·巴菲特警告说，高科技泡沫中已经产生了类似的现象。

its absolute rate of return than on how that rate compares with those of rivals. If one fund posts higher earnings than others, money immediately flows into it. And because managers' pay depends primarily on how much money a fund oversees, managers want to post relatively high returns at every moment. One way to bolster① a fund's return is to invest in slightly riskier assets. Such investments generally pay higher returns because risk-averse investors would otherwise be unwilling to hold them. Before the current crisis, once some fund managers started offering higher-paying mortgage-backed securities, others felt growing pressure to follow suit, lest their customers desert them.

Warren E. Buffett warned about a similar phenomenon during the tech bubble. Mr. Buffett said he wouldn't invest in tech stocks because he didn't understand the business model. Investors knew him to be savvy, but the relatively poor performance of his Berkshire Hathaway fund during the tech stock run-up persuaded many to move their money elsewhere. Mr. Buffett had the personal and financial resources to weather that storm. But most money managers did not, and the tech bubble kept growing. A similar dynamic precipitated② the current problems. The new mortgage-backed securities were catnip for investors, much as steroids are for athletes. Many money managers knew that these securities were risky. As long as housing prices kept rising, however, they also knew that portfolios with high concentrations of the riskier assets would post higher returns, enabling them to attract additional investors. More important,

---

① bolster [ˈbəulstə] vt. 鼓励
② precipitate [priˈsipiteit] vt. 促使

巴菲特表示，他不会投资高科技股，因为他不理解这种商业模式。投资者虽然知道他精明过人，但是在科技股节节攀高的阶段，他的伯克希尔-哈撒韦基金差强人意的表现足以使很多人把资金挪到其他地方。巴菲特先生靠个人和金融资产渡过了这场风暴。但是，大多数基金经理却无处逃生，而且高科技泡沫还在不断增长。一个类似的动态快速引发了当前的问题。新的抵押贷款支持证券是引诱投资者的猫薄荷，就像类固醇对运动员的诱惑一样。许多基金经理人知道，这些证券是有风险的。然而，他们也清楚，只要房屋价格不断上升，高度集中且风险较高的资产投资组合将会拥有更高的回报，从而使这些证券进一步吸引投资者。更重要的是，他们假设，如果事情出错，数量上仍然具有安全性。

前得克萨斯州参议员菲尔·格兰姆和其他金融业放松管制的支持者坚持认为，市场力量会提供充分的保护，以防止过度的风险。放债人显然不想做没有回报的贷款，借款人有明确的动力为这些优惠条件买单。因为所有人都赞同这种观点，即金融市场的竞争相当激烈，格兰姆先生援引熟悉的"看不见的手"这一理论，说服了许多其他的立法者。但是，当报酬在很大程度上取决于相对表现时，"看不见的手"就会失效。当其他才能似乎并不强于他们的人赚取明显高得多的回报时，有很大比例的投资者根本无法袖手旁观。人性的这一事实使"看不见的手"这个抵挡过度金融风险的庇护所摇摇欲坠。

我们究竟该何去何从呢？许多人主张对市场上了解甚少的衍生证券增加更大的透明度。更严格的信息披露规则会是一件好事，但他们不可能阻止未来的危机，不像对相关健康风险的行为进行披露

they assumed that if things went wrong, there would be safety in numbers.

PHIL GRAMM, the former senator from Texas, and other proponents of financial industry deregulation insisted that market forces would provide ample protection against excessive risk. Lenders obviously don't want to make loans that won't be repaid, and borrowers have clear incentives to shop for favorable terms. And because everyone agrees that financial markets are highly competitive, Mr. Gramm's invocation of the familiar invisible-hand theory persuaded many other lawmakers. The invisible hand breaks down, however, when rewards depend heavily on relative performance. A high proportion of investors are simply unable to stand idly by while others who appear no more talented than them earn conspicuously higher returns. This fact of human nature makes the invisible hand an unreliable shield against excessive financial risk.

Where do we go from here? Many people advocate greater transparency in the market for poorly understood derivative securities. More stringent disclosure rules would be good but would not prevent future crises, any more than disclosing the relevant health risks would prevent athletes from taking steroids. The only effective remedy is to change people's incentives. In sports, that means drug rules backed by strict enforcement. In financial markets, asset bubbles cause real trouble when investors can borrow freely to expand their holdings. To prevent such bubbles, we must limit the amounts that people can invest with borrowed money.

(904 words)

会防止运动员服用类固醇，唯一有效的补救措施是改变人们的激励机制。在体育运动中，这意味着严格执法，支持药物服用规则。在金融市场，当投资者可以自由借款、以扩大其持股能力时，资产泡沫就会造成真正的麻烦。为了防止这种泡沫，我们必须限制人们用借贷的方式进行投资的数额。

知识链接

The Wealth of Nations 《国富论》。1776年3月，英国经济学家亚当·斯密发表了《国民财富的性质和原因的研究》，简称《国富论》。《国富论》共分五卷，论述了国富的源泉——劳动，增进劳动生产力的手段——分工，因分工而起的交换和作为交换媒介的货币，商品的价格，以及价格构成的成分——工资、地租和利润。

The invisible hand 在《国富论》中，亚当·斯密在说明为什么对进口或对使用自己的资本进行限制为不必要时，使用了"看不见的手"一词："因此，当每一个人企图尽可能地使用他的资本去支持本国工业，从而引导那种工业使它的产品可能有最大的价值时，每一个人必然要为使社会的每年收入尽可能大而劳动。的确，他一般既无心要去促进公共利益，也不知道他对此正在促进多少。他宁愿支持本国工业而不支持外国工业，只是想要确保他自己的安全；他指导这种工业去使其产品能具有最大的价值，他这样做只是为了他自己的利益，也像在许多其他场合一样，他这样做只是被一只看不见的手引导着，去促进一个并不是出自他本心的目的。"

Catnip 猫薄荷。猫薄荷是一种有兴奋作用的天然无毒植物，并含有铁、硒、钾、锰、铅等微量元素及维生素、矿物质和叶绿素。

题　记

　　次级抵押贷款是一把双刃剑。它是对那些被认为具有较高信用风险的借款人发放的贷款，这些贷款通常缺乏坚挺的信用记录，或者具有与高违约率相关的其他特点。次级抵押贷款不仅促成了住房市场的繁荣和兴旺，使那些过去没有资格获得贷款的家庭现在能够拥有住房，而且催生了次级市场的成长，抵押贷款放贷人因此更容易降低交易成本，以及更为广泛地分散风险。但是，低标准放贷以及追逐高风险贷款又导致借款人、特别是信用较低的借款人逾期还款的可能性大大增加。次级贷款的逾期还款比例越高，次级市场放贷机构面临的风险也就越大。当一场发生在美国、因次级抵押贷款机构破产、投资基金被迫关闭、股市剧烈震荡引起的风暴席卷全球之时，次贷这把双刃剑随后给美国乃至世界造成了2008 年的金融大灾难。

The Subprime Mortgage Market

The recent sharp increases in subprime mortgage loan delinquencies①
and in the number of homes entering foreclosure② raise important
economic, social, and regulatory issues. Why have delinquencies and
initiations③ of foreclosure proceedings risen so sharply? How might the
problems in the market for subprime mortgages affect housing markets and
the economy more broadly?

Subprime mortgages are loans made to borrowers who are perceived
to have high credit risk, often because they lack a strong credit history or
have other characteristics that are associated with high probabilities of
default. Having emerged more than two decades ago, subprime mortgage
lending began to expand in earnest in the mid-1990s, the expansion
spurred in large part by innovations that reduced the costs for lenders of
assessing and pricing risks. In particular, technological advances
facilitated credit scoring by making it easier for lenders to collect and

---

① delinquency [di'liŋkwənsi] *n.* 行为不良
② foreclosure [fɔː'kləuʒə(r)] *n.* 丧失抵押品赎回权
③ initiation [iniʃi'eiʃən] *n.* 开始

次级抵押贷款市场

近来，次级抵押贷款违约和失去抵押品赎回权的家庭数量激增，引发了重大的经济、社会和监管问题。 为什么违约和失去抵押品赎回权的诉讼大幅上升？ 次级抵押贷款市场可能会怎样影响房地产市场和更大范围地影响经济呢？

次级抵押贷款是对那些被认为具有较高信用风险的借款人发放的贷款，这些贷款通常缺乏坚挺的信用记录，或者具有与高违约率相关的其他特点。 次级抵押贷款于20多年前应运而生，20世纪90年代中期大肆扩张，如日中天，创新性地降低了放贷人的成本评估和定价风险，在很大程度上刺激了这种扩张。 特别值得一提的是，当放贷人收集和传播潜在借款人的信誉信息更加容易之时，技术进步借此推动了信用评分。 此外，放贷人还发展了新的技术，利用这些信息来确定担保标准、设定利率和管理他们的风险。

次级抵押贷款市场的成长和发展已经强化了这些创新效果。 与以往放贷人在贷款偿还之前还一直把抵押贷款放在他们的账簿上相比，监管的改变和其他方面的进展使放贷人可以更轻而易举地将抵

disseminate information on the creditworthiness[1] of prospective borrowers. In addition, lenders developed new techniques for using this information to determine underwriting standards, set interest rates, and manage their risks.

The ongoing growth and development of the secondary mortgage market has reinforced the effect of these innovations. Whereas once most lenders held mortgages on their books until the loans were repaid, regulatory changes and other developments have permitted lenders to more easily sell mortgages to financial intermediaries, who in turn pool mortgages and sell the cash flows as structured securities. These securities typically offer various risk profiles and durations to meet the investment strategies of a wide range of investors. The growth of the secondary market has thus given mortgage lenders greater access to the capital markets, lowered transaction costs, and spread risk more broadly, thereby increasing the supply of mortgage credit to all types of households.

These factors laid the groundwork for an expansion of higher-risk mortgage lending over the past fifteen years or so. Growth in the market has not proceeded at a uniform pace, but on net it has been dramatic. About 7-1/2 million first-lien subprime mortgages are now outstanding, accounting for about 14 percent of all first-lien mortgages. So-called near-prime loans — loans to borrowers who typically have higher credit scores than subprime borrowers but whose applications may have other higher-

---

① creditworthiness *n.* 信誉

押贷款卖给金融中介机构，继而与后者合伙经营抵押贷款，以结构证券的形式出售现金流。 这些证券通常都提供多样化的风险预测和期限，以满足各个领域的投资者的各种投资策略。 次级市场的成长也因此使抵押贷款放贷人更容易进入资本市场，降低交易成本，以及更为广泛地分散风险，从而为所有类型的家庭增加抵押贷款信贷供给。

在过去约 15 年的时间里，这些因素为风险较高的抵押贷款放贷的扩张奠定了基础。 虽然市场成长的步调不一，但是按净值计算却发生了戏剧性的变化。 目前大约有 750 万笔第一留置权次级抵押贷款有待偿还，约占所有第一留置权抵押贷款的 14%。 所谓近优贷款，即与次级借款人相比，较高信贷评级借款人获得的贷款，但这些贷款的实施可能存在其他的高风险，因为它们额外地增加了 8% 到 10% 的抵押贷款。

次级抵押贷款放贷的扩大使那些过去没有资格获得贷款的家庭拥有住房，同时也使 20 世纪 90 年代中期的住房拥有率获得了增长。 现在，69% 的家庭拥有住房。 住房拥有率的增长基础很广泛，但根据记录，从百分比来看，少数民族家庭和人口普查区的低收入家庭获益最大。 新的业主和他们的社区都受益于这一趋势。有些研究指出了房屋所有权对加强社区建设的不同方式。 例如，与租客相比，业主更可能维护他们的财产和参加社会组织。 房屋所有权还帮助许多家庭积累了财富，积累的资产净值可以作为一项财政

risk aspects — account for an additional 8 to 10 percent of mortgages.

The expansion of subprime mortgage lending has made homeownership possible for households that in the past might not have qualified for a mortgage and has thereby contributed to the rise in the homeownership rate since the mid-1990s. Right now, 69 percent of households owned their homes. The increase in homeownership has been broadly based, but minority households and households in lower-income census tracts have recorded some of the largest gains in percentage terms. Not only the new homeowners but also their communities have benefited from these trends. Studies point to various ways in which homeownership helps strengthen neighborhoods. For example, homeowners are more likely than renters to maintain their properties and to participate in civic organizations. Homeownership has also helped many families build wealth, and accumulated home equity may serve as a financial reserve that can be tapped as needed at a lower cost than most other forms of credit.

Broader access to mortgage credit is not without its downside, however. Not surprisingly, in light of their weaker credit histories and financial conditions, subprime borrowers face higher costs of borrowing than prime borrowers do and are more likely to default than prime borrowers are. For borrowers, the consequences of defaulting can be severe — possibly including foreclosure, the loss of accumulated home equity, and reduced access to credit. Their neighbors may suffer as well, as geographically concentrated foreclosures tend to reduce property values in the surrounding area.

储备，与大多数其他形式的信贷相比，在需要使用的时候，它们的成本较低。

然而，更广泛地获得抵押贷款信贷也存在下行风险。不足为奇的是，考虑到次级借款人相对较差的信用记录和财务状况，与最优借款人相比，他们面临较高的借款成本，也更容易违约。对借款人来说，违约的后果不堪设想，可能包括丧失抵押品赎回权，损失积累的资产净值，以及减少获得信贷的机会。他们的邻居也可能遭受损失，因为地理上集中的抵押品赎回权的丧失，会减少周边地区的财产价值。

总的来说，近几年抵押贷款信贷的质量一直很可靠。但是，对可调利率的次级抵押贷款来说，这种表述不再正确。可调利率的次级抵押贷款目前占第一留置权次级抵押贷款的 2/3，占所有未偿还的第一留置权抵押贷款的 9%。这些抵押贷款的严重拖欠比率急剧上升，包括相应的止赎权、90 天付款或逾期未付等，目前已经达到 11% 左右。在一些近优抵押贷款的品种中，严重拖欠的比例也有所上升，不过较之次级市场的抵押贷款，这些品种的比率仍然要低得多。拖欠比例的上升在丧失抵押品赎回权中已经开始显现。今年的第四季度，约有 31 万例抵押品赎回权丧失，而在之前的两年中，按季平均大约只有 23 万例。自第四季度开始，次级抵押贷款丧失的比例就占到了抵押品赎回权中的一半。

多方面的原因导致可调利率次级贷款（ARMs）严重拖欠的比例

In general, mortgage credit quality has been very solid in recent years. However, that statement is no longer true of subprime mortgages with adjustable interest rates, which currently account for about two-thirds of subprime first-lien mortgages or about 9 percent of all first-lien mortgages outstanding. For these mortgages, the rate of serious delinquencies — corresponding to mortgages in foreclosure or with payments ninety days or more overdue — rose sharply and recently stood at about 11 percent. The rate of serious delinquencies has also risen somewhat among some types of near-prime mortgages, although the rate in that category remains much lower than the rate in the subprime market. The rise in delinquencies has begun to show through to foreclosures. In the fourth quarter of this year, about 310,000 foreclosure proceedings were initiated, whereas for the preceding two years the quarterly average was roughly 230,000. Subprime mortgages accounted for more than half of the foreclosures started in the fourth quarter.

The sharp rise in serious delinquencies among subprime adjustable-rate mortgages (ARMs) has multiple causes. "Seasoned" mortgages — mortgages that borrowers have paid on for several years — tend to have higher delinquency rates. That fact, together with the moderation in economic growth, would have been expected to produce some deterioration in credit quality from the exceptionally strong levels seen a few years ago. But other factors, too, have been at work. After rising at an annual rate of nearly 9 percent, house prices have decelerated, even falling in some markets. At the same time, interest rates on both fixed- and adjustable-rate mortgage loans moved upward, reaching multi-year

急剧增加。"久经风雨"的抵押贷款，即借款人已经偿还了数年之久的陈年老账，往往还有较高的拖欠比例。 随着经济增长的调整，相对于过去几年异常强大的水平来说，人们预料这一现象会造成信贷质量的某些恶化。 但是其他因素也会起作用。 年利率涨到近 9% 之后，房价增长已经减速，在某些市场甚至在下跌。 与此同时，固定利率和可调利率抵押贷款都在上升，达到多年的最高点。 在房价停滞不前的情况下，那些指望还款上升之前再融资的可调利率抵押贷款的借款人或许已经没有足够的家庭财产资格来获得新的贷款。 此外，几乎没什么财产的业主们可能会对他们的房产弃之不顾，尤其是那些并不拥有房屋、除了单纯的资金考虑之外对房产没什么感情的买房自住投资者。 地区经济问题也起到了一定作用。 例如，最高拖欠率和抵押品赎回权丧失的某些州就是那些汽车工业裁员最严重的地区。

某些抵押贷款的发行人还在对次级机构的困境推波助澜。 尽管发行贷款的潜在步伐开始减缓，但是由于投资者对高收益证券的需求依然强劲，某些放贷人明显放松了承销标准。 所谓的风险分层也变得越来越普遍，即将弱势借款人的信用记录与其他风险因素结合起来，诸如不完全的收入证明文件或非常高的累计贷款与价值比率等。 这些更为宽松的标准可能是"早期还款违约"显著增加的一个重要因素，在可调利率次级贷款中，这些违约在发行几个月后即显露出来。

highs. Some subprime borrowers with ARMs, who may have counted on refinancing before their payments rose, may not have had enough home equity to qualify for a new loan given the sluggishness① in house prices. In addition, some owners with little equity may have walked away from their properties, especially owner-investors who do not occupy the home and thus have little attachment to it beyond purely financial considerations. Regional economic problems have played a role as well; for example, some of the states with the highest delinquency and foreclosure rates are among those most hard-hit by job cuts in the auto industry.

The practices of some mortgage originators have also contributed to the problems in the subprime sector. As the underlying pace of mortgage originations began to slow, but with investor demand for securities with high yields still strong, some lenders evidently loosened underwriting standards. So-called risk-layering — combining weak borrower credit histories with other risk factors, such as incomplete income documentation or very high cumulative loan-to-value ratios②— became more common. These looser standards were likely an important source of the pronounced rise in "early payment defaults" — defaults occurring within a few months of origination — among subprime ARMs.

(1,070 words)

---

① sluggishness ['slʌgiʃnəs] *n.* 停滞
② loan-to-value ratio *n.* 抵押贷款乘数

知识链接

Subprime mortgage 次级抵押贷款。次级抵押贷款指一些贷款机构向信用程度较差和收入不高的借款人提供的贷款。利息上升会导致还款压力增大。如果很多本来信用不好的用户感觉还款压力加大，出现违约的可能，就会对银行贷款的收回造成影响。

题　记

　　公司在刀光剑影、激烈竞争的资本市场上只有三种选
择：进攻，不安的共存，或者自己成为低成本者。这种适者
生存的商业模式导致了可口可乐决斗百事可乐，索尼公司大
战飞利浦和松下电器，阿维斯出租汽车公司博弈赫兹租车公
司，保洁公司智取联合利华，卡特彼勒顶撞日本小松公司，
亚马逊公司轻拳出击易趣，叮当兄对抗叮当弟。但一个正确
的框架能帮助公司了解什么样的战略能更好地起作用。市场
有为金字塔顶端的客户提供红酒、香水和化妆品的奢侈品
牌，也有像苹果公司那样长于设计领先潮流的产品，像吉列
和 3M 公司那样善于创新，提供独特的产品组合，或者像星
巴克那样运用体验式的销售模式。小型的公司更是善于将这
些策略组合在一起使用，走低价格的路线出奇制胜，狼吞虎
咽地掠夺老牌企业的盘中大餐。低成本的竞争者正在改变资
本市场竞争的性质。

Strategies to Fight Low-Cost Rivals

It's easier to fight the enemy you know than one you don't. With gale-force winds of competition lashing every industry, companies must invest a lot of money, people, and time to fight archrivals. They find it tough, challenging, and yet strangely reassuring to take on familiar opponents, whose ambitions, strategies, weaknesses, and even strengths resemble their own. CEOs can easily compare their game plans and prowess① with their doppelgängers'② by tracking stock prices by the minute, if they desire. Thus, Coke duels Pepsi, Sony battles Philips and Matsushita, Avis combats Hertz, Procter & Gamble takes on Unilever, Caterpillar clashes with Komatsu, Amazon spars with eBay, Tweedledum fights Tweedledee.

However, this obsession with traditional rivals has blinded companies to the threat from disruptive, low-cost competitors. All over the world, especially in Europe and North America, organizations that have business models and technologies different from those of market leaders are mushrooming. Such companies offer products and services at prices

---

① prowess ['prauis] *n.* 非凡的才能
② doppelgänger ['dɔpəlˌgæŋə] *n.*(德语)长相很相似的人

低成本竞争战略

明枪易躲，暗箭难防。 随着竞争风暴席卷每个行业，公司必须投入大量的财力、人力和时间打击主要竞争对手。 他们发现，与熟悉的对手较量既艰难且具有挑战，但又不可思议地让人感到安慰，对手的抱负、战略、弱点、甚至优势与他们自己的方方面面类似。如果他们愿意的话，首席执行官们每分钟都可以通过跟踪股价与类似的公司比较他们的制胜策略和杰出的技能。 例如，可口可乐决斗百事可乐，索尼公司大战飞利浦和松下电器，阿维斯出租汽车公司博弈赫兹租车公司，保洁公司智取联合利华，卡特彼勒顶撞日本小松公司，亚马逊公司轻拳出击易趣，叮当兄对抗叮当弟。

然而，传统竞争对手的这种困扰却使公司对来自制造混乱、低成本的竞争对手的威胁熟视无睹。 纵观世界，尤其是在欧洲和北美，企业模式和技术不同于那些市场领导者的机构如雨后春笋般涌现。 这些公司提供的商品和服务的价格大大低于老牌企业的价格体系，他们通常根据放松监管力度、全球化和技术创新来定价。 20 世纪 90 年代初期，第一次价格大战已经狼吞虎咽地掠夺了好几家企业的盘中大餐，如美国好市多公司、戴尔公司、西南航空公司和沃尔玛。 现在，大西洋两岸的第二波浪潮滚滚而来，包括德国的阿尔迪

dramatically lower than the prices established businesses charge, often by harnessing the forces of deregulation, globalization, and technological innovation. By the early 1990s, the first price warriors, such as Costco Wholesale, Dell, Southwest Airlines, and Wal-Mart, had gobbled up the lunches of several incumbents[①]. Now, on both sides of the Atlantic, a second wave is rolling in: Germany's Aldi supermarkets, India's Aravind Eye Hospitals, Britain's Direct Line Insurance, the online stock brokerage E* Trade, China's Huawei in telecommunications equipment, Sweden's IKEA furniture, Ireland's Ryanair, Israel's Teva Pharmaceuticals, and the United States' Vanguard Group in asset management. These and other low-cost combatants are changing the nature of competition as executives knew it in the twentieth century.

What should leaders do? I'm not the first academic to pose that question, nor, I daresay, will I be the last. Several strategy experts, led by Harvard Business School's Michael Porter in his work on competitive strategy and Clayton Christensen in his research on disruptive innovations, and Tuck School's Richard D'Aveni in his writings on hypercompetition, have described the strategies companies can use to fight low-cost rivals. But that body of work doesn't make the phenomenon less interesting — or render the threat any less formidable. For, despite the buckets of ink that academics have spilled on the topic, most companies behave as though low-cost competitors are no different from traditional rivals or as though they don't matter.

Over the past five years, I've studied around 50 incumbents and 25

---

① incumbent [in'kʌmbənt] *n.* 任职者

超市、印度的仁爱眼科医院、英国的直通车保险公司、网络股票经纪转口贸易、中国的电讯设备商华为、瑞典的家具商宜家家居、爱尔兰的瑞安航空公司、以色列的梯瓦制药以及美国的先锋集团资产管理公司。正如 20 世纪的主管们所知道的一样，这些公司以及其他低成本的竞争者正在改变竞争的性质。

领导者们应该做些什么呢？我不是首位提出这个问题的学者，我敢说，我也不会是最后一位。以哈佛商学院迈克尔·波特为首的几位战略专家已经描述了公司可以用来抵制低成本竞争者的策略，迈克尔·波特在他的著作中论述了竞争策略，克莱顿·克里斯坦森研究了破坏性创新，塔克商学院的理查德·D. 戴维尼在他的著作中阐述了超强竞争理论。但是，大量的作品使这种现象愈发活灵活现，或者使威胁变得不那么令人生畏。因为尽管学者们对这个话题挥毫泼墨，但大多数公司依旧把低成本竞争者与传统竞争者同样对待，似乎认为他们无关紧要。

在过去的 5 年里，我研究了大约 50 家传统企业和 25 家低成本企业。我的研究表明，忽视低成本的竞争者是一个错误，因为这终将迫使公司腾出整个市场。当市场领导者确实做出反应时，他们往往会发起价格战，致使自己比挑战者更受伤。公司意识到这种事实的时候，通常用两种方式中的一种来改变流程。有些公司偏重防守，试图区分他们的产品，这是一个在一系列严格的条件下才能起作用的策略。另一些公司则采取攻势，推出他们自己的低成本业务。只要公司可以使传统业务与新业务产生协同作用，这种所谓的双重战略就会取得成功。如果他们不能，公司最好是把他们转交给供给商解决，即使困难重重，也要转交给低成本的竞争者。但是，

low-cost businesses. My research shows that ignoring cut-price rivals is a mistake because it eventually forces companies to vacate entire market segments. When market leaders do respond, they often set off price wars, hurting themselves more than the challengers. Companies that wake up to that fact usually change course in one of two ways. Some become more defensive and try to differentiate their products — a strategy that works only if they can meet a stringent① set of conditions. Others take the offensive by launching low-cost businesses of their own. This so-called dual strategy succeeds only if companies can generate synergies between the existing businesses and the new ventures. If they cannot, companies are better off trying to transform themselves into solution providers or, difficult though it is, into low-cost players. Before I analyze the various strategy options, however, I must dispel some myths about low-cost businesses. That is the sustainability of low-cost businesses.

Be it in the classroom or the boardroom, executives invariably ask me the same question: Are low-cost businesses a permanent, enduring threat? Most managers believe they aren't; they're convinced that a business that sells at prices dramatically lower than those incumbents charge must go bankrupt. They cite the experience of U. S. airlines, which, after the industry's deregulation in the 1980s, succeeded in beating off cut-price providers such as People Express. What they forget is that low-cost airlines soon reemerged. By slashing fares and cutting frills②, entrants like Southwest Airlines and JetBlue have grabbed a chunk

---

① stringent [ˈstrɪndʒənt] *adj.* 严格的
② frill [frɪl] *n.* 褶边

在我分析各种各样的策略选择之前，我必须要解开低成本企业的一些谜团，那就是可持续性的低成本企业。

无论是在教室还是在会议会，高管们总是问我同样的问题：低成本企业是永久的、持续的威胁么？大多数管理者认为，情况并非如此。他们相信，销售价格比那些成熟企业低得多的公司必然要破产。他们列举了美国航空的经历。美国航空在20世纪80年代行业管制放松的情况下，成功击败了人民快捷航空等低价供应商。他们所遗忘的是，低价航空公司很快又再度出现。通过大幅降低票价和削减附加值战略，西南航空和捷蓝航空之类的新晋参与者已抢下一大块美国的国内航空旅行市场。他们与前辈不同，他们也在轻轻松松地赚大钱。

成功的价格战斗士通过使用以下几种战术领先于更强大的对手：他们只关注一个或少量的消费者群体；他们交付的基本产品或提供的优势超过了竞争对手；他们利用超高效的运营坚持天天低价，以保持成本不断下降。这就是总部设在埃森、拥有美国乔氏连锁超市的零售商阿尔迪如何在竞争残酷的德国市场蓬勃发展的原因。阿尔迪的优势始于其产品范围的大小。相对于拥有25 000种产品的传统超市而言，典型的阿尔迪批发商店是一个相对较小、15 000平方英尺的小店，里面只有700件产品，95%是商店的品牌。连锁店销售的每件产品都超过了竞争对手的销量，这使阿尔迪能够就更低的价格和更高的质量与供给商谈判。事实上，阿尔迪的许多私人标签产品在竞争和品味测试中都是最驰名的产品。产品的少量交易还使公司的供应链灵活敏捷。另一种效率源于一个事实，即阿尔迪在闹市区和房地产价格相对低廉的地区的街头都设立了连

of America's domestic air travel market. Unlike their predecessors, they're making money hand over fist, too.

Successful price warriors stay ahead of bigger rivals by using several tactics: They focus on just one or a few consumer segments; they deliver the basic product or provide one benefit better than rivals do; and they back everyday low prices with superefficient operations to keep costs down. That's how Aldi, the Essen-headquartered retailer that owns Trader Joe's in the U.S., has thrived in the brutally competitive German market. Aldi's advantages start with the size of its product range. A typical Aldi outlet is a relatively small, 15,000-square-foot store that carries only about 700 products — 95% of which are store brands — compared with the 25,000-plus products that traditional supermarkets carry. The chain sells more of each product than rivals do, which enables it to negotiate lower prices and better quality with suppliers. In fact, many of Aldi's private-label products have bested branded products in competitions and taste tests. The small number of products also keeps the company's supply chain agile①. Another efficiency stems from the fact that Aldi sets up outlets on side streets in downtown areas and in, where real estate is relatively inexpensive. Since it uses small spaces, the company's start-up costs are low, which enables it to blanket markets: Aldi now owns 4,100 stores in Germany and 7,500 worldwide.

Aldi doesn't pamper② customers. Its stores display products on pallets rather than shelves in order to cut restocking time and save money.

---

① agile ['ædʒl] *adj.* 敏捷灵活的
② pamper ['pæmpə] *vt.* 纵容

锁店。 由于连锁店使用的空间小，公司的启动成本低，这使得它成为地毯市场。阿尔迪在德国拥有4 100家专卖店，在世界范围拥有7 500家专卖店。

阿尔迪从来没有纵容过客户。 为了减少补充存货的时间和节约资金，阿尔迪专卖店将产品陈列在托盘上，而不是摆放在货架上。消费者可以自己带购物袋或者在商店里买购物袋。 阿尔迪是要求消费者为购物车支付可退还押金的首批零售商之一。 消费者将购物车返还到指定的位置，为员工节省了搜集购物车的时间和精力。 同时，阿尔迪的基本设施安置得恰到好处。 它有好几条收银线，所以即使在营业高峰期，等待的时间也不会太久。 它的数据输入机快如闪电，收银员可以迅速处理每位顾客的购物清单。 大多数零售商遵循当地的定价，但每个国家中的每一家阿尔迪店都使用相同的价格，从而强化了作为消费者冠军连锁店的形象。 阿尔迪被德国人选为国家排名第三的最值得信赖的品牌，仅次于西门子和宝马。 阿尔迪销售的产品比竞争对手要便宜得多。 该公司对供应商的价格增加了约8%，用于支付交通、房租、市场营销和其他营业间接成本，以及约5%的员工成本。 因此，阿尔迪的平均涨价幅度为13%，而大多数欧洲零售商的涨价幅度为28%至30%。 全德国89%的家庭每年至少到访阿尔迪一次，这一点不会令人感到惊讶。 根据欧洲市场调查公司的报告，阿尔迪的连锁店占德国超市业务20%的份额。

阿尔迪的故事表明，低成本营销商的财务数据与那些知名公司的财务数据截然不同。 与传统的厂商相比，他们赚取的毛利较少，但是他们的经营模式却为他们带来了较高的营运利润率。 这些营运利润率又被企业高于平均水平的资产周转率放大，结果导致令人印

Customers bring their own shopping bags or buy them in the store. Aldi was one of the first retailers to require customers to pay refundable deposits for grocery carts. Shoppers return the carts to designated areas, sparing employees the time and energy needed to round them up. At the same time, Aldi gets the basics right. There are several checkout lines, so wait times are short even during peak shopping hours. Its scanning machines are lightning fast, which allows clerks to deal quickly with each shopper. Most retailers follow local pricing, but every Aldi store in a country charges the same price, which reinforces the chain's image as a consumer champion. Germans voted Aldi the country's third most-trusted brand, behind only Siemens and BMW. Aldi sells products far cheaper than rivals do. To suppliers' prices, the company adds about 8% to cover transportation, rent, marketing, and other overhead costs, and about 5% for staff costs. Thus, Aldi's average markup is 13% while that of most European retailers is 28% to 30%. Not surprisingly, 89% of all German households made at least one trip to an Aldi every year, and according to European market research firms, the chain had a 20% share of Germany's supermarket business.

As Aldi's story suggests, the financial calculations of low-cost players are different from those of established companies. They earn smaller gross margins than traditional players do, but their business models turn those into higher operating margins. Those operating margins are magnified by the businesses' higher-than-average asset turnover ratios, which result in impressive returns on assets.

(1,159 words)

象深刻的资产回报率。

知识链接 🔍

Caterpillar 卡特彼勒是全球财富 500 强公司之一，总部所在地在美国，主要经营工业农业设备。

Tweedledum and Tweedledee 叮当兄和叮当弟。叮当兄和叮当弟是《爱丽丝镜中奇遇记》中的两个人物，他们是一对双胞胎，通常用来形容半斤八两、难以区分的两个人。

ALDI 阿尔迪集团。阿尔迪取自 Albrecht 和 discount 的前两个字母，意为由阿尔布莱希特家族经营的廉价折扣商店，它是德国一家以经营食品为主的连锁超市。它的前身是 1948 年阿尔布莱希特兄弟接管其母在德国埃森市郊矿区开办的食品零售店。1962 年该店进行了改组，第一家以阿尔迪命名的食品超市在多特蒙德诞生。如今，阿尔迪由阿尔布莱希特家族的泰欧和卡尔兄弟二人所有，分别经营阿尔迪在北德地区的北店和南德地区的南店。多年来，北店又逐步扩展到丹麦、法国、荷兰、比利时和卢森堡；南店则进入了英国、爱尔兰、奥地利、澳大利亚和美国。

题 记

　　东盟自由贸易区在应对区域经济一体化的快速发展中应运而生，而印度同东盟10国集团新签署的贸易协定无疑为双方带来了双赢的结果。一方面，作为一个经济集团，东盟已经认识到印度对东南亚地区经济增长的实际和潜在的贡献，当东盟开始争取自己在东亚政治空间的核心位置之际，便不失时机地把印度设想成一个渴望获得投资的伙伴。另一方面，印度前总理纳拉辛哈·拉奥早就提出了"向东看政策"，寻求发展与东盟和北部邻国的关系，已经逐步减少了主要东盟国家最重要的出口项目的进口关税，发挥着区域成员和经济一体化主导者的潜在作用。较高的市场一体化水平、良好的贸易环境、相似的经济发展水平、相似的语言文化和国家接壤等相互交织的因素，形成了东盟与印度交往背后的推动力。

The Driving Force behind the ASEAN's Engagement with India

By coincidence, Singapore conferred its Honorary Citizen Award on Ratan Tata, "an exemplary business leader, " just a day after India and the Association of South East Asian Nations (ASEAN) announced a trade pact in the City-State.

The trade-in-goods agreement, slated for① signature by the two sides in December, will set the stage for talks on a liberalized flow of services and investments in either direction. And, while Mr. Tata had, as noted in connection with the award, "helped propel Singapore's economy, " the City-State has remained a key prime mover on the ASEAN side for its diversified engagement with India. Another coincidence was that Singapore's Nanyang Technological University conferred its honorary degree of doctor of engineering on the former President, A. P. J. Abdul Kalam, on the eve of announcement of the trade pact. Singapore will co-chair the ASEAN-India panel on services; and the City-State has, for long, recognized the actual and potential contributions of Indian

---

① slated for 任命为

东盟与印度交往背后的推动力

    无独有偶，就在印度和东南亚国家联盟（东盟）各成员国在新加坡签署贸易协定的一天后，这个城市型国家授予"模范商业领袖"拉丹·塔塔荣誉公民称号。

    双方原定于在 12 月签署的货物贸易协定，将可以为双方服务和投资的自由交流谈判打好基础。此外，尽管前述奖项的获得者塔塔先生"帮助推动了新加坡的经济"，但由于新加坡与印度有各种各样的合作，这个城市国家仍然是东盟方面的关键主导者。另一个巧合是，在宣布贸易协定的前夕，新加坡南洋理工大学授予印度前总统阿布杜·卡拉姆名誉工程博士学位。新加坡将共同主持东盟-印度小组的服务工作。长期以来，这个城市型国家已经认识到印度的专业人士对东南亚地区经济增长的实际和潜在的贡献。

    这种象征意义和真实希望的强烈交织是最近几年东盟与印度交往背后的推动力。显然，双方的专家，更多的是印度专家，热衷于梳理贸易协议中的一方或另一方为了做交易而让步的迹象，而这个艰苦的谈判近 6 年来踌躇不前。相对的收益和损失使这个问题变得

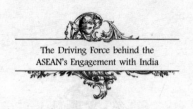
professionals to the economic growth of Southeast Asia.

The powerful mix of such symbolism and substantive hopes is the driving force behind the ASEAN's engagement with India in recent years. Obviously, experts on both sides, more so in India, are keen to comb the trade pact for signs of a caving-in by one party or the other for the sake of doing the deal, which was hanging fire for nearly six years of hard parleys①. The issue of relative gains and losses becomes more acute, because neither India nor the 10-state ASEAN enthusiastically described the pact, soon after it was announced, as "a win-win deal" for both. This nomenclature② is important, because the win-win approach has become a standard formula for political and other negotiations in the present post-Cold War period. Outwardly, the ASEAN will stand to gain more from this deal than India, at least to begin with. The available indications are that India has agreed to reduce, substantially and progressively, its import tariff on a few items of utmost export-importance to some key ASEAN states such as Malaysia, Indonesia, and Vietnam. These items are palm oil, coffee, tea, and pepper. And, as for petroleum products, Brunei's export lifeline, India has been equally accommodative. Surely, the 10 ASEAN countries have also, variously, committed themselves to giving a greater market access than available now in respect of Indian exports. At stake, as a fundamental question, though, is different from the standard analysis of economic transactions. And, within the economic domain itself, the ASEAN, aware of its relative gains, does expect New Delhi to

---

① parley [ˈpɑːli] *n.* 谈判
② nomenclature [nəuˈmeŋklətʃə] *n.* 术语

更加尖锐，因为印度和东盟 10 国谈到协议时都缺乏热情，协议宣布之后不久，就被双方视为"双赢协议"。 这个术语非常重要，因为在目前的后冷战时期，双赢的方法已经成为政治和其他协议的一个标准方案。 从表面上看，东盟从这笔交易中的获利肯定比印度多，至少是在刚开始的时候。 现有的迹象表明，印度已经同意大量且逐步地减少马来西亚、印度尼西亚和越南等主要东盟国家少数最重要的出口项目的进口关税。 这些项目是棕榈油、咖啡、茶和辣椒。此外，印度对文莱出口的生命线——石油产品，也维持着同样的宽松政策。 当然，东盟 10 国也以各种不同的方式，承诺对印度的出口给予比现在更大的市场准入。 然而，作为一个根本性的问题，经济交易分析标准的差异危如累卵。 此外，在经济领域的内部，东盟意识到了它的相对收益，就服务业出口而言，的确期待从制高点的角度与新德里协商。 与此同时，东盟把印度设想成一个渴望获得投资的伙伴。 而且，鉴于一些东盟国家在与基础设施投资相关的少数关键领域中的优势，这个团体擅长于以富有传奇色彩的规模突出自己的形象，渴望与印度达成条件苛刻的协议。 总的来说，最新的东盟-印度贸易协定将创造一个自由贸易区，包括现在的 17 亿人口和 23 000 亿美元的国内生产总值，可以被认为是带有政治色彩的经济外交的胜利。

尽管美国作为全球的超级大国仍然是"友谊"的"中心"，但随着印度谋求国家整体潜力的崛起，区域合作伙伴的重要性就不能被

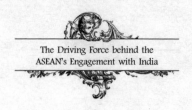
negotiate from commanding heights insofar as its exports of services are concerned. At the same time, the ASEAN has envisioned India as an investment-hungry partner. And, given the strengths of some ASEAN states in a few critical areas of infrastructure-related investments, this group, which specializes in projecting its image in larger-than-life dimensions, is eager to strike a hard bargain with India. On balance, the latest ASEAN-India trade pact, which will create a free trade area of 1. 7 billion people and $ 2. 3 trillion Gross Domestic Product as of now, can be seen as the triumph of economic diplomacy with a political focus.

As India seeks to rise as a nation to its full potential, the importance of regional partners cannot be downplayed①, regardless of the "centrality" of "friendship" of the United States as the global superpower of the day. In fact, before the U. S. appeared on India's horizon as a "potential partner," the former Prime Minister, P. V. Narasimha Rao, had outlined the "Look-East policy" of developing linkages with the ASEAN and its northern neighbours. One of his reasons, in the early 1990s, was to gain for New Delhi some political and economic space in the then context of an "imploding" Soviet Union, which had, in its halcyon② days, stood by India as a strategic friend in need. The ASEAN, on the other hand, was also looking at that time to widen its own circle of friends. As an economic bloc, its priority then was to try and befriend India as a potential trading partner. Yet, given the political circumstances in which the organization was born, it was also

---

① downplay [daun'plei] *vt.* 减轻……的重要性
② halcyon ['hælsiən] *adj.* 平静的

淡化。 事实上，在印度将美国视做"潜在的合作伙伴"之前，前总理纳拉辛哈·拉奥就提出了"向东看政策"，寻求发展与东盟和北部邻国的关系。 在 20 世纪 90 年代早期，其中的一个原因是在前苏联"膨胀"的背景下，为新德里获得一些政治和经济空间。 在太平盛世之际，前苏联被印度视做危难中的战略性朋友。 另一方面，东盟也希望在此时扩大自己的朋友圈。 作为一个经济集团，东盟当时优先考虑的是尽力帮扶印度，将其视为一个潜在的贸易伙伴。 然而，鉴于该组织诞生时的政治环境，东盟也一直在小心翼翼地关注印度作为区域成员的潜在作用。 这种相对新晋的现实可以追溯到这样一个事实，即东盟本身正在缓慢地成长，同时伴随着战略意识的完善。 特别是近几年，它的确已经开始争取自己在东亚政治空间的核心位置。

东盟在这方面的未来仍然不甚明朗。 然而，在签订了这个协议之后，总的来说，努力使印度成为一个区域性的力量在政治领域内对大国并不构成威胁，反而为他们提供了经济领域内的机会。 在很大程度上，正是这种原因帮助东盟抓住了与中国签订主要贸易协定的机遇。 当然，此类协议尚属首次。 这并不意味着中国这个庞大的经济体无法承受与相邻小国家的经济体和一些雄心勃勃的中等权利追求者签订贸易协定的影响。 与东盟签订贸易协定的光明前景势不可挡，印度终于决定效仿中国，追随中国的足迹。 但这并不意味着印度的经济利益将不受这一协议的影响。 然而，作为东亚首脑会

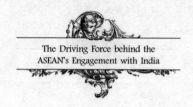
mindful, all the time, about India's potential role as a regional player. This relative new reality can be traced to the fact that the group itself is growing up, at a slow pace, as a strategically savvy① outfit as well. It has indeed begun, in more recent years, to try and position itself as the nucleus of the political universe in East Asia.

The ASEAN's future in this respect remains uncertain. However, the outfit has, by and large, managed to project itself as a regional force that would pose no threat to the big powers in the political domain and would, instead, provide them with opportunities in the economic sphere. To a large extent, it was this reasoning that helped the group to clinch a major trade pact with China. The accord was, of course, the first of its kind. This does not mean that China's mega economy cannot absorb the impact of a trade accord with a neighboring group of small countries and a few middle-power-aspirants. The lustre② of a trade pact with the ASEAN having become irresistible, following China's example, India has finally decided to follow suit. This does not mean that India's economic interests will not be served by this deal. However, as a dialogue partner of this group in the East Asian Summit and as a player eying high stakes, as evident in the current debate on India in the Nuclear Suppliers Group, New Delhi's choice becomes explicit.

(925 words)

---

① savvy ['sævi] *n.* 机智
② lustre ['lʌstə] *n.* 光芒

议这个团体的一个对话伙伴，作为见证高风险的参与者，新德里对核供应国集团就当前印度展开的争论心知肚明，它的选择变得明确起来。

知识链接 🔍

Ratan Tata 拉丹·塔塔。拉丹·塔塔是塔塔集团的掌门人，印度首富，掌控着96家印度跨国公司。拉丹执掌帅印之后，塔塔集团频繁穿梭于全球85个国家，向世界范围内的目标企业成功发动了30多场资本并购，其中有茶叶、汽车(知名品牌有捷豹等)、电信、酒店、软件等国际收购。

题　记

　　当世界格局朝着多极化发展时，多元化经营似乎成了企业做大做强、与国际接轨的一个门槛或标志。著名的通用电气公司在多元化经营方针的引导下，准确地掌握市场信息，促使企业在利润、成长和现金流等方面取长补短，根据市场需求研制新产品，并借助多元化的优势开拓新的增长点。通用电气买下了史密斯集团的航空业务，收购了伏特克·格雷的石油和天然气业务，控股雅培制药公司，涉足保安业务，发展生物技术……大型联合企业的多样化经营优势使通用电气公司形成了良好的整体业绩，释放出每位员工的能量、智慧和自信，以其多样性在世界市场上长久不衰。虽然任何事物都是"尺有所短"，但是，多元化经营的通用电气公司却灵活运用扬长避短的策略获得了更多、更好的机遇与发展。

Strength in Diversity Management

It is a hodgepodge① of the known biochemical pathways of the body — the way it makes DNA, for example, or turns sugar into energy. And it represents just a fraction of what goes on in living organisms. Mr. Hergersberg and his staff are trying to fill in some of the blanks, in hopes of finding genetic markers or other biochemical connections that could provide early alerts to cancer and other diseases. Many scientists are doing that. But Mr. Hergersberg is running a biotechnology lab at General Electric, a company that people associate more with engines and finance than with genetic research. He is aiming to bring G.E. ever closer to a business in clinical diagnoses, "And that," he said, "is a business G.E. definitely wants to be in."

So are security, energy services, "green" products and many other areas that Jeffrey R. Immelt, G.E.'s chief has singled out as the company's growth platforms. He has jettisoned② reinsurance and advanced materials, two slow-growth businesses, and the plastics business is on its way out. He is also bolstering some of G.E.'s older businesses — for

---

① hodgepodge [ˈhɔdʒpɔdʒ] *n.* 混淆
② jettison [ˈdʒetəsn] *n.* 投弃

多元化经营的优势

　　它是身体内已知的生化路径构成的大杂烩，例如，它是制造DNA或把糖转化为能量的方式。 它表现的只是生物体中正在运转的一小部分。 荷尔格斯伯格先生和他的工作人员正在试图填补其中的某些空白，希望找到遗传标记或其他的生化连接，能够提供癌症和其他疾病的早期警告。 许多科学家也正在忙于此类研究。 但是，荷尔格斯伯格先生却正在主持通用电气生物技术实验室的工作。 提到这家公司，人们会更多地联想到发动机和金融，而不是遗传研究。 他的目标是促使通用电气进一步靠近临床诊断业务。 他说："这是通用电气一定要涉足的商业领域。"

　　通用电气的首席执行官杰弗里·伊梅尔特挑出安全、能源服务、"绿色"产品和许多其他的领域作为公司的发展平台。 他放弃了转保业务和先进材料这两个增长缓慢的行业，同时还在退出塑料领域。 他也支持通用电气的一些老产业。 例如，通用电气花48亿美元买下史密斯集团的航空业务，这一收购增加了对蓬勃发展的航空产业的技术控制。 但他同时又出手19亿美元购买了伏特克·格雷的石油和天然气业务，并以81亿美元的价格从雅培制药公司购进诊断业务。

example, G.E. spent $ 4. 8 billion to buy the aerospace business of the Smiths Group, which adds control technology to the already thriving aerospace unit. But at the same time he also spent $ 1. 9 billion to buy the oil and gas operations of Vetco Gray, and $ 8. 1 billion to buy a diagnostics① business from Abbott Laboratories.

G.E.'s executives now face the task of integrating those mammoth acquisitions into the corporate fabric. But here at the company's Global Research Center, the impact may be even more immediate: more acquisitions mean more technologies to tap into, for use in other businesses. "The cross-business fertilization of research was marginal under Jack Welch, but Jeff has created an excitement and energy around the concept," said Noel M. Tichy, a professor at the Ross School of Business at the University of Michigan, who has written extensively about G. E. Examples abound. When G. E. decided to pursue the security business, its researchers immediately began adapting imaging technology from the health care division for use in scanning baggage. Another G.E. group is adapting lightweight carbon-and-plastic composites, originally developed for fan blades in aircraft engines, for use in windmill blades, some parts of power generators, and even for automotive parts. Investors often favor the shares of companies that focus on one business area — "pure plays" in Wall Street parlance — over those of conglomerates②. But scientists say that when it comes to research, the conglomerate structure is a strength.

---

① diagnostics [daiəg'nɔstiks] *n.* 诊断学
② conglomerate [kən'glɔmərit] *adj.* 多元化集团公司

　　通用电气的高管们现在面临着整合的任务，即如何将这些巨型收购融入企业的结构。 但这种影响对公司的全球研究中心可能更为直接：收购得越多，意味着引进的技术越多，当然也可以在其他行业里应用这些技术。 密歇根大学罗斯商学院的教授诺埃尔·M.蒂奇表示："杰克·韦尔奇认为，交叉行业相互作用的研究本无足轻重，但杰弗却为这个概念赋予了刺激和活力。"通用电气的涉及面很广，蒂奇教授写作时列举的例子比比皆是。 当通用电气决定涉足保安业务时，其研究人员立即开始将医疗保健部门的成像技术用于扫描行李。 通用电气的另一个小组用于风车叶片、发电机的一些零件，甚至是汽车零部件的轻型碳塑复合材料，原本是为飞机发动机开发的扇叶。 相对于综合性大企业，投资者往往青睐集中在某个业务范围内的公司股份，用华尔街的话来说就是"单一业务"。 但科学家们声称，根据研究的结果，大型联合企业的结构是一种优势。

　　到目前为止，生物技术实验室解析"基因句子"的能力仍然处于初级阶段，因此不必过分担心通用电气医疗集团之外的适用性。但是，许多较成熟的实验室可能很快会面临交互式方法不利的一面，即伊梅尔特先生坚持认为的：当通用电气退出一个行业时，公司的研究网络就会出现参差不齐的漏洞。 例如，塑料业务一旦被出售，通用电气将不得不和其他公司合作，制造和配销汽车塑料。 它必须向外部寻求无数的塑料配方和潜在的生产流程，而这些正是通用电气公司的研究人员在塑料电子方面已经修补了好几年的领域。而且，它将会失去科学家阿尼尔·杜嘎尔称之为的"塑料需求拉动的市场"。 阿尼尔·杜嘎尔正在开发塑料照明工程。 简单地说，它是为了满足那些寻找利用塑料新方法的客户。 尽管如此，在伊梅尔

For now, the ability to parse those "sentences" is far too rudimentary① for the biotechnology lab to worry much about applicability outside GE Healthcare. But many of the older labs may soon face one downside of the interactive approach that Mr. Immelt has insisted on: when G.E. exits a business, it can leave a jagged hole in the company's research network. Once the plastics business is sold, for example, G.E. will have to join with another company to manufacture and distribute automotive plastics. It will have to go outside for the myriad plastic formulations and potential manufacturing processes that G.E.'s researchers in plastics electronics have tinkered with for several years. And, it will lose what Anil Duggal, a scientist on the plastic lighting project, calls "the market pull from the plastics side" — the easy dialogue it has had with customers who are looking to use plastics in new ways. Still, under Mr. Immelt, G.E. has grown more amenable to joint projects with other companies. It folded its security business into a joint venture with Smiths Group, whose aerospace unit it purchased. And it has formed a research collaboration with Eli Lilly to find ways to detect and treat Alzheimer's disease.

At Niskayuna, just outside Schenectady, the emphasis is clearly on the science, not on the methods for commercializing it. The walls of the research center's lobby are adorned with pictures of dozens of G. E. scientists who each have more than 25 patents, with cases of medals and prizes they have won. And the anchor piece of the lobby is a desk — nothing special to look at, until you realize it was the one that Thomas

---

① rudimentary [ruːdiˈmentəri] *adj.* 未发达的

特的领导下，通用电气变得越来越易于和其他公司联合开发项目。它整合了公司的保安业务，购买了史密斯集团的航空航天部门，成立了合资企业。 它与礼来制药厂共建了一个研究协作机构，寻找检测和治疗阿尔茨海默氏病的方法。

纽约尼什卡纳通用电气全球研究中心就在斯克内克塔迪市外，它的工作重点显然是科学，而不是使之商品化的方法。 研究中心大厅的墙上，装饰着几十个通用电气公司科学家的照片和他们已获得的奖牌和奖项的镜框，每位科学家都有 25 个以上的专利。 大厅的镇殿之作是一张桌子，看上去并无特别之处，一旦你意识到这就是1892 年托马斯·阿尔瓦·爱迪生协助建立通用电气公司时用过的桌子，惊讶之情便溢于言表。 然而，实验室本身并没有停留在过去的辉煌之上，而是更多地着眼于虚幻的未来。 例如，几乎每一个实验室都在研究风能的某个方面。 复合材料实验室正在研究风车使用的那些轻型碳纤维叶片；电子专家正在寻求自动控制，以更好地协调需求和供应；电力研究人员正在研究更有效的方法，将风车产生的交流电转换为可靠的直流电能，与多种用途的电网无缝对接，当风速特别猛烈时，这种方法也许可以存储过剩的能量。 主管电力和推进系统实验室的可再生能源专家胡安·德·贝德奥表示："我们正与能源部、夏威夷政府、地方公共事业部以及我们可以合作的每个人协商，看看我们可以将什么样的技术更好地融入风力发电。"

但是，对通用电气公司来说，最重要的可能是实验室与企业的紧密合作。 小约翰·F.韦尔奇担任主席时，通用电气公司的高管们极少花时间视察尼什卡纳研究中心。 伊梅尔特先生担任主席期间，他们每年到访 4 次。 通用电气医疗集团的首席执行官约瑟夫·M.霍

Alva Edison was using when he helped found G.E. in 1892. The labs themselves are dealing more with the illusive future than the illustrious past, though. Almost every lab is working on some aspect of wind energy, for example. The composites lab is working on those lightweight carbon-fiber blades for windmills. The electronics specialists are seeking automatic controls to better coordinate demand and supply. The electric power researchers are studying more efficient ways to convert the alternating current generated by windmills to a reliable source of direct energy that can move seamlessly onto utility grids, and perhaps ways to store excess energy when the wind is blowing particularly hard. "We're working with the Department of Energy, with the state of Hawaii, with local utilities, with everyone we can to see what technologies we can incorporate into better wind power," said Juan de Bedout, a renewable energy specialist who manages the electric power and propulsion systems lab.

But perhaps most important for G.E., the labs are working closely with its businesses. G.E. executives rarely spent time at Niskayuna when John F. Welch Jr. was chairman; under Mr. Immelt, they visit four times a year. Joseph M. Hogan, chief executive of GE Healthcare, is a frequent visitor to the bioscience labs, while Scott C. Donnelly, the chief executive of the aviation business — and the former director of the research center — closely follows the composite work. The frequent visits help the labs parcel out their results to many of the businesses simultaneously. In the nanotechnology lab, for example, abracadabra moments occur often. A pool of black liquid contains tiny iron particles that jump up to a hovering magnet and form little "solid" spikes that, when touched,

根是生命科学实验室的常客；而前研究中心主任、现任航空业务的行政长官斯科特·C.唐纳利则密切关注复合材料的工作。 频繁的造访有助于实验室将研究成果同时分配到很多企业。 例如，在纳米技术实验室，经常出现莫名其妙的瞬间。 一些黑色液体含有微小的铁粒子，粒子跳到盘旋的磁铁上，形成小小的"固体"尖峰，触摸时却仍然是液体。 数英尺之外，研究人员在硬质表面努力复制防水能力，这种能力是纳米颗粒传授给荷叶的。 另一项实验涉及纳米摄影机。 在身体周围安置纳米摄影机，然后将他们连在一起使用，拍摄的器官图片比大多数影像设备的旋转单相机拍摄的效果更清晰。 这些试验的结果可能产生比磁共振成像更为清晰的图像，不失为较好的飞机除冰方式，甚至可以被生物恐怖分子用来检测物质。 换句话说，他们可能为通用电气的卫生保健、航空航天和保安等各种各样的业务提供产品。 负责纳米技术研究项目的玛格丽特·布洛姆声称："纳米技术让我们在众多的领域内去做我们以前从来没有做过的事情。"

通用电气希望，生物技术可以对公司产生类似的影响。 在某种意义上，它把通用电气带入未知的领域。 通用电气一直在回避进入人体的产品，因为即使是很小的失误也可以造成可怕的后果。 但是，如果荷尔格斯伯格先生带领的全体成员成功了，通用电气将获得大量的物质，用以研究诊断成像。 荷尔格斯伯格先生停了下来，他认为低风险并不等同于无风险。 他表示，"这种物质可能不会长期留在体内，并不足以引起不良反应。"不管怎样，这是一个争论未决的问题。 他认为，"诊断和预防是未来的趋势。 这就是我们要做的"。

turn out to still be liquid. A few feet away, researchers work to replicate on hard surfaces the water-repellent ability that nanoparticles impart to lotus leaves. Yet another experiment involves nanocameras that when positioned around a body and used in tandem, can take a much sharper picture of an organ than is yielded by the rotating single cameras in most imaging devices. Those experiments might yield results that could lead to sharper images from M.R.I.'s, better ways to de-ice airplanes, and even to ways to detect substances that might be used by bioterrorists. In other words, they could yield products for G.E. businesses as diverse as health care, aerospace and security. "Nanotechnology is letting us do things we never did before, in a huge number of areas, " said Margaret Blohm, who runs the nanotechnology research program.

G.E. hopes biotechnology can have a similar impact at the company. In a sense, it takes G.E. into uncharted territory. G.E. has always avoided products that enter the human body, since even small mistakes can be dire. But if Mr. Hergersberg's crew is successful, G.E. will have an arsenal of substances for use in diagnostic imaging. Mr. Hergersberg stops short of equating low risk to no risk. "The substances probably wouldn't stay in the body long enough to trigger adverse reactions, " he said. It is a moot point, anyway. "Diagnoses and prevention are the future, " he said, "and that's where we have to be."

(1,218 words)

知识链接

G. E. 通用电气公司（General Electric）。通用电气是美国、也是世界上最大的电器和电子设备制造公司，它的产值占美国电工行业全部产值的1/4左右。通用电气公司的总部位于美国康涅狄格州费尔菲尔德市。公司由多个多元化的基本业务集团组成，产品品种繁多，据称有25万多种品种规格。它除了生产消费电器、工业电器设备外，还是一个巨大的军火承包商，制造宇宙航空仪表、喷气飞机引航导航系统、多弹头弹道导弹系统、雷达和宇宙飞行系统等。

题 记

　　在商界竞争日益激烈的今天，商品销售已成为各企业发展的瓶颈制约因素。为了达到预期的销售目标，首席执行官们制定了科学的销售计划，严格遵循着他们自己的黄金销售原则：即使受到伤害，也要坚持诚实；以一种独特的方式与人接触；简单而直接地表达自己的意图；真诚地表达感觉；出错的时候说声对不起；与人交谈时眼睛一定要正视对方；尽早取得承诺；勤问必有所得；重新定义"不"字；提出行动的要求。事实上，多数首席执行官都是从第一线销售人员起家的，成功的销售员和成功的首席执行官具有许多相同的特性。如果你想和首席执行官谈生意，如果你想成为成功的销售人员，你就必须具备企业家的精神，并绝对维持黄金销售守则的完整性。

The Golden Selling Rules for CEOs

CEOs are honest, even when it hurts. This is one of those rules that you should carry into your day-to-day interactions with everyone. Never, ever lie to a CEO or anyone else. If you don't believe in what you're selling enough to tell the truth about it at all times, find something else to sell. CEOs can't afford to tell a lie. Why? Because there are too many ears listening to what they are saying, including stockholders, the media, employees, suppliers, customers, etc. CEOs know, that problem accounts are those that someone over-promised and under-delivered on. CEOs and those of us who sell to them must be totally ready, willing and able to stand behind every word that we write or that comes out of our mouths. If that means "walking" on a short-term opportunity today, so be it. You can always come back tomorrow. And when you do come back, you will be remembered as a person of integrity.

CEOs touch people in a special way. CEOs who sell have a "signature" that's all their own. They create a look and feel that others associate with them that's as unique as the logo on their products.

Know what you want, and keep it simple and straightforward. CEOs

首席执行官的黄金销售原则

即使受到伤害，首席执行官也要坚持诚实。 这是日常交往中每个人都应该遵守的原则之一。 绝对、永远不要对首席执行官或其他人撒谎。 如果你一直无法判断销售的东西是否足以告之实情，那就卖点其他的东西。 首席执行官们承担不起撒谎的代价。 为什么？因为太多的人在听他们究竟在说什么，包括股东、媒体、雇员、供应商、客户，等等。 首席执行官们知道，那些问题账目是有人过度承诺和交付不足造成的。 首席执行官和我们这些卖出商品的人必须做好充分的准备，愿意并能够对我们写下或说过的每个字都问心无愧。 如果这意味着"辞退"今天的短期机会，那就让它如此。 你通常第二天就可以转回来。 当你再回来时，在人们的记忆里，你就是一个正直的人。

首席执行官以一种独特的方式与人接触。 做销售的首席执行官拥有完全属于自己的"签名"。 他们为与他们打交道的人创建了一种外观和感觉，这种外观和感觉就像他们产品上的标识一样独一无二。

知道你想要什么，并保持简单和直截了当。 首席执行官采用的

are incredibly simple in their approach. Every single CEO I interviewed was able to quickly and accurately articulate what they want. Can you? For example: "Your opinion on how to use my proven ideas to increase the size of your entry point orders, compress your sales cycle and get add-on business from your existing customers."

Show your feelings. How are you today? Oh, I'm fine. No, actually I just got word that my cholesterol level is dangerously high and I must go on a very restrictive diet. How many times do you tell someone how you really feel? How many times when you take that step are your feelings acknowledged by the other person? CEOs who sell show their own feelings and respond to others' feelings, and they are always in the present moment and time. Most of us think that doing this takes too much time. Actually, you'll save a lot of time if you take the lead from the CEO, and here's why. If you take the time to make every interaction you have with everyone on your way to the CEO's office memorable, your return trip will be much easier. Your calls will be accepted, voice-mail messages returned and ideas entertained. In other words, you'll get top-of-mind. Making yourself and your interactions memorable isn't that hard — all you have to do is show your feelings in a sincere way and acknowledge the feelings of others in a sincere way.

Say you're sorry when you mess up. Too many salespeople seem to assume it's bad etiquette to admit you've made a mistake. Nothing could be further from the truth! CEOs know the importance of taking personal responsibility, and so should you. That means saying and meaning those

方法简单得让人难以置信。 我交谈过的每个首席执行官都能快速和准确地表达出他们想要的东西。 你能吗？ 例如，"如何用我的切实有效的观点增加你的入口点订单量，压缩你的销售周期，从你的现有客户中获得附加业务，对这些问题你意下如何"。

真诚地表达你的感觉。 你今天好吗？ 哦，我很好。 不，不好。 实际上我刚刚知道，我的胆固醇指标已经高到了危险的状态，我必须严格节食。 你有多少次告诉他人你的真实感觉？ 这种真情实感的表达又有多少次得到他人的承认？ 做销售的首席执行官常常会在现场及时表达自己的感觉和应对别人的感受。 我们大多数人认为，这样做太费时了。 实际上，如果学习首席执行官的方法，你会节省大量的时间，原因如下。 如果你在前往办公室的路上花时间决定好与每个人的每一种令人难忘的交流方式，你的回程会容易得多。 人们会接受你的决定，回复你的电话留言，考虑你的想法。换句话说，你将获得最佳建议。 让你自己和你的行为给人留下难忘的印象并非那么困难——你所要做的只是用真实的方式表现你的情感，并用真实的方式认同他人的情感。

当你出错的时候说声对不起。 太多的销售人员似乎认为，承认自己犯了错误是件不体面的事。 没有什么比这种想法更不靠谱的了！ 首席执行官们知道承担个人责任的重要性，你也应知道。 这意味着当某事出错或即将出错时，就要说出和表达出"对不起"这样一些令人难堪的话。 应该是由你来传递这种信息，而不是其他的任何人。 理由是：其他人或许与你的动机不一样。

dreaded words "I'm sorry" when something goes wrong or is about to go wrong. You, not anyone else, should be the person to deliver this message, and here's why: Someone else may have a different agenda than you.

Look at people when you talk to them. Many of the interviews I conducted were done in person. In every case, the CEO always gave me a generous amount of eye contact. Why? Making appropriate eye contact is a necessary ingredient of effective listening. Besides, if you know what to look for, watching someone's eyes can tell you a lot about their feelings of what's being said. Generally speaking, the right kind of eye contact demonstrates a sincere purpose. Let's say that during a conversation with a CEO, they're giving you a consistent amount of eye contact. When you get to your third call objective — do you see any reason that you wouldn't do business with us? — they break their eye contact while answering. This is what I would call "out of integrity." It could very well be that there's something going on that he/she may not be at liberty to discuss with you. And the opposite of this is also true. Watch your eye contact when you give responses to questions. The best way to get your eyes to match your words is to always speak the truth. Remember, eyes don't lie — words do.

Get commitment early-on. This doesn't mean that you should invent meaningless questions or statements designed solely to get buyers bobbing①

---

① bob[bɔb] *vt.* 使上下快速摆动

　　与人交谈时眼睛一定要正视对方。 我亲自做过很多访谈。 无论哪种情况，首席执行官总是与我有着大量的目光交流。 为什么？ 进行适当的目光交流是有效倾听的一种必要成分。 此外，如果你知道想要寻找什么，注视别人的眼睛就可以帮你大量了解他们表达出的感情。 一般而言，正确的目光交流传递着真诚的目的。 举例来说，在与首席执行官交谈的过程中，他们会始终如一地与你保持目光接触。 当你达到第三个期待已久的目标时，即你会找到拒绝和我们做生意的理由吗？ 他们在回答时会中止目光接触。 这就是我称之为的"出于诚实"。 有时发生的事情很有可能使他/她无法自由与你交谈。 反之亦然。 对问题做出反应时注意目光接触。 眼睛与言语表达的最佳配合方式是永远讲真话。 请记住，眼睛不会说谎，言语谎话连篇。

　　尽早取得承诺。 这并不是说你应该虚拟一些毫无意义的问题或声明，只是故意让买者像没有思想的摇头娃娃一样上下点头。 我的意思是，首席执行官往往在早期从为他们完成工作或执行任务的人那里"大宗买进"承诺。 这是一种转移所有权的方式，而另一方毫无疑问地需要承担责任。 既然这是首席执行官的强硬领导和销售风格，那么当你要求承诺时，你就可以放心，他们会完全理解你们正在做什么，以及他们正在扮演什么角色。

　　勤问必有所得。 无论什么时候向首席执行官索求任何东西，你都会得到一些回报。 也许它与你的请求不完全匹配，但是你毕竟有所收获。 我成功的销售生涯就建立在简单的信仰之上，即你要求得

their heads up and down like mindless dashboard① olls. What I am talking about is that a CEO will always get early "buy in" from anyone who is to perform a task or mission for them. It's a way of transferring ownership so responsibility is unquestionably with the other party. Since this is a strong leadership and selling style of a CEO, you can rest assured that when you ask for it, they will understand exactly what you're doing and what part they are to play.

Ask and you shall receive. Whenever you ask a CEO for anything, you will get something in return. It may not be exactly what you asked for, but you will get something. I've built a successful sales career on the simple belief that the more you ask and the sooner you do so, the more and sooner you will sell.

Redefine the word no. I have an ironclad② policy about the word no — I never accept, at face value, any interruption that contains the word! You shouldn't either. Instead, you should ask yourself "Exactly what is this person saying no to?" Government agencies, school districts, county, state and municipalities③ and certain nonprofit organizations are governed by strict laws and policies that they must buy the lowest-price provider of any service they are in search of. Of course, there are ways around these requirements, such as being the only

---

① dashboard ['dæʃbɔːd] n. (汽车上的)仪表盘
② ironclad [aiən'klæd] adj. 坚固的
③ municipality [mjuːnisi'pæliti] n. 自治区

越多，这样做得越快，你就会卖得越多越快。

重新定义"不"字。 我对"不"字有一条铁定的原则，即我从不根据表面价值接受任何包含"不"字的干扰。 你也应该这样。相反，你应该扪心自问："这个人到底为什么说不？"政府机构、学区、县、州和自治区以及某些非营利的组织都受到严格的法律和政策管治，他们正在寻求的任何服务，都必须购买最低价格供应商的产品。 当然，满足这些需求有多种方式，比如说，成为某一特殊服务的唯一供应商，这就是通常称之为的"单一来源"合同。 但是一般说来，如果你不是最低价格供应商，你就不必做简短的列表。 如果不做简短的列表，你就不可能做销售。 这是一种经典的方式，它可以改变竞争环境，让首席执行官考虑真正的经营成本是什么。 在我多年的销售生涯中，我用这种回答应对"不"字，将高价的计算机系统销售到"低价取胜"的领域。

首席执行官们总是呼吁人们采取行动，你也应该这样。 这是第一次会议上问题的关键的一部分。 当谈到指定的承诺时，有些销售人员习惯于一种松弛的方法。 正如你到目前为止所了解的那样，但这不是首席执行官的风格。 首席执行官喜欢"行动"这个词，因此，他们经常要求自己的团队行动起来。 你可以对他们这样要求。我提到的行动是为首席执行官把一切整理得井然有序。 这些步骤是在首席执行官的管理下必然发生的结果。

provider of a particular service — what's typically called "sole-source" contracts. But generally speaking, if you're not the lowest-price provider you don't make the short list. And if you don't make the short list, you can't make the sale. This is a classic way to change the playing field and get this CEO to look at what the real cost of ownership is. For many years of my sales career, I sold the highest-price computer systems into the "lowest-price wins" world using this response to the word "no."

CEOs always issue a call to action, and you should, too. This is the part of the first meeting where the rubber meets the road. Some salespeople take a laid-back approach when it comes to specifying commitments. As you have learned so far, that's not the approach of a CEO. CEOs love the word action. They constantly ask it of their own team, so therefore; you can ask it of them. The action that I am referring to is one that puts everything in the proper order for the CEO — the steps that are necessary for results to happen in this CEO's organization.

(1,172 words)

知识链接

CEO 首席执行官（Chief Executive Officer）。首席执行官是在一个企业中负责日常经营管理的最高级管理人员，他向公司的董事会负责，而且往往是董事会的成员之一。首席执行官在公司或组织内部拥有最终的执行经营管理决策的权力。在较小的企业中，首席执行官可能同时又是董事会主席和总裁；但在大企业中，这些职务往往是由不同的人担任的，避免一个人在企业中扮演过大的角色、拥有过多的权力，同时也可以避免公司本身与公司的拥有人（即股东）之间发生利益冲突。

题　记

　　全球化正在迈入多方位的发展阶段，许多新兴市场的企业开始走上自己的跨国之路，以寻求获得深远的管理经验和发展机会，赢得全球竞争力。全球化时代的一个特征就是新兴市场的企业数目不断增长，尤其是来自被称为"金砖四国"经济体的巴西、俄罗斯、印度和中国，快速上升已成定势。美国最脍炙人口的啤酒品牌百威，已经被一家比利时-巴西的企业集团收购；好几家美国金融机构的龙头老大为了避免破产，不得不屈膝向阿拉伯各国和中国政府的主权财富基金求助；联想集团买下了美国国际商用机器公司的ThinkPad个人笔记本电脑业务；印度和中国的快速增长率已经转移了经济活动的平衡点，远远超越了早期崛起的人口较少的经济体日本和韩国。全球化的多方位发展阶段为商业贸易提供了提高全球生存水平的巨大潜力。

Multidirectional Phase of Globalization

Globalization used to mean, by and large, that business expanded from developed to emerging economies. Now it flows in both directions, and increasingly also from one developing economy to another. Business these days is all about "competing with everyone from everywhere for everything".

One sign of the times is the growing number of companies from emerging markets that appear in the Fortune 500 rankings of the world's biggest firms. It now stands at 62, mostly from the so-called BRIC economies of Brazil, Russia, India and China, and is set to rise rapidly. On current trends, emerging-market companies will account for one-third of the Fortune list within ten years, predicts Mark Spelman, head of a global think-tank run by Accenture, a consultancy.

There has been a sharp increase in the number of emerging-market companies acquiring established rich-world businesses and brands, starkly①

---

① starkly [ˈstɑːkli] *adv.* 明显地,毫无掩饰地

全球化的多方向发展阶段

　　总体而言，全球化在过去常常意味着商务交易从发达国家向新兴的经济体扩展。 如今，它在这两个方面都十分活跃，同时越来越多地从一个发展中国家向另外一个发展中国家迁移。 当今商务贸易的全部理念就是"与世界各地的每个人进行全方位的竞争"。

　　这个时代的一个特征就是新兴市场的企业数目不断增长，他们越来越多地出现在《财富》500强世界最大公司的排名中。 目前已有 62 家企业上榜，大部分来自被称为"金砖四国"经济体的巴西、俄罗斯、印度和中国。 快速上升已成定势。 埃森哲咨询公司管理的全球智库负责人、高级顾问马克·斯伯尔曼预计，根据目前的趋势，新兴市场的企业将在 10 年之内占据《财富》500 强名单的三分之一。

　　新兴市场企业的数量已经急剧上升，他们收购了发达国家的老牌企业和品牌，赤裸裸地显示 "全球化"不再仅仅是"美国化"的另一种表述。 在过去的一年中，美国最脍炙人口的啤酒品牌百威，已经被一家比利时-巴西的企业集团收购。 同时，好几家美国金融机构的龙头老大为了避免破产，不得不屈膝向阿拉伯各国和中国政府

demonstrating that "globalization" is no longer just another word for "Americanization". Within the past year, Budweiser, America's favourite beer has been bought by a Belgian-Brazilian conglomerate. And several of America's leading financial institutions avoided bankruptcy only by going cap in hand to the sovereign-wealth funds (state-owned investment funds) of various Arab kingdoms and the Chinese government.

When a company has its leading position in a domestic market buoyed by GDP growth rates that dwarf those in the country, it tends to afford a piece of Big one, just like Lenovo bought the ThinkPad from IBM in 2005, paid around \$1.75 billion. The GDP growth rates are lifting the incomes of millions of people to a level where they start to splash out on everything from new homes to cars to computers. The sheer size of the consumer markets now opening up in emerging economies, especially in India and China, and their rapid growth rates, will shift the balance of business activity far more than the earlier rise of less populous economies such as Japan and South Korea and their handful of "new champions" that seemed to threaten the old order at the time.

Globality is creating huge opportunities — as well as threats — for developed-world multinationals and new champions alike. The macroeconomic turbulence[①] that the world is now going through after almost a decade of smooth growth will probably not alter the picture

---

① turbulence ['tə:bjuləns] n. 波动

的主权财富基金（国有投资基金）求助。 当一家公司受国内生产总值增长率的支撑而在国内市场处于领先地位并使该国的其他公司相形见绌之时，它往往会购买一块更大的蛋糕，如同联想集团以大约17.5亿美元买下美国国际商用机器公司的 ThinkPad 个人笔记本电脑业务一样。 国内生产总值增长率提高了数百万人的收入，使得他们达到开始随意花钱置业的水平，包括新家、汽车和电脑。 现在，消费者市场的绝对规模在新兴市场中已经逐渐开放，尤其是在印度和中国，他们的快速增长率将转移经济活动的平衡点，远远超越了早期崛起的人口较少的经济体，如日本和韩国，以及似乎对当时的旧秩序形成威胁的少数"新盟主"。

　全球化为发达国家的跨国公司和类似的新盟主创造着巨大的机会，同样也对他们造成了威胁。 宏观经济经历了将近 10 年的平稳增长后，当今世界迎来了动荡不安的局势，这可能不会从根本上改变经济格局，但会使之复杂化。 尽管所有人都在谈论"关联系统分离"，但新兴经济体的增长近期已经趋于放缓阶段，因为他们面对的是越来越谨慎的美国消费者。 此外，油价和食品价格的上涨对许多新兴国家造成了通货膨胀的压力，而这些国家大多享受了随着高速经济增长而维持多年的稳定和低价。 快速发展带来了污染和水资源匮乏等副作用，这些都是需要应对的问题。 高盛投行的鲍伯·贺梅兹认为，"在全球化仅关注劳动生产率的很长一段时期之后，全球经济受到了挑战，尤其是新兴市场的经济，它将越来越多地提高资源生产率，更有效地使用燃料、原材料和水"。

fundamentally, but it will complicate it. Despite all the talk of "decoupling①", emerging economies have recently been growing more slowly because of their exposure to increasingly cautious American consumers. Moreover, high oil and food prices are creating inflationary pressures in many emerging countries that had enjoyed years of stable, low prices along with extraordinary economic growth. The side-effects of rapid development, such as pollution and water shortages, also need to be tackled. "After a long period in which globalization has been all about labor productivity, the business challenge everywhere, and especially in emerging markets, will increasingly be to raise resource productivity — using fuel, raw materials and water more efficiently," says Bob Hormats of Goldman Sachs, an investment bank.

Assuming that the upbeat growth forecasts for emerging markets remain broadly on track and the developed economies get back on their feet, what will be the main competitive battlegrounds of global business? One is those new consumers, who often demand products at far lower prices and often in more basic forms or smaller sizes than their developed-country counterparts. Emerging-market firms with experience of serving these consumers think they are better placed to devise such products than their developed-world competitors. The innovations in business models that designed to consumers' demand allow goods and services to be delivered in fundamentally different ways and at much lower. Although multinational

---

① decoupling [ˌdiːˈkʌplɪŋ] n. 解耦

　　假设新兴市场的增长前景保持乐观，大体步入正轨，发达国家的经济体重新自立，那么全球经济的主要竞争战场在哪里呢？　其中一部分是那些新的消费者，相比发达国家的消费者，他们通常要求产品以更低的价格、更基本的形式或更小的尺寸出售。　新兴市场的公司拥有为这些消费者服务的经验，他们认为，他们可以比发达国家的竞争者更好地设计出这样的产品。　这些为消费者需求所设计的商业模式创新使商品和服务以完全不同的方式和低得多的价格交付使用。　尽管发达国家的跨国公司必须与各种各样的遗产转让成本抗衡，包括财务上的（退休金、医保责任）、组织上的（总部离新市场很远）以及文化上的（思维的旧模式），他们也有自己的优势。　其中最大的优势可能在于大量的管理经验，而这往往是新兴市场的公司不足之处。　当一家公司面临全球化发展时，它必须竭尽全力融合公司内部风格迥异的文化。　许多内情报告中写进了这样一条："不管在什么情况下，都可以假设人们的动机善良，刻意地理解他人和被理解，尊重文化差异"是促进"跨文化有效团队工作"的途径。简而言之，联想集团之类的中国公司正在大踏步地前进，他们在全球化时代为成功的跨国公司树立了榜样。

　　新盟主的出现是否以牺牲优质态势为代价、并能够反映资本主义不良形式的发展吗？　担忧者指出，通过企业并购和国有资产的投资，国家在全球经济中扮演的角色正在快速扩张。　根据国家干预经济的令人惋惜的历史来看，部分预测者认为，过于膨胀的全球化并非是个好兆头。　如果仅仅是因为正在发生的事是全新的体验，无论

companies in developed countries must grapple① with legacy costs of various kinds — financial (pensions, health-care liabilities), organizational (headquarters far away from new markets) and cultural (old ways of thinking) — they have advantages too. The greatest of these may be a deep well of managerial experience, which emerging-market firms often lack. When a firm grows globally, a huge effort has to be made to integrate the different cultures within it. "In all situations: assume good intentions; be intentional about understanding others and being understood; respect cultural differences," reads one of many tip sheets to promote "effective teamwork across cultures". In short, firms in China like Lenovo are well on their way to becoming role models for successful multinational company in the age of globality.

Could the rise of the new champions reflect the advance of bad forms of capitalism at the expense of good forms? The worriers point out that, through corporate acquisitions and the investments of sovereign-wealth funds, the role of the state in the global economy is rapidly expanding. Given the lamentable history of state intervention in business, some predictors figure out that expanding too much globally does not bode well. Such fears are not easily dismissed, if only because what is happening is so new that there is not much evidence either way. Sovereign-wealth funds insist that they are interested only in getting a good return on their money and will not meddle in politics. Perhaps they will turn out to be sources of

---

① grapple ['græpl] vi. 与……格斗

哪种方式都没有前车之鉴，这种担心恐怕真难以消除。 国有资金主张，他们只对资金的高回报感兴趣，不会插手政治。 令人钦佩的是，与发达国家越来越多的短期机构投资者相比，也许他们是良好的公司治理和耐心资本的来源。 但也许不是。

联想集团提供了一个鼓舞人心的例子。 尽管联想最大的股东在中国，但是它对美国国际商用机器公司个人电脑业务的收购看上去并没有带来任何令人不安的后果。 但是，也有可能这个股东受到其联合投资者的限制，联合投资者是两个美国主要的私募股权公司。此外，联想也许并不能代表新盟主，而俄罗斯天然气工业股份公司却当之无愧，这使俄罗斯政府可以对海外业务从中作梗。 如同联想总裁杨元庆先生指出的，在《财富》500强上榜的29家中国企业中，联想是"唯一一家完全由市场驱动的"企业。 大部分其他的企业都在享受着垄断势力或者在自然资源行业运营，与消费类电子产品相比，存在着更大范围的政治影响力和腐败。 至少，政府所起的作用越来越大，这种现象造成了一种感觉，即来自新兴经济体的盟主和投资者的竞争是不公平的，富裕国家的公司可能输给那些运营欠佳的竞争者，他们享受着补贴资金，或者有特权获得资源供应。所以，确实存在着风险，不良资本在未来几十年将会泛滥成灾。 但是，与此同时的最新看法是，全球化的多方向发展阶段为商业贸易提供了提高全球生存水平的巨大潜力。

good corporate governance and patient capital, in admirable contrast to the growing number of short-term institutional investors in developed countries. But perhaps they will not.

Lenovo offers an encouraging example. Even though its largest shareholder is in China, its acquisition of IBM's PC business does not seem to have had any troubling consequences. But maybe the shareholder was restrained by its co-investors, two of America's leading private-equity firms. Besides, the new champions may be typified not by Lenovo but by, say, Gazprom, through which the Russian state can make mischief abroad. As Mr. Yang Yuanqing, Lenovo's chairman, points out, of the 29 Chinese firms in the Fortune 500, Lenovo is the "only one that is truly market-driven". Most of the rest enjoy monopoly power or operate in the natural-resources industries, where there is far more scope for politics and corruption than in consumer electronics. At the very least, the growing role of states creates a sense that the competition from emerging-economy champions and investors is unfair, and that rich-country firms may lose out to less well-run competitors who enjoy subsidized capital, or privileged access to resource supplies. So there is a real risk that bad capitalism will spread in the coming decades. Yet at the same time this latest, multidirectional phase of globalization offers enormous potential for business to raise living standards around the world.

(1,067 words)

知识链接

BRICs 金砖四国。"金砖四国"来源于英文 BRICs 一词，指巴西（Brazil）、俄罗斯（Russia）、印度（India）和中国（China）四国，因这四个国家的英文名称首字母组合而成的"BRICs"，其发音与英文中的"砖块"（bricks）一词非常相似，故被称为"金砖四国"。其中，巴西被称为"世界原料基地"；俄罗斯被称为"世界加油站"；印度被称为"世界办公室"；中国被称为"世界工厂"。"金砖四国"的国土面积占世界领土总面积的 26%，人口占全球总人口的 42%。随着四国经济的快速增长，其国际影响力与日俱增。

题 记

在高级金融人士的圈子里，数 10 亿美元的交易可以在鸡尾酒和甜点的觥筹交错之间落下帷幕，一项曾经被称之为并购融资的鲜为人知的交易近来成为商家最热门的游戏。在公司蓄意收购者横行霸道、华尔街被短期利益困扰之际，融资收购提供了良好的商业模式。美国零售商梅西百货公司策划了史上最雄心勃勃的融资游戏，美国家庭国际公司并购了包括从美国东海岸到西海岸的五金器具店铺和本·富兰克林连锁便利店，玫琳凯化妆品公司的董事长买进了公司的全部股权，美国最大的品牌服装制造商李维·斯特劳斯获得了一群公司高管和公司创始人后裔的投资。当管理者一次次地获得、支付和归还资金时，他们也在为公司制造生命的血液，从而使失败的企业重获生机，使有活力的企业持续繁荣。

The Popular Game of Going Private

In the world of high finance, where billion-dollar deals can be struck between cocktails and dessert, the hottest play these days is a once obscure transaction known as the leveraged buyout. In such operations, corporate officers are turning publicly held firms into private businesses that are free from the demands of short-term investors and the unwanted attention of corporate raiders. In the process many of them are making vast progress. All that is needed to play this lucrative① game is mountains of borrowed money — or leverage, in financial jargon — which lenders seem eager to provide. A record $ 10. 8 billion was spent to take companies private last year, vs. just $ 636 million three years ago. This year's pace is even more furious.

One of the largest and most ambitious buyouts yet was proposed by executives of Macy & Co., the eleventh-biggest U. S. retailer. Led by Chairman Edward Finkelstein, a group of top officers offered $ 70 a share, or $ 3. 58 billion, for Macy's stock that had been selling for

---

① lucrative [ˈljuːkrətiv] *adj.* 获利多的，赚钱的

走向私有化的流行游戏

在高级金融人士的圈子里，数 10 亿美元的交易可以在鸡尾酒和甜点的觥筹交错之间落下帷幕，一项曾经被称之为融资收购的鲜为人知的交易近来成为商家最热门的游戏。 在这样的交易中，公司的管理人员将上市公司转为私营企业，这些私营企业摆脱了短期投资者的要求和企业掠夺者的不必要的关注。 在这个过程中，他们中的很多人取得了很大的进步。 玩这种有利可图的游戏只需要借入大量的资本，用金融行话来说就是杠杆作用，即出借方似乎迫不及待地提供的资金。 去年，公司私营化的资金创纪录地达到 108 亿美元，而三年前仅为 6.36 亿美元。 今年的融资速度甚至更加疯狂。

美国排名第十一的零售商梅西百货公司的高管们提议的并购无疑是最大和最雄心勃勃的融资之一。 爱德华·芬克尔斯坦董事长导演了这场游戏。 一群高级管理人员为梅西股票提供每股 70 美元或 35.8 亿美元的资金，而此前的卖出价约为每股 50 美元。 事实上，梅西百货的高管们正在与华尔街的高盛集团合作，为募集所有的资金做准备。 高价收购显然是有计划地击退竞争对手的投资，避免公

about $ 50 a share. The Macy's executives were working with the Wall Street firm of Goldman Sachs to line up virtually all that money. The high buyout price, apparently designed to repel rival offers and avoid a bidding war for the company, drove up the value of other retailing issues as investors speculated that a wave of buyouts was about to break over the department-store industry. Indeed, merchandising firms are much in vogue with acquisition-minded managers. One day after the Macy's announcement, officers of Household International agreed to pay $ 700 million for the Chicago-based conglomerate's retailing units, which include Coast-to-Coast hardware and the Ben Franklin variety chain. Even small Wieboldt Stores, a 102-year-old Chicago concern, also announced a $ 37. 4 million deal that turned the firm into a private company. Consumer-product companies have been going private as well. Mary Kay Ash, chairman of Mary Kay Cosmetics, began a $ 300 million buyout of her company. San Francisco-based Levi Strauss, the largest brand-name clothing maker in the U.S., was acquired for $ 1. 48 billion by a group headed by corporate executives and descendants of the company's founder.

Some skittish① firms turn to buyouts to escape unwelcome suitors. "Management has often used them as a weapon to defend against hostile takeovers, " says Burton Malkiel, dean of the Yale School of Organization and Management. Directors of Storer Communications, a major cable-TV operator, voted to take the company private for $ 93. 50

---

① skittish ['skitiʃ] *adj.* 容易激动的,轻佻的

司间的竞购战，以此抬高其他零售业务的价值，因为投资者推测，收购的浪潮即将袭击百货行业。 的确，商品销售类企业有收购头脑的经理多如牛毛。 梅西百货宣布收购一天之后，美国家庭国际公司的官员们同意为总部设在芝加哥的大型企业零售集团支付 7 亿美元，收购包括从美国东海岸到西海岸的五金器具店铺和本·富兰克林连锁便利店。 即使是经营了 102 年的芝加哥小商店韦伯尔特，也宣布融资 3 740 万美元成立私营公司。 消费品公司也加入了私营化的行列。 玫琳凯化妆品公司的董事长玫琳·凯·艾施以 3 亿美元买进全部股权。 总部位于旧金山的美国最大的品牌服装制造商——李维·斯特劳斯，获得了一群公司高管和公司创始人后裔 14.8 亿美元的投资。

一些不太稳定的企业求助于并购基金，以逃避不受欢迎的起诉者。 耶鲁大学组织与管理学院的院长伯顿·麦基尔说："管理层常常把他们当做武器，抵御恶意收购。"一家主要的有线电视运营商斯托尔通信公司的董事们采取投票表决的方式，以每股 93.50 美元将该公司私有化，没有接受一家较小的有线电视公司康卡斯特 95~96 美元/股的出价。 露华浓公司推行了一条相似的路线，它安排了一场复杂的 18 亿美元的交易，这笔交易将会拆分化妆品公司，但可以逃脱佛罗里达食品零售商派泰·普莱特的掌心。 当法院驳回露华浓公司以 5.25 亿美元的廉价出售两个分公司的计划之时，公司蒙受了巨大的损失。 这项裁决使派泰·普莱特继续享有接管权。

a share, rather than accept a $ 95-to- $ 96 bid from Comcast, a smaller cable company. Revlon pursued a similar path when it arranged a complex $ 1. 8 billion transaction that would break up the cosmetics firm but keep it out of the hands of Pantry Pride, a Florida retailer. Revlon suffered a setback when a court struck down its plan to sell two divisions for a bargain price of $ 525 million as part of the proposed deal. The ruling allowed Pantry Pride to continue its take-over effort.

Management buyouts are evolving into offensive weapons too. "They can be viewed as offers made by internal raiders, " notes Alfred Rappaport, professor of accounting at Northwestern University's Kellogg School of Management. In one snarled① battle, investors, led by the former chairman of a Beatrice acquisition, offered nearly $ 5 billion for Beatrice, which once rejected the bid. Now Beatrice may be turning to outsiders for help. Said one Chicago lawyer: "Their investment bankers are burning up the phone lines looking for a white knight." Beatrice received word of a different kind of proposal that the firm may wish to ponder. It came from Warren Avis, founder of the Avis car-rental company. The entrepreneur, who sold Avis, said he wants to buy it back from Beatrice, which has owned the business for little more than a year. Avis said he has assembled a group of private, international investors who hope to acquire the auto concern, which operates in more than 100 countries and is worth an estimated $ 400 million.

---

① snarl [snɑːl] *vt.* 咆哮着说

　　管理层的收购也正在演变成攻击性的武器。 美国西北大学凯洛格管理学院会计学教授阿尔弗雷德·拉巴波特指出："他们可以被看做内部入侵者发动的攻击"。 在一个纠缠不清的战场上，比阿特丽斯公司的前主席领导的投资者出资近 50 亿美元收购了比阿特丽斯，但比阿特丽斯曾拒绝过此项交易。 现在，比阿特丽斯可能会转向外界寻求帮助。 一位芝加哥的律师说："他们的投资银行家打爆了电话，四处寻找白衣骑士"。 比阿特丽斯收到了不同的建议，公司也许希望深入探讨这个问题。 建议来自艾维士汽车租赁公司的创始人华伦·艾维士。 这位出售了艾维士的企业家认为，他希望从比阿特丽斯回购艾维士，因为他经营公司才一年多的时间。 艾维士说，他已经邀请了一群个体国际投资者，他们希望收购这家汽车机构，艾维士汽车租赁公司在 100 多个国家运营，估价 4 亿美元。

　　管理层收购是热点，并且是不断增长的热点，因为他们到目前为止产生了无数的赢家，即使有输家也少得可怜。 典型的交易包括银行家、机构投资者、专门从事收购的华尔街公司以及被兼并公司的经理们。 要启动一项交易，高管们求助于华尔街的专家安排融资。 一家专门从事收购的投资公司阿德勒和谢肯公司的执行合伙人伦纳德·谢肯说："我们关注三方面的事情：公司以往的恒定利润、可预见的未来利润和质量管理。"一旦做出收购决定，谢肯会轮流拜访银行和养老基金及保险公司之类的大型投资者，这些机构可以给他提供贷款。 银行对外国、钻探石油的人和其他风险债务人放贷时

Management buyouts are hot and growing hotter because they have so far produced countless winners and few if any losers. A typical deal involves bankers, institutional investors, Wall Street firms that specialize in buyouts and the managers of acquired companies. To start a transaction, the executives turn to Wall Street experts to arrange financing. "We look for three things," says Leonard Shaykin, managing partner of Adler & Shaykin, an investment house that specializes in buyouts. "They are consistent past profits, predictable future profits and quality management." Once he decides to work on a deal, Shaykin makes the rounds of banks and large investors like pension funds and insurance companies, which put up the loan money. Banks are leery① of lending to foreign countries, oil drillers and other risky debtors, but they are happy to provide up to 70% of the cost of a buyout because of the large fees and lucrative interest rates that such business brings. The rest of the credit comes from selling so-called junk bonds — IOUs with relatively poor quality ratings — and other securities that offer high yields. Like the banks, investors count on getting their money back from earnings of the acquired firm or from the sale of its assets. "Lenders look for a business that is very stable," says a California moneyman. "The company ought to generate lots of cash."

The popularity of buyouts has received an added boost from the U.S. tax code, which permits investors to deduct the interest on their debts.

---

① leery ['liəri] *adj.* 机敏的，狡猾的

十分谨慎，但他们乐意提供高达 70% 的收购费用，因为这种交易会带来大笔酬金和利润丰厚的利率。 其他的贷款来自销售所谓的垃圾债券，如质量相对低劣的评级借据，以及提供高产出的其他债券。投资者像银行一样，靠收购公司的盈利或变卖它的固定资产收回他们的资金。 加利福尼亚州的一位金融投资者说："贷方希望做一桩稳定的交易。 公司应该能够衍生大量的现金。"

美国税法助长了收购的流行，它允许投资者扣除债务利息。 这使得大额借款具有吸引力，因为债务人可以使用借据避税，从而收取部分费用交给山姆大叔。 耶鲁大学的麦基尔认为，"我们的税法明确鼓励这种活动"。 接二连三的收购已经令人忧心忡忡：如果利率攀升或经济陷入萧条，公司可能会被巨额债务击垮。 其他的批评人士直言，公司私有化是浪费稀缺资本。 一家曼哈顿投资公司——M.J.惠特曼有限公司的总裁马丁·惠特曼说："作为金融家，我认为这是一种轻而易举的致富之道。 但作为爱国的公民，我认为，国家的货币供应量应该有更好和更富有成效的用途，而不是创造偿还股东的债务。"然而，负债累累的交易有其捍卫者。 华盛顿美国企业研究所财政政策研究主管约翰·金表示："我认为举债经营不是一件坏事。 极少有人买房不贷款的，这是现代金融的一个非常重要的工具。"在公司蓄意收购者横行霸道、华尔街被短期利益而不是长期战略困扰之际，融资收购通常提供了良好的商业模式。

That makes heavy borrowing attractive, since debtors can use IOUs as tax shelters and thus charge part of their cost to Uncle Sam. "Our tax laws clearly encourage this kind of activity," says Yale's Malkiel. The spate① of buyouts has raised fears that companies may be crushed by their huge debts if interest rates climb or the economy falls into a recession. Other critics call going private a waste of scarce capital. "As a financier, I regard it as an easy way to get rich," says Martin Whitman, president of M.J. Whitman & Co., a Manhattan investment firm. "But as a citizen who loves his country, I think there are better and more productive uses of the nation's money supply than to create debt to pay off stockholders." Yet the debt-laden deals have their defenders. "I don't think leverage is a bad thing," says John Makin, director of fiscal-policy studies at Washington's American Enterprise Institute. "Very few people would own a house without it. It is a very important tool of modern finance." At a time when corporate raiders are on the rampage and Wall Street has become obsessed with short-term gains rather than long-term strategy, buyouts are often just good business.

(1,105 words)

---

① spate [speit] *n.* 大量,许多

知识链接

Macy & Co. 梅西百货。美国梅西百货公司是美国联合百货公司旗下公司（1994 年美国联合百货公司收购了梅西百货公司）。它是美国的著名连锁百货公司，梅西百货公司是美国的高档百货商店，主要经营服装、鞋帽和家庭装饰品，以优质的服务赢得美誉，其旗舰店位于纽约市海诺德广场（Herald Square）。1924 年梅西百货公司在第 7 大道开张时曾被宣传为"世界最大商店"。梅西百货公司还有 2 个全国性旗舰店，分别设在旧金山的联合广场和芝加哥州街。其公司规模虽然不是很大，但在美国和世界有很高的知名度。

Uncle Sam 山姆大叔。山姆大叔通常指美国政府或者美国人。

题 记

　　无论你决定投身其中，还是决定置身事外，首次公开募股中投资人获取的收益和风险一如既往地刺激着你的神经。巴菲特有句名言似乎应验了首次公开募股投资人的不择手段：当市场疯狂时，多数人都是舞会中的灰姑娘，明知在舞池中多待一会，现出原形的几率就越高，但多数人还是舍不得错过这场盛大舞会的高潮部分。首次公开募股的投资人涵盖的范围很广，既有天使投资人，也有早期和中期阶段的风险投资人；既有增长型私有股权人，也有清购存货的艺术家。首次公开募股的禁售期使投资人犹如热锅上的蚂蚁，焦躁不安，诚惶诚恐，却不知打开门来迎接运气，赚他个盆满钵满；首次公开募股的使命感使投资人感受到精神力量的伟大，他们不仅成为首次公开募股的忠实拥趸，而且凭借持有策略拥有了丰厚的盈余。

The Investors for IPO

It's shaping up to be a bleak year for IPOs. BG Medicine pulled its initial public offering, citing market conditions. Elixir Pharmaceuticals also put its IPO plans on ice. But the idea of IPOs was alive and well, when I had the pleasure of moderating a great discussion — Are You Ready for IPO? — before some 300 guests at MIT's Kresge auditorium and who knows how many others who watched on a special TV broadcast at 45 locations worldwide.

We dissected① the current climate for IPOs, bleak no matter how you slice it, the spectrum of investors — from angels, to early and mid-stage VCs, to growth private equity folks like Goldstein and Evans, who typically invest in established, profitable companies looking to move to the next level, to buyout artists who use as much debt as possible to purchase companies that typically are not growing very fast. Along the way, we heard some riveting tales from Bush and Goodman about what it was actually like to go on the IPO road show, the wheeling and dealing with

---

① dissect [di'sekt] *vt.* 仔细分析和研究

首次公开募股中的投资人

就首次公开募股的表现而言，这是暗淡的一年。 BG 医药公司以市场行情为由，从首次公开募股中抽身。 易胜制药也搁置了首次公开募股计划。 但是，首次公开募股的观点依然完好无损，我有幸主持了一次伟大的讨论：你为首次公开募股做好准备了吗？ 大约有300 位来宾在麻省理工学院的克雷斯吉大礼堂参加了讨论，说不定还有很多人在世界各地的 45 个地方观看过这个特别的电视节目。

我们仔细考察了当前的市场环境，对首次公开募股来说，无论你如何细分，前景都十分渺茫，投资人涵盖的范围很广，既有天使投资人，也有早期和中期阶段的风险投资人；还有像哥德斯坦和埃文斯之类的增长型私人股权人，他们通常投资老牌盈利公司，希望进入下一个级别；也有清购存货的艺术家，他们尽可能多地使用债权，通常购买增长不那么快的公司。 在首次公开募股的过程中，我们还从布什和古德曼那里听到这样一些引人入胜的故事，包括继续坚持首次公开募股路演的实际情况如何、不择手段地与投资银行家打交道、私人飞机和黑色轿车、禁售期以及其他的很多问题。 在我们的讨论接近尾声时，布什突然抛出一些他已经写下的笔记，让周围的人蠢蠢欲动，他对那些有一天可能会寻求自己的首次公开募股

investment bankers, the private jets and black sedans, lock-up periods, and a lot more. Somewhere near the end of our discussion, Bush whipped out some notes he had taken and delighted the crowd dispensing some key advice to entrepreneurs who might one day seek their own IPO.

Now, to put his comments in perspective, it's important to know that Bush is anything but demure. Like when I said: "People often ask you how you are related to the President, and I'm told that's not the right question: How is the President related to you?" And he said: "Yeah, you're goddamn right. The President is my cousin, and he lobbied hard for the role and succeeded in the end. We took him. Sometimes we think about putting him back." I figured pearls of wisdom from such a character were too good to pass up, so I snatched① his notes and convinced the MIT Enterprise Forum's Greg Wymer to let me listen to a private video feed of the broadcast so I could get things exactly right. The result is a slight hodgepodge② and condensation of what he wrote and what he said at various times during the event. It all started when we were talking about investment bankers — and that seems to have set him off:
"The investment bankers are really charming and incredibly good negotiators ... they're very savvy, very svelte③ kind of smooth talkers, and you can see a lot of use for that after you've been, you know, kind of

---

① snatch [snætʃ] vt. 抓住
② hodgepodge [ˈhɒdʒpɒdʒ] n. 混合物
③ svelte [svelt] adj. 清晰的

的企业家们给出了一些关键性的建议。

现在，为了正确地领悟他的看法，重要的是要明白，布什绝对没有假装正经。就像当我问他："人们经常会问，你跟总统有什么关系，我会说，这个问题问得不好，正确的问法是：总统跟你有什么关系？"然后他回答说："呵呵，你说得太对了。总统是我的堂兄，他为了这个职位煞费苦心地四处游说，最终成功上位。我们只得承认这个事实。有时，我们还在考虑让他重回原位。"我感受到这种人身上焕发出的智慧的光芒，简直无与伦比，不容拒绝，所以我很快接收了他的建议，对麻省理工学院企业论坛的古瑞格·怀墨让我听的一段电台播放的私人视频深信不疑，这样我就可以完全正确地处理事情。结果是他在这个事件中的不同时期表现不一，他所写的和他所说的显得有点杂乱无章和过分简洁。当我们谈论投资银行家的时候，这一切就开始了。他似乎就是这样突然开始讲了起来："投资银行家真是有魅力，是令人难以置信的谈判好手……他们非常精明，非常和蔼，是那种能说会道的人，你和他们接触之后就会发现，你可能在很大程度上被他们玩弄于股掌之间，你知道，就是那种被他们切成了碎片的感觉。我希望有人，抑或是我们的律师，抑或是别的什么人，已经给我列了一张清单。我能给你列个清单吗？"

关于禁售期的表态。禁售期指的是公司上市后，公司内部的关键人士不得抛售自己的股票。"有一个禁售期，他们说，'通常是 180天。情况就是如此。'好吧，绝对不需要 180 天。它可以根据你的谈判结果而定。现在，你不应该急于出售你的股权，这是荒谬的买卖。但是，你应该谈判，因为有多种监视你的窗口，当你宣布你打

filleted by them. I wish that somebody, either our lawyer, or somebody, had given me a list. Can I give you the list?"

On lockup (the period after a company goes public when key insiders can't sell their stock) . "There's a lockup and they say, 'It's always got to be 180 days. It's just what's done.' Well it absolutely does not have to be 180 days. It can be whatever you negotiate. Now you shouldn't go and rush the sell, it's ridiculous to sell. But you should negotiate that, because there are windows where you're allowed to sell that can't be too near when you're announcing how you did. This makes sense to me. But you don't want to lock yourself up in an artificial way because what happens is — and I didn't get this — the lockup then gets used as a mechanism for them to come back and sell you a secondary offering for another fee. You get out of the lockup if you hire them to do a secondary, and you don't get out of it if you don't. Well, I didn't know that. There's something called a 10b5-1 plan — this plan can't be launched until your lockup is over, but it has to burn in for a certain number of months, and so you add to your lockup. There's no reason why they couldn't let you start your 10b5-1 plans so that by the time the lockup is over you get to start selling. These don't seem to matter until you're right there and you know you've bought a house, or you're feeling like, 'Jesus, everybody else is doing this dance, and I'm sitting here' — not just you but your whole team, is like 'Dude, what the heck, we're all walking LBOs, and everybody else has made a zillion dollars.' And I think you have to stand up to those guys just on

算如何做的时候，他们不会允许你刚拿到股权就抛空。 这对我很有意义。 但是，你肯定不想让自己被人为地锁定，因为发生的情况是，他们因此把股权锁定当成工具，回笼证券并再次收费二次发行。 当然，我没有碰到过这种情况。 如果你雇人进行第二轮融资，你就摆脱了股权锁定；如果你没有这么做，你就无法摆脱股权锁定。 当然，我对这一点还不是很清楚。 有一个所谓的 10b5-1 计划，该计划要到你的禁售期结束时方可启动，但它会让人在好几个月里焦虑不安，让你与股权牢牢绑定。 他们没有理由不让你启动你的 10b5-1 计划，所以禁售期一旦结束，你就可以开始销售股票。 直到你真正进入状态时，才发现这些似乎很重要，你要知道，你已经买了房，或者你仿佛有这种感觉：'天啊，每个人都在欢呼雀跃地做着这件事，而我却坐在这里无动于衷。'不仅是你，还有你的整个团队，似乎都在大发感慨：'老兄，真见鬼，我们都在做杠杆收购，而其他人赚的美元已经达到了天文数字。'我认为，你必须勇敢地抵抗那些只知道按原则办事的家伙。"当运气敲门时，不妨打开门来迎接吧。

坚持你的使命。"拥有使命感是如此重要，我们已经从社会使命中获益匪浅。 事实上，我们相信，我们在此是为了把经营诚信纳入卫生保健。 我们这一代人没有太多实实在在的机会获得精神使命，因此，我们发现，如果你能够在工作场所感受到这样的使命，你就会从芸芸众生中获得同样的伟大、内在的伟大。 我们需要大量地依靠这种伟大的力量，因为它的作用不言而喻。""虽然建议并不总是正确，但所有的建议都非常重要。 因此，就算是错误的建议，也不要轻易地否决。"古德曼提出了一条有益的忠告：不要急躁莽撞。

principle." Open the door when luck knocks.

Hang onto your mission. "It's just so important to have a mission. We have benefited tremendously from a social mission. We actually believe we are here to put operational integrity into health care. There's not a lot of real opportunities for spiritual mission in our generation, and so we find if you can provide that in the workplace you will get that same kind of bigness, inner bigness, from people. And we've needed to rely on that a lot, and it's worked." "No advice is ever right, but all of it is incredibly important. So just because it's wrong, don't blow it off." And a bonus from Goodman: Don't rush. "Be ready before you go. The business needs to be ready, the team needs to be ready, and the board needs to be ready. And get lots of great advisers around you."

(891 words)

"在首次公开募股之前做好准备。 企业需要做好准备，团队需要做好准备，董事会需要做好准备。 而且，身边还要有很多资深顾问。"

知识链接 🔍

IPO 首次公开募股(Initial public offering)。首次公开募股指某公司(股份有限公司或有限责任公司)首次向社会公众公开招股的发行方式。有限责任公司首次公开募股后会成为股份有限公司。对应于一级市场，大部分公开发行股票由投资银行集团承销而进入市场，银行按照一定的折扣价从发行方购买到自己的账户，然后以约定的价格出售。

题　记

房地产经济泡沫是引发美国金融风暴的催化剂之一。而房地产市场不仅是民生所系，也是观察一个国家经济运行的晴雨表。为了拯救楼市，美国政府通过整顿金融市场、加大财政投入等多种措施来试图挽救这场危机。专家们希望，住房价格的回升能够增加公众对范围更广的经济领域的信心，刺激银行再次放贷。曾几何时，信用卡的狂轰滥炸让美国人应接不暇，现在却是一卡难求。信贷束缚使大大小小的公司奄奄一息，房地产市场形成了一种恶性循环：信用紧缩意味着购房更加困难；房屋买卖一旦陷入困境，房价随之进一步下跌；房价止跌无门又导致取消抵押品赎回权越来越多。也许美国政府可以借鉴罗斯福新政，针对当前的实际，顺应广大人民群众的意志，大刀阔斧地实施一系列旨在克服危机的政策措施。

Mending Housing Market

Washington's financial bailout plan is now law. So the credit spigot will start flowing again, banks will resume lending, and an economic recovery can begin, right? Wrong. Experts say the most important thing that needs to happen before the government bailout even has a chance of working: Home prices must stop falling. That would send a signal to banks that the worst has passed and it's safe to start doling① out money again. The problem is the lending freeze has made getting a mortgage loan tough for everyone except those with sterling credit. That means it will take several months or longer to pare down② the glut③ of houses built when times were good — and those that have come on the market because of soaring foreclosures④— before home prices start appreciating. Housing is a critical component to the U.S. economy and by extension the availability of credit. Roughly one in eight U.S. jobs depends on housing directly or

---

① dole[dɔl] *vt.* 少量地发放
② pare down 减少
③ glut [glʌt] *n.* 供应过多
④ foreclosure [fɔː ˈkləuʒə] *n.* 丧失抵押品赎回权

整顿住房市场

华盛顿的财政救助计划现在已经成为法规。于是，信贷水龙头将再次打开，银行将会恢复贷款，经济复苏即将开始，对吗？不对。专家们指出，在政府救助可能生效之前，还需要一个非常重要的条件：住房价格必须停止下跌。这将给银行发送一个信号，最坏的时期已经过去，再次少量发放贷款是安全的。问题是，贷款冻结已经使所有人的抵押贷款变得困难重重，这些人还不包括那些拥有英镑贷款的人。也就是说，在经济状况不错时，我们需要花费数月或者更长时间来减少建房的供给，即在房价开始回升之前，削减那些由于丧失抵押品赎回权的房主数量不断上升而流向市场的建房贷款。住房供给是美国经济中的关键部分，它影响着获得信贷的可能性。美国大概有八分之一的工作直接或间接地依赖于住房，包括建筑工人、银行信贷员以及华尔街的大经纪人。住房价格的回升将会增加公众对范围更广的经济领域的信心，同时，专家们希望，它能刺激银行再次放贷。

瓦乔维亚证券所的资深经济专家加里·泰耶尔认为，"传统上，住房确实可以带领经济走向复苏。我认为，要在这个经济周期实现持续复苏，住房同样也将会是关键。"与此同时，诸如艾丽西娅·埃

indirectly — from construction workers to bank loan officers to big brokers on Wall Street. A turnaround in housing prices would boost confidence in the wider economy and, experts hope, goad banks into lending again.

"Housing traditionally does lead the economy through a recovery. I think it's going to be critical for a sustained recovery in this cycle, too, " said Gary Thayer, senior economist at Wachovia Securities. In the meantime, people like Alicia Elliott are adjusting to a new American reality: Life without credit. The 21-year old Morgantown, W. Va., resident just bought a used mobile home, borrowing $ 4,000 from friends and family because she couldn't get a bank loan. "I tried to. Couldn't do it. It's just hard to get a loan, " said Elliott, who works as a cashier at a Lowe's Cos. store. She used to get bombarded with offers for credit cards. Now she can't even get one. "I get denied one after another after another. It doesn't matter if you have a co-signer or not, " she said. Trey Simmons, a 31-year-old barber at a Dallas hair salon, said he worries tighter lending standard will squash his goal of buying a home. "Credit is a privilege everybody can't get, " Simmons said. "I had credit at a young age and messed up." He now operates on a strictly cash basis. "If I don't have it, " he said, referring to cash, "I don't spend it."

The dilemma boils down to a matter of trust. "Credit, by definition, means trust and faith, and for many reasons trust and faith have been damaged, " said Sung Won Sohn, an economics professor at California State University, Channel Islands. Sohn said the near certainty

利奥特之类的人正在调整，以适应一种新的美国现实：没有借贷的生活。 这个来自弗吉尼亚州摩根镇只有 21 岁的居民，从亲戚朋友处借了 4 000 美元，买了一间二手移动房，因为她不能从银行获得贷款。 家居装饰连锁公司劳氏集团商店的收银员埃利奥特说："我尝试过。 但还是不能做到。 贷款太难了。"曾几何时，信用卡的狂轰滥炸让她应接不暇。 现在却是一卡难求。 她说："我被一家又一家的银行拒之门外。 不管你有没有担保人都是一样。"在达拉斯发艺沙龙工作的 31 岁的理发师特利·西蒙斯表示，他担心更严格的借贷标准将会压制他的买房目标。 西蒙斯声称："贷款并非是每个人享有的特权。 我小时候贷过款，结果弄得一团糟。"他现在执行一套严格的现金支付制。 他对现金的看法是："如果我没有现金，我就不花钱。"

这种两难的境地归结为信誉问题。 加州州立大学海峡岛分校的经济学教授宋·桓·索恩认为："根据定义，信誉指的是信任和诚信，有很多因素已经破坏了这种信任和诚信。"索恩指出，经济萧条已经成为近期的必然趋势，这使全国各地数千家中、小型银行不敢借款给埃利奥特之类的人，他们认为这样做的风险太大，难以承受。 索恩曾经担任过银行的执行官。 他说："银行知道，经济状况正越来越恶劣，所以他们将会继续保持警惕。"尽管如此，政府仍然希望通过向抵押债务坏账和其他不良资产投入数十亿美元的举措，银行最终能够厘清他们不稳定的资产负债表，撬开金库，再次向金融系统投入资金。 这个救援计划同样使联邦被保险存款的限额从 10 万美元上升到 25 万美元，此举将提高银行的储备金，并进一步推动贷款的顺利进行。

of a recession makes it too risky for the thousands of small and medium-sized banks across the country to lend to people like Elliot. "Banks know the economy is getting worse, so they will keep being cautious," said Sohn, a former banking executive. Still, the government hopes that by scooping up billions of dollars in bad mortgage debt and other toxic assets, banks eventually can clean up their shaky balance sheets, crack open the vaults and send money washing through the system again. The rescue plan also raises the federally insured deposit limit from $ 100,000 to $ 250,000, a move that could boost banks' reserves and further grease the lending wheels.

Rep. Barney Frank, D-Mass., the Financial Services Committee chairman and a key negotiator over the past weeks, said the measure was just the beginning of a much larger task Congress will tackle: overhauling housing policy and financial regulation in a legislative effort comparable to the New Deal. In the meantime, the Treasury Department is moving swiftly to get the plan started. Treasury Secretary Henry Paulson said he did not wait for final approval of the measure to begin preparation. He has been lining up outside advisers as his staff works out details on a multitude of complex issues. But several hurdles could trip up the plan. For starters, even when the Treasury starts buying bad assets, some banks may hoard the cash they receive in return until they see how the plan pans out. That has the potential to make the lending logjam worse, said Vincent R. Reinhart, former director of the Federal Reserve's monetary affairs division. "They may sit on the sidelines and wait to see the bailout get

　　来自马萨诸塞州的民主党众议员巴尼·弗兰克是财经事务委员会的主席,同时也是过去几周谈判中的关键代表,他指出,这项措施只是一个开始,国会将酝酿一个更大的任务:即彻底改革住房政策和金融监管,其立法效果与罗斯福新政旗鼓相当。 与此同时,财政部正在快速地启动这项计划。 财政部长亨利·鲍尔森指出,他不会等到计划最终获批之后才开始准备工作。 他已经邀请了一批外部顾问作为他的工作人员,从细节入手解决大量的复杂问题。 但是,有几个障碍可能会使这个计划受阻。 首先,即使政府开始购买不良资产,有些银行在了解这个计划如何奏效之前,仍然可能会囤积他们收到的资金作为回报。 美国联邦储备局金融事务部门的前任负责人文森特·R.莱因哈特指出,这很有可能使贷款困境更加糟糕。 他说:"他们可能会隔岸观火,看是否能通过紧急救助得到一定的拉动力。 问题是,如果每个人都做旁观者,就没有人参与到游戏中来。这就要承担风险。"

　　这也造成了一种恶性循环:信任的缺失意味着无法获得借贷;信用紧缩意味着购房更加困难;房屋买卖越困难,房价将进一步下跌;房价进一步下跌,取消抵押品赎回权就会越多。 美国的住房价格已经从最高峰时期下跌了20%,仍然有可能继续下跌,需求回升之前必须触底。 期待已久的底价可能还需要一年或者更长的时间。科威国际不动产公司的总裁吉姆·吉尔斯拜表示,他希望较低的价格与政府的行动相结合,能够启动萧条期的需求。 他承认,联邦政府的救助计划"将会给人们带来信心,即抵押资金可供使用。"工作是另一个大问题。 信贷束缚使大大小小的公司奄奄一息,这些公司的命运取决于借贷有规律地流动,以支付员工的工资和维持公司的

some traction. The problem is if everybody sits on the sidelines, nobody gets in the game. It's a risk, " he said.

It also creates a vicious cycle: No trust means no lending; tight credit means it's harder to buy a home; the more difficult it is to buy or sell a home, the further home prices will fall; and the further prices drop, the more foreclosures there will be. U.S. home prices — down 20% from their peak — still have further to fall, and must hit bottom before demand picks up. The long-awaited bottom in prices could be a year or more away. But Jim Gillespie, chief executive of Coldwell Banker Real Estate, said he hopes that lower prices, combined with the government's actions will jump-start stagnant demand. The federal bailout plan, he said, "will give people reassurance that mortgage money is available." Jobs are another big concern. The stranglehold on credit has choked companies big and small that depend on regular inflows of borrowed money to pay employees and stay afloat.

The Labor Department said that employers cut 159,000 jobs, the fastest pace of losses in more than five years. Experts say that number will grow as the effects of the credit gridlock course through the economy in coming days and weeks. The nation's unemployment rate is now 6. 1% , up from 4. 7% a year ago. Over the last year, the number of unemployed people has risen by 2. 2 million to 9. 5 million. The unemployment rate could rise to as high as 7. 5% by next year, economists predict. If that happens, it would mark the highest since the recession. Boosting employment is critical to kick-starting lending because "if jobs are

运转。

美国劳工部宣称，雇主们削减了 15.9 万个工作岗位，流失速度是五年多来最快的。专家们宣称，由于贷款阻塞在未来一段时间对经济体的影响，这个数字还会上升。国家的失业率已经从一年前的 4.7% 上升到现在的 6.1%。在过去的一年里，失业人数已经从 220 万上升到 950 万。经济学家们预计，失业率在下一年度可能会上升，高达 7.5%，如果事情真的发展到这一步，失业率将会成为自大萧条以来的最高纪录。莱因哈特认为，扩大就业是启动贷款的关键手段，因为"如果工作岗位不断增加，收入则会随之增长；如果收入不断增加，那么大众消费量就会随之增加"。消费者和商家都如此紧缩开支，以至于一些分析者担心，经济将会止步不前或萎缩。劳工部的报告显示，工人的工资上涨缓慢，这就意味着他们面临经济更加窘迫的消费状况，特别是住房之类的昂贵消费品。这就与经济萧条期的经典定义相吻合：即一个萎缩经济体的两个连续段。

值得庆幸的是：人们仍然珍藏着一丝乐观和希望。克利夫兰市商业区莫里亚蒂俱乐部的业主摩根·卡瓦诺夫已经在尝试卖掉他的另一个酒吧，以减轻工作负荷，但是有意的买家都不愿意提高价格。既然政府的救援法令已经亮起了绿灯，他希望他将可以完成这项交易。白宫批准救助计划之后，卡瓦诺夫立即电话告诉有意购买者："救助计划已经获准。我们也得有所作为。"他啪地关上手机，环视着这间有着 75 年历史的爱尔兰酒吧，在历尽沧桑的红褐色吧台后微笑。卡瓦诺夫表示，他打算再次申请借款。这就是进步。

143

growing, then incomes are a growing, and if incomes are growing then people are consuming, " Reinhart said. Consumers and businesses have retrenched① so much that some analysts fear the economy stalled or shrank. The Labor Department report showed wage growth for workers is slowing, meaning they'll be more hard-pressed to spend, especially for something as expensive as a home. That would meet the classic definition of a recession — two consecutive quarters of a shrinking economy.

One bright spot: optimism hasn't been totally squashed yet. Morgan Cavanaugh, proprietor of Moriarty's Pub in downtown Cleveland, has been trying to sell another bar he owns to ease his workload, but the prospective buyer hasn't been able to raise the money. Now that the bailout legislation has the green light, he's hopeful he'll get a deal done. "It passed. Let's work something out, " Cavanaugh told the man over a cellphone just after the House approved the plan. He flipped the phone shut and smiled from behind the weathered mahogany bar of his 75-year-old Irish pub. He's going to put the loan request in again. It's looking up, Cavanaugh said.

(1,181 words)

---

① retrench [ri'trentʃ] *vi.* 紧缩开支

知识链接

Wachovia Securities，***LLC*** 美联证券。美联证券公司是美联银行（Wachovia）的全项服务零售经纪公司，通过在 49 个州和 5 个拉丁美洲国家内的 693 间办事处为客户服务，并通过 33 间国际办事处提供全球服务。2008 年，联邦反垄断监管机构批准富国银行以 117 亿美元的价格收购美联银行。

Coldwell Banker 科威国际不动产。科威国际不动产成立于 1906 年，是全球历史最悠久的房产中介连锁品牌，在全球 6 大洲的 48 个国家和地区拥有 3 900 家门店，101 000 名专业经纪人。

题 记

　　经营策略是企业面对激烈的变化和严峻的环境，为求得长期生存和不断发展而进行的总体性谋划。营销策略是企业市场营销部门根据战略规划，在综合考虑外部市场机会及内部资源状况等因素的基础上，确定目标市场，选择相应的市场营销策略组合，并予以有效实施和控制的过程。星巴克从卖咖啡伊始，至今仍在世界范围内从事咖啡业务。通过持续不断地推出新的咖啡品种、定位体验、高价位等营销策略和战术性活动，星巴克取得了令人羡慕的利润。另一方面，曾经庞大的电子之家西屋电气，在进入娱乐业的重组中败下阵来，具有讽刺意味的是，它现今仍然保留着从前的阴影，利用剩余核能技术的核心发电。一家新公司的经营策略也许看起来很有希望，但如果缺乏良好的营销策略它可能还是回天乏力。

Marketing Strategy and Business Strategy

There is a time for business strategy and a time of marketing strategy, Kotler Marketing Group (KMG) has seen this process for six years. Business strategy is always oriented to changing a company's business portfolio in order to achieve a desired level of profitability. It inherently drives the business away from its current core business toward diversified businesses that will yield greater profit and for which the company has some core competence or the assets to acquire new competency. It questions the business that the company is in and restructures the company for a new business portfolio. Marketing strategy is very different. It is always oriented to changing the marketing portfolio of the company, not its core business. It inherently drives the company to optimize the profitability of its core and adjacent① businesses, with better marketing strategy and tactics. It questions the marketing and sales organization of the company, and the relation of the different parts of the

---

① adjacent [ə'dʒeisənt] *adj.* 邻近的

经营策略与营销策略

企业有时采用经营策略，有时采用营销策略，科特勒咨询集团观察这个进程已达 6 年之久。 为了达到盈利能力的预期水平，经营策略通常要适应公司业务组合的变化。 它自动将企业驱离当前的核心业务，朝多元化的方向发展，这样便可产出更大的利润，企业要么具备某些核心竞争力，要么具备斩获新能力的资产。 备受质疑的是，公司的业务是处于新的投资组合状态，还是为了新的投资组合而重组公司。 营销策略则迥然不同。 它始终定位于改变公司的营销组合，而不是公司的核心业务。 它自动驾驭公司，运用更好的战略和战术，使其核心和相关业务的盈利能力达到最优化。 但公司的营销和销售机构以及公司不同部门与营销和销售之间的关系却饱受诟病。 经营策略和营销策略双方对公司的生命周期都起着至关重要的作用。 但营销策略长期以来通常是企业深陷困境的第一道防线。如果新的营销策略和实施并不管用，企业可能就需要改变经营策略和进行重组。 问题是企业喜欢本末倒置。 他们首先假设最糟糕的状态，然后运用经营战略。 他们首先应该查明，营销秩序是否井

company to marketing and sales. Both disciplines of business strategy and marketing strategy are important to the life cycle of a company. But marketing strategy is always the first line of defense when a business that has been around for a long time fids itself in deep trouble. If new marketing strategy and implementation do not work, then it may be time for business strategy and restructuring. The trouble is that businesses tend to put the cart before the horse. They assume the worst first and reach for business strategy. They should first see if their marketing house is in order. In most cases it is not, because companies rarely focus on marketing department or exercise true marketing functions. Let's break this down further.

What are Business Strategy and Marketing Strategy? Business strategy generally has four parts: Strategy audit; Strategic selection of core business portfolio and capability; Core business strategies; and Organizational change. Marketing strategy also has four parts: Customer audit and customer market segments trends; Strategic target segments, capability, positioning, value proposition and branding; Tactical plans for product line, distribution and sales, promotion, and pricing; and Implementation.

The Business strategy audit always starts with a financial analysis of revenue, profitability and resources. Then it moves to an industry and competition position analysis. In other words, it starts with money trouble and links it to average decline in the industry. By contrast a marketing audit starts with market share analysis by customer segment and links this

然。 在大部分情况下，情况并非如此，因为公司很少关注营销部，或发挥真实的营销功能。 让我们进一步打破这种惯例。

什么是经营策略和营销策略？ 经营策略一般包括四个方面：战略审计；核心业务组合和能力的战略选择；核心业务战略；组织变革。 营销战略同样包括四个方面：客户审计和客户市场细分趋势；战略目标细分、能力、定位、价值取向和品牌；生产线、分发和销售以及促销和定价的战术性计划；项目实施。

企业的策略审计通常从收支、获利和资源的财务分析开始。 然后，转入产业和竞争定位分析。 换句话说，先从财务困难开始，再与行业的平均衰退相联系。 与此相反，营销审计通过客户细分开始市场占有率分析，将市场份额与相关变化的客户需求、欲望、偏好和公司定位的变化动态相联系。 换句话说，先从客户困难入手，再考虑市场份额下降和市场上不断变化的消费者动态。 注意这些区别。 业务审计一旦完成，公司将从当前核心业务转向新的核心机遇。 这是一种商业模式的变化。 相反，市场营销审计一旦完成，公司会发现，它将失去原来目标下的市场份额和价值，在其核心产业内部寻找新的目标细分。 它其实并没有改变它的核心业务，仅仅只是改变了营销模式。

经营策略在抢救当前核心业务的同时，也会继续选择未来的核心业务组合。 另一方面，营销策略选择有吸引力的客户目标，研究新产品的特征和设计需求，客户愿意接触和感受这些产品的新方

to changing trends in customer needs, wants and preferences and company positioning with respect to these changes. In other words, it starts with customer trouble and links it market share decline and changing customer trends in the marketplace. Notice the difference. By the time the business audit it done, the company is thrust① away from its current core business to new core opportunities. That is a change in the business model! By contrast, by the time the market marketing audit is done the company sees that is has lost market share and value in old target and discovers new target segments within its core industry. It does not have to change its core business, only its marketing model.

Business strategy then proceeds to selecting a future core business portfolio, while salvaging② current core businesses. Marketing strategy, on the other hand, selects attractive customer targets and researches there needs and wants for new product features and design, new ways customers want to access and feel about these products and the price they will exchange for these new values. The company does not have to depart from its industry or business. It just has to become more customer focused. Business strategy then propounds tactical camp long-term strategies (3-5 years) for the new core business portfolio. Marketing strategy, on the other hand, uses R&D to launch new products and related services, new distribution polices and improved networks and sales management, new

---

① thrust [θrʌst] *vi.* 推挤
② salvage ['sælvidʒ] *vt.* 抢救

式，以及他们交换这些新价值的价格。 公司没有必要放弃它的产业或业务，只需要进一步做到以消费者为中心。 经营策略此时为新的核心业务组合提出战术特别的长远战略（3~5年）。 另一方面，营销策略运用研发推出新产品和相关服务、新的分销渠道和改进了的网络和销售管理、新的品牌活动、促销策略和新价格政策。 这些都是可以迅速改进获利能力的短期和近期战术（1~2年）。 此时，经营策略进入为新的长期业务组合而重组公司的阶段。 这是昂贵和不可逆转的趋势，它需要一种新的长期负债结构。 营销战略的实施需要根据整体市场预算来改善组织结构和资源投资。 公司监控他们的营销成功并保持灵活性，以便对他们的表现进行调整。 营销战略的实施不需要对组织和财政结构做任何改变。

让我们看看这种区别的一些经典范例。 耐克和星巴克从开始就从未改变过他们的经营策略。 耐克未曾制造过一双鞋子，但它却始终如一地致力于营销研究，为促销、分销和定价制定新的设计和令人难以置信的项目。 星巴克从卖咖啡伊始，至今仍在世界范围内从事咖啡业务。 通过持续不断地推出新的咖啡品种、定位体验和高价位等营销策略和战术性活动，星巴克取得了令人羡慕的利润。 另一方面，曾经庞大的电子之家西屋电气，在进入娱乐业的重组中败下阵来，具有讽刺意味的是，它现今仍然保留着从前的阴影，利用剩余核能技术的核心发电。 公司可能拥有太多的经营策略，但缺乏足够良好的营销判断力。 贝尔-豪威尔在战略转移进入国防工业之前，

brand campaigns and promotion and new pricing policies. These are short-term and near-term tactics (1-2 years) that can improve profitability quickly. Business strategy then proceeds to restructure the company for its new long-term business portfolio. This is costly and irreversible①. It requires a new long-term debt structure. Marketing implementation will requires organizational improvement and resource investment in its holistic marketing budget. Companies monitor their marketing success and retain the flexibility to make adjustments in performance. Marketing implementation does not require organizational and financial restructuring.

Let's look at some classic examples of this difference. Nike and Starbucks have never changed their business strategy from day one. Nike never manufactured a shoe, but has devoted itself consistently to marketing research for new designs and fabulous programs of promotion, distribution and pricing. Starbucks started in the coffee business and is still in the coffee business all over the world. Through consistent marketing strategies and tactical campaigns of new types of coffee, location experience, and high prices it has racked up enviable profits. On the other hand, Westinghouse, once a great electrical powerhouse, restructured itself unsuccessfully into entertainment and remains today a shadow of its former self, ironically generating electricity from its remaining nuclear technology core. It may have had too much business strategy and not enough marketing good sense. Bell & Howell was once a

---

① irreversible [iri'vɜːsəbl] *adj.* 不可逆转的

曾经是一家了不起的摄影器材公司。索尼进入娱乐业的战略多元化似乎事与愿违，因为它已经失去了电子产品方面的技术优势。美国国际商用机器公司今天面临的强大挑战是其全球服务业务的停滞。国际商用机器公司做了一个战略性的改变，将其业务从设备转入商业服务。但是这个部门现在停滞不前，于是国际商用机器公司计划在欧洲解雇1.5万名员工。太阳微系统公司和惠普公司正在挑战国际商用机器公司历史性的技术领导力。但幸好国际商用机器公司在新行业运行良好。

这并不表示公司一成不变地恪守核心业务、拒绝多样化就是明智之举。毕竟，施乐公司和宝丽莱公司坚持复印机和照相机业务，最后还是倾家荡产。通用汽车公司坚持生产汽车和卡车同样濒临破产的边缘。但这些公司不同于丰田和本田公司，因为他们未曾关注过它的客户。通用多年来早已让出了营销巨人的宝座。或许更好的营销策略可以拯救这些公司。

知识链接

Kotler Marketing Group 科特勒咨询集团（KMG）。科特勒咨询集团是目前最大的、服务最广的、专注于发展战略特别是营销战略领域的全球顶尖咨询公司之一。它的总部设在美国华盛顿，在英国、瑞典、加拿大、澳大利亚、韩国、法国、巴林和中国设有办事机构，并在美国芝加哥设有"大客户

great camera company before it strategically shifted its business to defense industries. Sony's strategic diversification into entertainment appears to have backfired as it has lost its technology edge in electronics. IBM is facing a mighty challenge today with the stagnation① of its global services businesses. IBM made a strategic change in its business from equipment to business services. That sector is now stagnating, as IBM plans to lay off 15,000 workers in Europe. Sun Microsystems and HP are challenging IBM's historic technology leadership. But IBM had a good run at a new business.

This does not mean that it is always wise to stay with your core business and not diversify. After all, Xerox and Polaroid stuck with copiers and camera and failed. GM has stuck with car and trucks and is about to fail. But these companies, unlike Toyota and Honda, never paid much attention to its customers. GM has not been a marketing giant for many decades. Better marketing strategy may have saved them.

(1,030 words)

---

① stagnation [stæg'neiʃən] *n.* 停滞

管理研究中心"和"科特勒企业大学（KMG Enterprises University）"。

Westinghouse 　西屋电气公司。西屋电气公司（Westinghouse Electric Corporation）是世界著名的电工设备制造企业。1886 年由乔治·威斯汀豪斯在美国宾夕法尼亚州创立。总部设在宾夕法尼亚州匹兹堡市。西屋电气公司在世界 26 个国家和地区设有 250 家工厂，现有职工 12.5 万人，持股人达 13.5 万。其主要业务领域涉及发电设备、输变电设备、用电设备和电控制设备、电子产品等门类共 4 000 多种产品，其中发电设备、输变电设备尤具特色。

题　记

在一个侥幸大于理性、贪婪战胜恐惧的市场上，谁也不知道击鼓传花掌控经济的鼓点何时停下，更多人愿意玩到最后，都以为自己能参加完最后一段"猜谜"游戏再功成身退。尽管大多数人认识到时间所剩无几，有必要重组金融体系并改善几个关键资产和保险市场的流动性，有必要保护纳税人并允许政府分享好处，但许多人把道德风险看做是限制干扰程度、特别是惩罚股东的理由却不禁让人大跌眼镜。即使股东的道德风险、资金实力、决策的科学性是决定公司治理效率、盈利能力、内部风险管理机制的主要因素，但激励倒错随时可能触发危机。让股东接受惩戒性的处罚如同将反道德危机战略转变成一种酶化剂，它可以被抑制剂与激活剂所调控。控制酶的作用，可以在生物体内维持一个稳定的内部环境；刺激酶的作用，也许会导致处理道德风险时适得其反。

"Exemplary Punishment"
Could Backfire

Hank Paulson's "bailout" plan unleashed① a flurry of alternative proposals, as most people recognize that time is running out. There is an urgent need for a significant intervention to break an accelerating downward spiral that is threatening the very survival of the financial core of the world economy. Most proposals, including the one just agreed to by Congress, have in common a few general principles. First, they recognize the need to recapitalize the financial system and to improve the liquidity of several key asset and insurance markets. Second, there is agreement on the need to protect taxpayers by giving the government a share of the upside as well. Third, most see moral hazard as a reason to limit the extent of intervention and, in particular, to punish shareholders. Not doing so, the argument goes, would make future crises more likely as it would encourage the financial sector to repeat the excesses that caused the crisis in the first place.

We share the first two "principles" but are less persuaded by the third one. The main problem of the standard moral hazard view is its

---

① unleash [ˈʌnˈliːʃ] vt. 把(感情、力量等)释放出来

"惩戒性处罚"可能适得其反

汉克·保尔森的"救市"计划释放出一连串可供选择的建议，因为大多数人认识到，时间所剩无几。 人们迫切需要一次重大的干预行动，以打破威胁世界经济金融中心生存的螺旋式加速下降。 大多数提议在一些通行的原则上达成共识，包括国会刚批准的一个提案。 首先，人们认识到有必要重组金融体系，并改善几个关键资产和保险市场的流动性。 其次，大家一致赞同有必要保护纳税人，同时允许政府分享好处。 最后，许多人把道德风险看做是限制干扰程度、特别是惩罚股东的理由。 他们争辩说，如果不这样做，将加大未来爆发危机的可能性，因为这将鼓励金融部门重复过分荒诞的行为，而这正是导致危机的首要原因。

我们赞成前两个"原则"，但对第三个原则却有所保留。 标准道德风险观的主要问题是它漠视危机中产生的激励问题。 在现实生活中，危机与许多模型不同，它并非转瞬即逝，而是要延续一个时间段。 这一时间维度为危机中的各类战略决策创造了充分的机会。 痛苦不堪的代理商不得不决定何时以及是否放弃他们的资产，因为他们知道，对正确时机的误算将付出非常昂贵的代价。 投机商和战略玩家们不得不决定，何时加强螺旋式下降，何时稳住它。 政府不

disregard for the incentive problems it generates within crises. In real life, unlike in many of our models, crises are not an instant but a time period. This time dimension creates ample opportunity for all sort of strategic decisions within a crisis. Distressed agents have to decide when and if to let go of their assets, knowing that a miscalculation on the right timing can be very costly. Speculators and strategic players have to decide when to reinforce a downward spiral, and when to stabilize it. Governments have to decide how long to wait before intervening, fully aware that delaying can be counterproductive, but that the political tempo may require that a full-blown crisis becomes observable for bickering to be put aside. Each of these agents is in the game of predicting what others are likely to do. In particular, the likelihood of a bailout and the form this is expected to take, change the incentives for both distressed firms and speculators within the crisis. These incentives are central, both to the resolution of the current crisis as well as for the severity of the next crises.

A standard advice stemming from the moral hazard camp is to subject shareholders to exemplary punishment (the words used by Secretary Paulson during the Bear Stearns intervention) . This is sound advice in the absence of a time dimension within crises. With no time dimension, all shareholders were part of the boom that preceded the crisis and as soon as the bailout takes place the crisis is over; the next concern is not to repeat the excesses that led to the crisis. Punishing shareholders means punishing those that led to the current crisis, and it is better that they learn the lesson sooner rather than later. However, this advice can backfire when we add back the time dimension. Now, the expectation that shareholders will be exemplarily punished if the crisis worsens delays the decision to inject much needed capital by stabilizing investors. As a concrete

得不决定，等待多久才开始干预，因为他们已充分认识到，拖延可能会适得其反，但政治节奏可能需要危机全面展开时才变得清晰可见，此时即可搁置争吵。 这些监管人中的每一位都投入到这场游戏之中，预测其他人可能在干什么。 人们特别期望紧急救助和这种形式有可能采取或改变激励措施，以解救处于危机中的问题企业和投机商。 这些激励措施对于解决当前的危机和处理接下来的严重危机都至关重要。

持道德风险观的人给出了一个标准意见，就是让股东接受惩戒性的处罚（这是财政部长保尔森干预贝尔斯登时使用的字眼）。 当危机中的时间维度缺失之时，这是个中肯的意见。 没有时间维度，所有股东都是危机前经济繁荣的一部分，一旦紧急救助生效，危机就会结束；下一个关注点是不要重复引发危机的过剩。 惩罚股东意味着惩罚那些导致目前危机的人，他们应该更好地吸取教训，宜早不宜迟。 然而，当我们重新考虑时间维度时，这一建议可能会适得其反。 现在，如果危机恶化，期待对股东实施惩戒性处罚就会延误稳定的投资者注入大量急需资金的决定。 这有一个具体的例子，与过去相比，主权财富基金现在不再那么急于向美国的金融体系注资。 相反，摇摆不定的投机商和沽空型投资者却看到了惩戒性处罚政策加强了他们的策略价值。 由于这两个原因，危机变得更加严重，因为在恐慌和混乱爆发期间，不确定性和风险陡增，股票市场变得极端片面。 反道德危机战略转变成一种酶化剂。

救助计划的许多细节尚待确定，就如何安排这些细节而言，这种观点导致了几种观察结果。 一个目标是必须对战略投资者发出信号，阻止投机等待，因为他们正在一旁观望，等待价格止跌。 这

example, sovereign wealth funds are now much less eager to inject equity into the US financial system than they once were. Conversely, destabilizing① peculators and short sellers see the value of their strategy reinforced by the policy of exemplary punishment. For both reasons, crises become more acute, as the equity market becomes extremely one-sided when uncertainty and risk rise during bouts of panic and confusion. The anti-moral hazard strategy turns into a crisis enzyme.

This perspective leads to several observations regarding how the details of the bailout, many of which are yet to be determined, should be arranged. One objective must be to signal to strategic investors waiting in the sidelines that prices will stop falling and thus discourage speculative waiting. Speculators will not expect that prices of securities will be lower than those established at the Treasury's auction (if indeed an auction is used), at least in the period that immediately follows the auction. Thus the date of the auction provides a clear deadline to any speculative waiting. Announcing a timetable for purchasing a given list of securities may therefore have a salutary effect on prices even before the actual purchases take place. To the extent possible, the first securities to be purchased should be those where the evidence of mispricing is greatest. For instance, certain AAA-rated tranches of subprime mortgage backed securities have been trading at prices that are hard to justify except by the extreme illiquidity of the market. If these securities were first on the Treasury's list this would signal to speculators that the possible gains from speculative waiting will soon disappear. One risk is that if some of the holders of a particular security are especially distressed, this may lead to

---

① destabilize [di'stebəˌlaiz] vt. 使打破平衡

样，至少在紧接着拍卖的时期，投机者不会期望证券价格低于财政部拍卖时设置的价格（如果确实是使用了拍卖的方式）。 因此，拍卖日期给任何投机等待都提供了一个明确的截止期限。 为购买某一给定的债券清单公布一个时间表可能会因此对价格产生有益的影响，这种影响甚至会发生在实际购买之前。 在可能的范围内，首先被购买的证券将是那些标价错误最大的证券。 除非在市场的极度非流动性价格下交易，某些 AAA 评级的部分次级抵押贷款支持的证券交易时价格难以确认。 如果这些证券首次在财政部的清单上出现，这种现象就会提示投机者：投机等待的可能收益将很快消失。 一种风险是，如果某一特定证券的有些持有者感到特别沮丧，这可能导致财政部以跳楼价购买证券。 在某种程度上，纳税人在此次购买中获得的利润减轻了这种风险。 不过，令人担忧的是，如果对其剩余资产按市价计值后别无所得，以过于低廉的价格完成购买将损害其他的证券持有者。 部分避免出现这种情况的一种方法是承诺购买足够大量的各种证券，使任何特定证券持有者的沮丧对拍卖价格的影响降到最低。

最后，财政部的计划包括尚未明确的规定，即是否给予政府在其援助公司内的股权。 据推测，这将稀释现有股东的持股量。 在这种政策生成的危机激励机制中，一种方法是给予那些在危机之初筹集新资金的公司以特别考虑（例如，较低的股本稀释）。 必须明确，我们的立场并不是忽视道德风险标准，相反，我们认为，在制定政策解决这个问题时，我们更加警惕激励倒错，因为这种做法可能会触发危机。"惩戒性处罚"的方式就是沿着这些路线误导政策的一个例子，导致雷曼崩溃可能是另外一个例子，但也有许多危机后

fire-sale prices when the Treasury purchases the securities. To some extent, this risk is mitigated① by the profits the taxpayers would make on this purchase. Still, there is a concern that purchases at excessively low prices would harm other security-holders, if nothing else from having to mark-to-market their remaining holdings. One way to partially avoid this situation is to commit to purchasing a sufficiently large amount of each security to minimize the impact that any particular security-holder's distress will have on auction prices.

Finally, the Treasury's plan contains as-yet-unclear provisions for giving the government an equity stake in the companies it assists. Presumably this will involve diluting the holdings of current shareholders. One way to take into account the within-crisis incentives this policy generates would be to give special consideration (for instance, lower dilution) to firms that raised fresh capital since the start of the crisis. To be clear, our position is not that the standard moral hazard concerns should be disregarded. Instead, our argument is that it is important that when designing policies to address it, we are more mindful of the perverse incentives that they may trigger within crises. The "exemplary punishment" approach is one example of a misguided policy along these lines, letting Lehman go under may have been another one, but there are many post-crisis regulatory responses that could deal with moral hazard without backfiring during the crisis.

(1,034 words)

---

① mitigate ['mitigeit] vt. 减轻

的监管对策可以在危机期间处理道德风险而不会适得其反。

知识链接

Bear Stearns Cos.　贝尔斯登公司。贝尔斯登公司是一家全球领先的金融服务公司，成立于 1923 年，总部位于纽约，原是美国华尔街第六大投资银行，全球 500 强企业之一。公司致力于为全世界的政府、企业、机构和个人提供服务，主要业务涵盖机构股票和债券、固定收益、投资银行业务、全球清算服务、资产管理以及个人银行服务。在 2008 年的金融危机中，摩根大通收购了贝尔斯登。2010 年伊始，摩根大通决定不再继续使用"贝尔斯登(Bear Stearns)"的名称。

Sovereign Wealth Funds　主权财富基金。主权财富(Sovereign Wealth) 与私人财富相对应，是指一国政府通过特定税收与预算分配、可再生自然资源收入和国际收支盈余等方式积累形成的、由政府控制与支配的、通常以外币形式持有的公共财富。得益于国际油价飙升和国际贸易扩张急剧增加，近年来主权财富的管理成为一个日趋重要的议题。国际上最新的发展趋势是成立主权财富基金，并设立通常独立于央行和财政部的专业投资机构管理这些基金。

题　记

　　互联网产业在移动互联网、云计算、物联网、三网融合和电子商务等五个新兴关联领域的影响力正在与日俱增，互联网及电子商务产业的物理空间聚集和虚拟空间拓展规律不仅改变了企业发展布局和科学规划的价值观，而且以一种数字化电子方式的崭新商业模式完成了互联网技术与商务服务业流通技术的交叉整合。仔细观察电子商务的技术路线图，你会发现日臻完善的电子商务彻底改变了人们的经营理念：访问控制、企业整合和随需应变的电子商务这三个阶段是一个自然的进程，他们引导企业在各个阶段同相协调地向前推进；反应能力、可变因素、专注程度和弹性能力是随需应变企业的四种经营特征，他们可以使企业获得全球共享的和从端对端进行管理的计算资源。这种非常灵活并允许相对容易的部署新能力的基础结构正是随需应变的企业所依赖的技术环境。

The Technology Roadmap
for E-business

IBM has defined e-business on demand as an enterprise whose business processes — integrated end-to-end across the company and with key partners, suppliers, and customers — can respond with speed to any customer demand, market opportunity, or external threat. Are you wondering just what this means for you? Developers and IT professionals will be expected to build the technical infrastructure to support the integrated business processes of e-business on demand. To help you get up to speed, this article describes the e-business on demand environment and gives you the technology roadmap to get there.

It's all about return on investment. In the beginning, the Internet linked scientists in academia, government, and research. It evolved to provide e-mail and then the World Wide Web, which was good for communicating market messages but didn't have a lot of business value. Technology quickly evolved and enabled computing on the Internet, driving business processes. But this capability has come with a cost — it has required serious investment in technology. And when a business invests in information technology, it expects to derive benefits from its

电子商务的技术路线图

美国国际商务机器公司将随需应变的电子商务定义为这样一种企业，它的经营过程通过公司终端对终端的整合，与核心合伙人、供应商和客户相连，可以迅速地应对任何顾客需求、市场机遇或者外部威胁。你想知道它对你意味着什么吗？开发商和信息技术的专业人士有望建立技术基础设施，以支持整合电子商务的经营过程。为了帮助你熟悉了解这些技术的详细情况，本文描述了随需应变的电子商务环境，并给出了实现电子商务的技术路线图。

电子商务与投资回报息息相关。在开始的时候，互联网就将学术界、政府和研究机构的科学家套了起来。它亦步亦趋，先是提供电子邮件，然后开发了万维网，这种做法有利于沟通市场信息，但没多大的商业价值。技术进步的日新月异使互联网的计算信息处理技术成为可能，从而推进了商业流程。但这种能力伴随着成本耗损，即它需要大量的技术投资。当一家企业投资于信息技术时，它会期望从投资中受益。降低成本的问题永远不会消失。

信息技术承诺的与它所兑现的存在着差距。如果你是开发商，就会知道整合分散的异构系统和网络是一项复杂的工作。这种复杂性是现今困扰首席信息官的头号问题。仅仅是试图整合各种技术就

investment. Issues of cost reduction never go away.

There's a gap between what IT promises and what it delivers. You're a developer — you know that integrating disparate①, heterogeneous② systems and networks is complex. This complexity is the number one issue troubling CIOs today. Just trying to get technologies to work together eats up more than 40 percent of IT budgets. That means almost half the IT investment goes toward things that don't directly drive business value. Because it's complex, it can take months, maybe a year, before an IT investment delivers any value. Because it's complex, skills are in short supply, and it will get harder to hire the people to integrate, implement, and maintain technologies.

Of course, the industry grappled with cost of ownership and utilization long before the Internet and e-business introduced a new era of computing. Now we have the Web, but the promise of complete business integration efficiency still lies in the next generation of e-business technology infrastructure. And this is where you — the developer — come into play.

Just what is e-business on demand? You are in an e-business on demand environment when your organization connects its core business systems to key constituencies using intranets, extranets, and the Web, allowing you to build and enhance business relationships through the thoughtful use of network-based technologies; and leverage Internet technologies to transact and interact with customers, suppliers,

---

① disparate ['dispərit] *adj.* 不同的
② heterogeneous [ˌhetərəu'dʒiːniəs] *adj.* 由不同成分形成的

耗尽了 40% 以上的信息技术预算，这意味着几乎半数的信息技术投资不会直接带来商业价值。因为它是如此复杂，所以信息技术投资可能要花费几个月、也许一年的时间才能收回商业价值。因为它是如此复杂，而且技术供不应求，所以更加难以雇人整合、执行和维护这些技术。

当然，自互联网和电子商务开创计算机信息处理技术的新纪元以来，行业在很长一段时间内纠结于经营成本和使用成本的处理。虽然我们现在有了万维网，但是对于完整的经营整合效率的承诺仍然要以下一代的电子商务技术为基础。这就是你这个开发商将要参与的游戏。

究竟什么是随需应变的电子商务？当你的组织机构将它的核心经营系统与使用企业内联网、外联网和万维网等关键区域相连时，你就处于随需应变的电子商务环境之中，通过对基于网络的技术深思熟虑的使用，它允许你建立和加强经营关系，它允许你充分利用互联网技术与客户、供应商、合作伙伴以及员工交流和互动，实现和保持竞争优势。完善随需应变的电子商务是一个自然的进程，一般来说要经历以下三个阶段：

访问控制：启用简单的网络发布和交易系统单点解决方案，使核心业务系统参与交易。

企业整合：利用万维网整合企业的业务流程。链接内联网和外联网系统，包括企业之间和超越企业边界。

随需应变的电子商务：利用万维网动态地适应客户和市场需求。改变经营模式。用新方式整合人员、技术和流程。

随需应变的电子商务在各个阶段同相协调地向前推进。互联网

173

partners, and employees to achieve and sustain a competitive advantage; Getting to e-business on demand is a natural progression that typically goes through three stages:

Access: Enable transactions against core business systems using simple Web publishing and point solutions.

Enterprise integration: Use the Web to integrate business processes across enterprises. Link internal and external systems, both across enterprises and beyond enterprise boundaries.

E-business on demand: Use the Web to adapt dynamically to customer and market requirements. Change business models. Combine people, technologies, and processes in new ways.

E-business on demand evolves in phases. In each phase, the Internet transforms the business processes.

Access to digital information: This phase is all about publishing content, most of it of the static "look-up" variety. Simple database queries allow us to check a bank account, look up airline flight information, or see where our overnight package is. It's pretty easy to get in the game here. All an enterprise needs is a home page. All an individual needs is a browser.

Real transactions, real e-business: Don't just look at your bank account — move some money. Don't just check a flight departure time — book your seat. Trade a stock, buy a book, apply for a loan, renew your driver's license, and take a college course. Doing this requires more than a Website — this requires behind-the-scenes integration of technologies and business processes.

The advanced stage of e-business: In a fluid system of customers,

在各阶段改变了业务流程。

获取数字信息：发布信息涵盖此阶段的全部内容，人们需要采用各种各样的手段静态"查找"大多数信息。简单的数据库查询允许我们核对银行账号，查询航空信息，或者查找我们昨晚的行李在哪里。参与这场游戏容易至极，一个主页就能满足企业的全部需求，一个浏览器就能满足个人的全部需求。

真正的交易，真正的电子商务：不要只盯着你的银行账户——让钱流通起来。不要只检查航班的起飞时间——预订你的座位。交易股票，购书，申请贷款，更新驾驶证。这样做远超过了一个网站的承受能力，它需要技术和业务流程的幕后整合。

电子商务的高级阶段：在一个客户、供应商、合伙人和员工流动的系统中，互联网是沟通、交易和联系的主要方式。商业流程由人工操作转向自动运行。一种关系在单个交易完成之时便宣告结束。环境按实时计算。你构造了网络社区，所以公司可以更快地创造新产品和服务，接触新客户，在经济上增加新的伙伴关系，动态地改变现有关系，同时参与多方电子商务模式，并通过参与这些关系的各方改善信息获取。

对通过这些阶段不断发展的企业来说，投资收益是什么呢？他们是客户支出增长的份额，是更好的资产收益率，是税收机遇，还是更好的股东利润。每个行业部门都有整合终端对终端的共同需求，以便产品、服务（私营部门和政府）、单据、形象、决策和解决方案全都可以随需应变。谁将拥有竞争优势呢？是最先到达这个阶段的企业，是知道如何让它发生的软件和服务供应商。

任何与全球化相连的企业，都必须有能力处理发展过程中遇到

suppliers, partners and employees, the Internet is the primary way to communicate, transact, and connect. Business processes shift from manual to automatic. A relationship could last only as long as a single transaction. The environment is real-time computing. You form networked communities so that organizations can create new products and services faster, reach new customers and economically add new relationships, dynamically change existing relationships, simultaneously engage in multiple e-business models, and improve access to information by constituents involved in these relationships.

What's the return on investment for an enterprise that progresses through these phases? They are an increased share of customer spending, a better return on assets, new revenue opportunities, and better shareholder return. Every industry segment has the common requirement to integrate end-to-end so that products, services (private sector and government), invoices, images, decisions, and answers are all available on demand. Who will have the competitive advantage? The enterprises that get there first, and the software and services providers that know how to make it happen.

Any globally connected enterprise must have the ability to handle whatever comes its way, such as changes in customer preferences or competitive actions, fluctuations in capital markets, labor situations, natural disasters, or political unrest. An advanced e-business must be able to respond to the unpredictable and the unforeseen and never question the ability of the infrastructure to deliver.

So what kind of computing environment is required for an on-demand business? What does "on demand" mean for the way a business

的任何问题，比如客户偏好的改变或者竞争行为的出现、资本市场的波动、劳动力的状况、自然灾害或者政治动乱等。先进的电子商务必须能够应对毫无征兆和无法预见的情况，并毫不怀疑基础结构部门释放出的能力。

那么，哪一类计算环境是随需应变的电子商务必需的呢？对购买和管理计算系统的电子商务而言，"随需应变"意味着什么？在解答这些问题之前，让我们看看随需应变企业的四种经营特征：

反应能力：能够察觉环境的变化，对不可预测的供给或需求波动、新出现的客户、合作伙伴、供应商和雇员需求或者通过竞争产生的出乎意料的变动做出动态反应。

可变因素：能够灵活地适应成本结构和交易流程，能够降低风险，在生产力、成本控制、资本效率以及财政可预测性等较高水平上推动经营绩效。

专注程度：致力于把精力集中在核心竞争力、差异化任务和资产上。能够利用关系密切的战略合作伙伴，管理从制造业、后勤、成就感到人力资源部门和财务运营等方面的任务。

弹性能力：准备应对电脑病毒、地震或突然激增的需求变化和威胁。

具备这些属性的电子商务需要足以支持它的技术，但这不是现在可以操作的数字环境。今天的环境种类繁多、分布广泛、垂直隔绝，一般来说，比以往的商务环境更为复杂。相同的信息技术是必不可少的业务能力，它既可以创建战略优势，也是一个主要障碍——这种易变、敏感和动态的业务成为人们多年来谈论的话题。

buys and manages its computing technology? Before tackling these questions, let's look at the four business characteristics of an on-demand business:

Responsive: Able to sense changes in the environment and to respond dynamically to unpredictable fluctuations in supply or demand, emerging customer, partner, supplier and employee needs, or unexpected moves by the competition.

Variable: Able to adapt cost structures and business processes flexibly, to reduce risk, and to drive business performance at higher levels of productivity, cost control, capital efficiency, and financial predictability.

Focused: Committed to concentrating on core competencies and differentiating tasks and assets; able to use tightly integrated strategic partners to manage tasks ranging from manufacturing, logistics, and fulfillment to human resources and financial operations.

Resilient: Prepared for changes and threats like computer viruses, earthquakes, or sudden spikes in demand.

A business with these attributes requires technology that can support it, but that's not the computing environment that's operating today. Today's environment is heterogeneous, widely distributed, vertically isolated, and generally more complex than businesses would like. The same IT that's essential to a business' ability to create strategic advantage, is also a major obstacle to becoming the kind of fluid, responsive, dynamic business that's been talked about for years.

(1,092 words)

知识链接 🔍

CIO 首席信息官（Chief Information Officer）。首席信息官是负责一个公司信息技术和系统所有领域的高级官员。他们具备技术和业务过程两方面的知识，将组织的技术调配战略与业务战略紧密结合在一起，并通过指导对信息技术的利用来支持公司的目标。

CIO：首席信息官（Chief Information Officer）...

题 记

　　当意大利经济学家菲尔弗雷多·帕累托的社会资源配置原则问世之时，社会总财富的增加引起了少数人的狂欢：20%的人掌握着80%的财富，贫富差距的鸿沟既印证着人与人的不同，也彰显着每个人都有与众不同的价值。时光荏苒，美国各阶层的人现在比以往任何时候都活得开心，但即便不考虑通货膨胀在个人财富上留下的蛾洞，普通员工和白领阶层之间的收入差距仍然在持续拉大。缩小收入差距已经成为半个多世纪以来的一个美国理想：美国自 1913 年以来实行了累进所得税，自 1916 年以来强制执行了累进遗产税，自罗斯福新政以来，通过了旨在缓解贫困的昂贵计划，美国国会现在又开始重新审查大量的所得税"优惠"政策。但所有这些关于贫富收入分配的政策收效甚微。穷人最现实的希望可能在于强劲的经济发展能够持续，因为这才是"抬高所有船只"的涨潮。

Incomes: The Unshrinking Gap

Vilfredo Pareto, a 19th century economist, had a theory: if A equals a given income, and B equals the number of people in a country with incomes greater than A; and if the logarithms① of A and B are plotted on the Cartesian y axis and x axis, respectively, the resulting curve will be inclined by approximately 56°. In other words, the rich get richer and the poor stay poor.

Pareto has now found an ally in the U.S. Government. Peter Henle, a Library of Congress labor specialist, has found in a new study that the share of wage and salary income going to people who are already well paid is gradually increasing, while the share paid to low-ranking workers is falling. Using Census Bureau figures, he estimates that the share of all job income that went to the top fifth of male wage earners rose from 38% to $40\frac{1}{2}$%. At the same time, the bottom fifth's share dropped from 5% to $4\frac{1}{2}$%.

Henle's study is the latest in a series of surprising findings on economic inequality in the U.S. During the past year and a half, the Census Bureau, the nonprofit Cambridge Institute in Massachusetts, and

---

① logarithm [ˈlɔgəriðəm] *n.* 对数

持续性收入差距

19世纪的经济学家维尔弗雷多·帕累托提出了一个理论：如果A等于给定的收入，B等于一个国家人口数量，他们的收入比A大。如果A和B的对数绘制在笛卡尔Y轴和X轴，最终曲线将分别产生大约56度的倾斜。 换言之，富者会越来越富，而穷人则依旧停留在贫困线上。

帕累托现在已经在美国政府中找到了盟友。 国会图书馆的劳动力专家彼得·亨勒在一项新研究中发现，在已经获得高收入的人群中，工资及薪酬收入所占份额正在逐渐增加，而支付给低级工人的薪酬比例却正在下降。 他利用人口普查局的数字估算出下列结果：前1/5男性工资收入者占有的全部工作收入份额从38％上升到40.5％。 与此同时，后1/5男性工资收入者占有的市场份额从5％降至4.5％。

在一系列关于美国经济不平等的令人惊讶的发现中，亨勒的研究是最新成果。 在过去一年半中，人口普查局、非营利性的马萨诸塞州剑桥研究所和麻省理工学院的经济学家莱斯特·梭罗和罗伯特·卢卡斯都发现，自第二次世界大战以来，美国工人的工资在最高和最低收入之间的差距相当大，国家对此几乎无所作为，更不用

M.I.T. Economists Lester Thurow and Robert Lucas have all found that since World War II the U.S. has made almost no progress toward closing the considerable income gaps between the nation's highest- and lowest-paid workers — let alone creating the classless society of popular myth. Unlike Henle, who based his conclusions on the wages of family breadwinners, the earlier researchers used figures reflecting total family incomes, including "transfer payments" like Social Security. But the results still showed persistent if not growing inequality. The bottom and top fifths of American families had about the same shares of total family income at present as they did in the past decades: 6% v. 42% .The three-fifths in the middle brackets received about the same share of income throughout the period: 52% . At present, the average family in the top fifth pulled in an income of about $ 23,000, or approximately eight times that of the typical family on the bottom. If personal income in the U. S. were distributed on an absolutely even basis, each family would receive more than $ 11,000.

The size of the gap between rich and poor has been something less than a flaming issue simply because all levels of Americans are better off now than they ever have been. Even discounting for the moth holes left in everyone's dollar by inflation, real buying power for the average factory worker with three dependents has increased about 11% in the past decade and more than 29% since World War II. President Nixon argued during the campaign that "the people on welfare in America would be rich in most of the nations of the world today, " and his line clearly impressed more voters than George McGovern's grumbling① about unfair tax favors

---

① grumbling [ˈgrʌmbliŋ] *adj.* 喃喃鸣不平的,出怨言的

说创建无阶级社会的流行神话了。 亨勒得出的结论基于养家糊口的人的工资，而早期的研究人员另辟蹊径，他们使用的数据反映了家庭的总收入，包括社会保障等"转移支付"。 但研究结果显示，即使不平等没有加剧，但收入差距仍然在持续拉大。 前 1/5 和后 1/5 的美国家庭目前的整体家庭收入与过去 10 年所占的份额持平，即 6% 比 42%。 在此期间，3/5 的中等收入家庭保持着 52% 的相同份额的收入。 目前，前 1/5 的家庭平均收入约为 2.3 万美元，大约是典型的低收入家庭的 8 倍。 在美国，如果个人收入绝对平衡地分配，每个家庭的进账会超过 1.1 万美元。

就是因为各阶层的美国人现在比以往任何时候都过得好，所以富人与穷人之间的差距大小已经不再是炙手可热的问题。 即便不考虑通货膨胀在个人收入上留下的蛾洞，赡养 3 名家庭成员的普通工厂工人的实际购买力在过去 10 年中增长了约 11%，比"二战"以来多出 29%。 尼克松总统在竞选期间辩称："在当今世界的大多数国家中，美国享受福利待遇的人是富有的。"毫无疑问，相比乔治·麦戈文为取悦富人而喋喋不休地抱怨税收不公，他的演说给选民留下了更为深刻的印象。

此外，一些经济学家认为，为了所有人的利益，普通员工和白领阶层之间的收入差距会持续拉大。 经济学家时代董事会成员艾伦·格林斯潘指出："如果不减少国家的实际收入增长，我认为你不可能缩小收入差距。 面对一群人人都在努力致富的人，你会收效甚微。 我们的整体激励结构取决于收入的增加。"

然而，即使不结束收入阶层的划分，缩小差距也已经成为半个多世纪以来的一个美国理想。 美国自 1913 年以来实行了累进所得

to the rich.

Some economists argue, moreover, that the income gap between broom closet and executive suite should continue to yawn wide, for everybody's sake. "I don't think you can narrow the income gap without reducing the nation's real income growth, " says Alan Greenspan, a member of TIME's Board of Economists. "You would get less effort out of a whole group of people who are striving to get rich. Our whole incentive structure depends on having income increments."

Yet narrowing, if not closing the income spectrum, has been a U.S. ideal for more than half a century. The nation has imposed a progressive income tax since 1913, enforced a graduated estate tax since 1916 and passed expensive programs designed to alleviate poverty since the New Deal. Why have these policies had so little effect on income distribution between rich and poor?

Analyst Henle blames the structure of the U. S. job market. The number of high-paying jobs, such as engineer, computer programmer and upper-level civil servant, he finds, has increased, and salaries in those categories have risen markedly. But the number of very low-paying jobs — janitor, dishwasher and hospital orderly, for example — has not declined. Henle gives two reasons: an influx over the past few years of postwar babies, who despite generally higher educational levels act as a drag on the lower end of the job market, and an increase in women and part-time workers, who often command relatively low pay. In other words, employers have found so many people available to be hired for relatively little money that they have not gone all-out to upgrade jobs and salaries.

Other economists point out that effective tax rates on top-bracket

税，自 1916 年以来强制执行了累进遗产税，自罗斯福新政以来，通过了旨在缓解贫困的昂贵计划。 为什么这些政策在贫富收入分配上收效甚微呢？

分析师亨勒将责任归咎于美国就业市场的结构。 他发现，工程师、计算机程序员和高级公务员等高薪工作人群的数量已经增加，这些类别的工作薪酬均显著上升。 但有些报酬极低的工作，如看门人、洗碗工和医院护工等，数量却没有下降。 亨勒给出了两个理由：一是战后婴儿潮在过去几年中大量涌入劳动力市场，尽管他们受教育的程度普遍较高，但仍然拖累了低端就业市场；二是妇女和兼职工作者增加，他们只要求相对较低的工资。 换句话说，雇主已经发现，既然他们可以花相对少的钱聘用如此多的人，就没有必要不遗余力地增加工作机会和提升薪酬。

其他的经济学家指出，自第二次世界大战以来，因为监管漏洞和降息的结合，高收入人群的有效税率一直在稳定下降；而由于递减的销售、工资和社会保险税的重要性日益增长，低收入税率已经有所增加。 另一位经济学家时代董事会成员约瑟夫·倍克曼已经发现，排名前 1% 的纳税人去年支付的联邦所得税的实际税率仅为26%，尽管他们收入的联邦税率档次在名义上高达 70% 。

很难发现收入再分配的方法是否可取、可行和在政治上可以接受。 美国国会的此轮会议将开始重新审查大量的所得税"优惠"政策，但历史上关闭漏洞的努力表明，他们为每一个被淘汰的方案创建了一个新的不平等。 最近几年的低出生率也许会造成本世纪末的人工短缺，届时将会抬高低薪工作的报酬。 联邦政府可以直接资助工作中的穷人，如尼克松政府当年首次提出的家庭援助计划，这可

individuals have been declining steadily since World War II, because of a combination of loopholes and rate reductions, while rates on lower incomes have increased because of the growing importance of regressive sales, payroll and Social Security taxes. Joseph Pechman, another member of TIME's Board of Economists, has found that the effective rate of federal income tax paid last year by the top 1% of taxpayers was only 26%, even though the nominal federal tax rates on their income brackets ranged up to 70%.

Whether or not they would be desirable, workable and politically acceptable methods of income redistribution are hard to find. Congress this session will begin re-examining scores of income tax "preferences," but the history of loophole-closing efforts is that they create a new inequity for each one eliminated. The low birth rates of recent years might create a shortage of workers later in the century that would jack up① pay in lowly jobs. Direct federal aid to the working poor, as contained in the Family Assistance Plan first proposed at the time by the Nixon Administration, could be an effective means of income redistribution, but the President has quietly withdrawn his support of the plan. For now, the most realistic hope of the poor probably lies in continuation of the strong economic advance that John Kennedy once compared to a rising tide that "lifts all the boats."

(991 words)

---

① jack up 提高

能是收入再分配的有效手段，但是总统悄悄地撤回了他对这项计划的支持。 现在，穷人最现实的希望可能在于强劲的经济发展能够持续，约翰·肯尼迪曾经将此比作可以"抬高所有船只"的涨潮。

知识链接 🔍

Vilfredo Pareto 维弗雷多·帕累托（1848—1923 年）。维弗雷多·帕累托生前任瑞士洛桑大学教授，是意大利经济学家、社会学家，洛桑学派的主要代表之一。帕累托的主要成就是运用立体几何研究经济变量间的相互关系，发展了瓦尔拉的一般均衡的代数体系；提出在收入分配为既定的条件下，为了达到最大的社会福利，生产资料的配置所必须达到的状态，这种状态称为"帕累托最适度"。

Robert Lucas 伯特·卢卡斯。经济学天才，理性预期学派的重量级代表。他倡导和发展了理性预期与宏观经济学研究的运用理论，深化了人们对经济政策的理解，并对经济周期理论提出了独到的见解。他于 1995 年获得诺贝尔经济学奖。

题 记

　　人们虔诚地认为，哈利·波特头上的那个闪电标志，其实更像个扭曲的"＄"标志。随着《哈利·波特》系列图书的问世，与之相关的电影、DVD、电视片、游戏、服装、文具、主题公园、主题旅游已经渗透到现代人的生活之中，形成了一个庞大的产业链，创造出上千亿美元的商业价值和文化价值。哈利·波特的旅行故事创造了一个难以复制的财富童话，它从生活在爱丁堡的一位单身母亲的脑海中诞生，成长为全球大众媒体的新宠，继而被赐予最富有的世界公民的封号。伦敦的一家出版社布鲁姆斯伯里因出版《哈利·波特》赚得盆满钵满，收购了因出版莎士比亚作品系列而闻名退迹的雅顿、法律类出版品牌托特尔以及板球爱好者的圣经品牌威斯登。哈利·波特不仅创建了一个产业，而且也改变了好莱坞：它开创了用新方法制作高成本电影的先河，电影的特许经营权从此演绎着商业色彩和艺术魅力交织的奇迹。

The Harry Potter Economy

A former Rolls-Royce factory north of London, a new kind of industry is churning①. Gothic walls are being moulded and costumes sewn. Women stitch hairs onto goblins. A sculptor creates a huge monument to wizarding might. Two men are employed to spackle the roof. This production line at Leavesden Studios, which has been running for almost a decade, will soon be switched off. "People talk about the effect of factories closing," says David Heyman, who produces the Harry Potter films. "When we stop filming next May, at least 800 people will be looking for work."

The recession has been accompanied by bold claims about businesses' economic importance. As carmakers teetered② many people put it about that one in ten American jobs depended on the industry which the figure turned out to include taxi drivers. Similarly adventurous claims have been made for telecoms and road-building. As a single-handed creator of jobs and wealth, though, few can match the writer Joanne Rowling.

---

① churning [ˈtʃɜːnɪŋ] *adj.* 搅拌的
② teeter [ˈtiːtə] *vt.* 使⋯⋯摇摆；使⋯⋯上下晃动

哈利·波特经济

北伦敦劳斯莱斯工厂的旧址上，一种新型的产业正在如火如荼地运行。 人们忙于铸造哥特式的城墙，缝制各种服饰。 妇女们把毛发缝在小精灵的身上。 为了显示魔法的威力，一位雕刻家创建了一尊巨大的纪念碑。 两个人被雇来粉刷屋顶。 利维斯登工作室的这条生产线已经运行了近 10 年，现在即将被关闭。 创作了哈利波特电影系列的戴维·海曼如是说："人们都在谈论工厂关闭的影响。当我们明年 5 月停止拍摄的时候，至少有 800 人会去找工作。"

企业经济的重要性向世人大胆地昭示，它与经济衰退如影相随。 由于汽车生产商处于摇摇欲坠的边缘，许多人认为，美国十分之一的工作依赖于这个产业，这一数字甚至还包括出租车司机。 与此类似的是，电信行业和道路建设行业也面临岌岌可危的境况。 的确，作家乔安妮·罗琳单枪匹马地创造了就业机会和财富的神话，几乎无人可以与之匹敌。

罗琳女士对经济的主要贡献包括 7 本关于魔法师的书。 哈利·波特是一个孤儿，生活在城郊一间沉闷得令人窒息的屋子里。 11 岁的时候，他惊讶地收到了一封加入霍格沃茨魔法学校的邀请函。 在那里，他知道了杀死他父母的凶手伏地魔，他是一个邪恶至极的魔

Ms. Rowling's chief contribution to the economy consists of seven books about a wizard. Harry Potter is an orphan who has been raised in a stifling① suburban house. At the age of 11 he is surprised to get an invitation to attend Hogwarts School of Witchcraft and Wizardry. There, he learns about Lord Voldemort, his parents' killer and a wizard of such wickedness that he is known as "He Who Must Not Be Named". Potter must confront this menace in between worrying about sport, homework and girls.

The story of Harry Potter's journey from the mind of a single mother living in Edinburgh to a global mass-media franchise is a fairy tale. Precisely, it is Cinderella — a story of greatness overlooked, chance discovery and eventual riches. Harry Potter might never have become known had an employee at Christopher Little's literary agency in London not taken a liking to the manuscript's binding and picked it out to read. It went on to be rejected by several publishers. Cinderella's transformation from kitchen grunt to belle is both delightful and disruptive. So it has proved for the companies involved with Harry Potter.

The first company to be transformed was Bloomsbury, a London publishing house. It was a somewhat unlikely home for a blockbuster children's book series. In general the firm's children's books division had generated just £732,000 in sales, compared with £4.7m for the reference division. Nigel Newton signed up the manuscript that was to become "Harry Potter and the Philosopher's Stone" after market-testing

---

① stifling ['staifliŋ] *adj.* 令人窒息的,沉闷的

法师,是个臭名昭著、"连名字都不能提的人"。 波特必须面对这一威胁,忧心忡忡地周旋于运动、家庭作业和女孩之间。

哈利·波特的旅行故事是一段童话,它从生活在爱丁堡的一位单身母亲的脑海中诞生,成长为全球大众媒体的系列影片。 准确地说,它是灰姑娘的故事,讲述了一个被完全遗弃的人发现机会、并一夜暴富的神话。 如果位于伦敦的克里斯托弗·里特文学代理机构的一位雇员没有翻阅捆扎在一起的手稿并将其挑出来阅读的嗜好,哈利·波特可能永远都不会为人所知。 它接连遭遇几家出版商的拒绝。 灰姑娘从厨房女佣摇身变为美女的情节既令人愉快又制造了混乱。 与哈利波特相关的公司已经证明了这一点。

伦敦的一家出版社布鲁姆斯伯里是第一家彻底转型的公司。 这是一家不太可能因儿童系列读物而引发轰动效应的公司。 一般来说,与相关部门 470 万英镑的盈利相比,该公司儿童读物部的销售额仅为 73.2 万英镑。 奈杰尔·牛顿在他的女儿身上进行了市场测试后,签下了后来成为《哈利·波特与魔法石》一书的手稿。

该公司根本想不到接下来将会发生什么样的事情。 布鲁姆斯伯里在《哈利·波特与魔法石》出版前不久曾发布过一份年度报告,完全没有提及即将出版的新书。 下一年度的报告庆祝了三大主题。它们是维尔·赛尔富的《巨猿》、布雷·摩尔的《魔法师的妻子》和安妮·迈克尔的《漂泊手记》。 该报告没有提及罗琳女士获得儿童颁发的"聪明豆奖"、且销量不错的一本书。 即使哈利·波特在当年春天就已经售出 76.3 万册,公司仍然重点推出其他的儿童读物,认为哈利·波特系列只是"出版业的冰山一角"。

事实上,哈利·波特读物确实是座冰山。 随着每本书的上市,

it on his daughter.

The firm had little idea of what was to come. Bloomsbury's annual report, written shortly before the publication of "Harry Potter and the Philosopher's Stone", contained no mention of the forthcoming book. The following year's report celebrated three big titles. They were "Great Apes" by Will Self, "The Magician's Wife" by Brian Moore and "Fugitive Pieces" by Anne Michaels. The report did mention that a book by Ms Rowling had won the Smarties prize, awarded by children, and was selling well. Even in the spring of that year, by which point the Harry Potter books had sold 763,000 copies, the company was still emphasising other children's books, referring to the Harry Potter series as "the tip of a publishing iceberg".

In fact the Harry Potter books were the iceberg. As each book appeared it drew new readers to the series and expanded sales of earlier books in a snowball effect. Thanks largely to the boy wizard, Bloomsbury's turnover, which had gradually increased from £11m to £14m, took off. The next year it stood at £21m. Two years later it was £61m. By the middle of this decade, with Bloomsbury's revenues above £100m, rival publishers were griping that there was no point bidding against the firm for a children's title. So far the books, which are published in America by Scholastic, have sold more than 400m copies worldwide. Not all were read by the young. Central to the books' success was a repackaging, with a darker cover, for adults embarrassed about being seen reading a children's book.

Mr. Newton says he became "fearful and respectful" of the

它不断将新的读者吸引到这个系列中来，继而扩大了早期读物的销售量，产生了滚雪球式的效应。多亏了这位闻名退迩的少年巫师，布鲁姆斯伯里的营业额从 1.1 千万英镑直线上升至 1.4 千万英镑。第二年即达到 2.1 千万英镑。两年后达到 6.1 千万英镑。到这个 10 年的中期，随着布鲁姆斯伯里的总收入超过 1 亿英镑，其出版行业的竞争对手均悔之莫及，抱怨自己无法在儿童题材方面与该公司竞争。到目前为止，学者出版社在美国发行的哈利·波特系列读物的销售量已经超过 4 亿套。并不是只有年轻人在读这些书。这套书成功的核心是再包装，他们的封面颜色较暗，使成年人不会因为被人看到阅读儿童书籍而感到尴尬。

牛顿先生认为，他变得对意外之财"恐惧和敬畏"。突然的打击可以击垮任何公司，但是这种危险在耀武扬威的传媒产业面前转瞬即逝。布鲁姆斯伯里在银行存入了大笔的钱，充分利用资产价格猛跌的优势挑选专业的出版商和学术出版商。它现在拥有因出版莎士比亚作品系列而闻名退迩的雅顿、法律类出版品牌托特尔以及板球爱好者的圣经品牌威斯登。学会与魔法师打交道之后，布鲁姆斯伯里返璞归真，重塑麻瓜（非魔法师）的形象。牛顿先生表示，可靠的商业小说行业拥有巨额的潜在利润，理想的方式是平衡这种风险和专业出版行业之间的高额利润率。

商业魔杖触摸到的下一个公司甚至更小。"鼎盛电影"是海曼先生创立的一家年轻的伦敦制作厂家，它一直在寻找可以拍成电影的图书。在另一个魔法故事几乎被忽略的时候，海曼先生的秘书挑出了《哈利波特与魔法石》。他把它交给华纳兄弟，这是他做的第一笔交易。虽然他的主要联系人莱昂纳尔·威格拉姆兴趣浓厚，但高

windfall. A sudden hit can destabilise any company, but the danger is acute in the swaggering media industry. Bloomsbury banked a lot of the money, and has taken advantage of the slump in asset prices to pick up specialist and scholarly publishers. It now owns Arden, most famous for its series of Shakespeare texts, the legal publisher, Tottel, and the cricketer's bible, Wisden. Having learned to handle magic, Bloomsbury is thus returning to its Muggle (non-wizard) roots. The ideal, Mr. Newton says, is to balance the risks — and large potential profits — of the trade fiction business with the dependability and high margins of specialist publishing.

The next company to be touched by the commercial magic wand① was even smaller. Heyday Films, a young London production outfit founded by Mr. Heyman, was looking for books that could be turned into films. In another tale of magic nearly overlooked, "Harry Potter and the Philosopher's Stone" was picked up by Mr Heyman's secretary. He took it to Warner Bros, with which he had a first-look deal. Although his main contact there, Lionel Wigram, was keen, senior executives did not share the enthusiasm. It took the studio until the next year to option the rights to the first books. Warner Bros commissioned a screenplay but then spent months negotiating with Steven Spielberg of DreamWorks, who was interested in directing. Only after he pulled out two years later, did the project roll forward.

Harry Potter is a wholly different product. Instead of A-listers the films

---

① wand [wɔnd] *n.* 魔杖

管们却没有能够分享这份热情。 直到第二年第一批书的版权问题解决之后，拍摄才正式启动。 华纳兄弟委任了一名编剧，然后又花了几个月的时间与梦工厂有意担任其导演的斯蒂芬·斯皮尔伯格谈判。 直到他两年后退出该项目，拍摄工作才继续向前推进。

哈利·波特是一个完全不同的产品。 这部影片没有启用一线明星，主演由迄今为止不太出名的童星和英国的戏剧人才担任。 艾伦·里克曼也许是最大腕的明星，他因以前出演过《虎胆龙威》中的恶棍而为美国电影观众（即使不是全部）所熟知。 随着时间的推移，他们已经褪去了商业色彩和艺术魅力。 如果有什么区别的话，真实的情况恰恰相反。 前两部影片问世之后，哈利·波特的电影特许经营权被交给非美国导演，使其与独立电影和电视的关系更加密切。

哈利·波特开创了用新方法制作高成本电影的先河。 大多数现代大片的特许经营权有两个共同点：一是基于书籍及漫画等广为人知的故事；一是由令人尊敬、但鲜为人知的导演执导。 成功的《蜘蛛侠》系列片由山姆·雷米执导，他是一位狂热的恐怖片电影制作人。 新西兰人彼得·杰克逊受命执导《指环王》，在哈利·波特上映一个月之后，《指环王》的第一集问世。 也许新模式最好的例子是复活的《蝙蝠侠》，它的特许经营权现在由独立电影导演克里斯托弗·诺兰掌管。 它再次为华纳兄弟收获了公众的好评和大量的金钱。 虽然这些特许经营权创造了明星，但他们全都游离于影星圈之外。

feature hitherto obscure child actors and British theatrical talent. Perhaps the biggest star is Alan Rickman, previously known to American cinema-goers (if at all) as the villain in "Die Hard". Over time they have faded neither commercially nor artistically. If anything the reverse is true. After the first two films the Harry Potter franchise was handed to non-American directors more associated with independent film and television.

Harry Potter was in the vanguard① of a new approach to big-budget film-making. Most modern blockbuster franchises have two things in common: they are based on known properties such as books and comics, and they are steered by respected but little-known directors. The successful "Spider-Man" films are directed by Sam Raimi, a cult horror-film maker. Peter Jackson, a New Zealander, was asked to steer "Lord of the Rings", the first instalment of which appeared a month after Harry Potter. Perhaps the best example of the new model is the revived "Batman" franchise, now in the care of an independent-film director, Christopher Nolan. It is again producing critical cheers and plenty of money for Warner Bros. None of these franchises revolves around a star actor, although all have created stars.

(1,129 words)

---

① vanguard ['vængɑːd] *n.* 先锋

知识链接 🔍

Cinderella 灰姑娘。灰姑娘辛德瑞拉是《格林童话》中一个从苦役生活中逃脱出来、并嫁给王子的童话主角。人们通常认为灰姑娘的故事向我们传达了这么一个人生历练过程：在任何嘲讽、刁难和欺凌之下，都要吃苦耐劳、忍辱负重；即使极度艰难困苦，只要心怀对美好未来的无限憧憬，保持善良与积极的心态，最终会获得幸福的生活。

题 记

　　全球需求和贸易萎缩的严重影响，只是"亚马逊平原上蝴蝶扇动的第一下翅膀"。欧洲经济在金融风暴的肆虐下似乎并未独善其身：美国经济疲软导致世界贸易低迷，坚挺的欧元汇率加剧了这种影响；英国、西班牙和爱尔兰等主要经济体的房地产泡沫逐渐破裂，现在已波及法国、丹麦和葡萄牙等其他国家；欧元区的国内生产总值正在加速萎缩，制造业和服务业的购买力已经降至历史最低水平；欧元区的消费物价连续上涨，膨胀指数达欧元区实行单一货币以来的最高水平；大规模的融资枯竭阻止中央银行采取更多的扶持政策，贷款方正在进一步压缩信贷规模。人们期待欧元区的出口商可以受益于石油输出国不断上升的进口需求，欧元对美元的汇率会缓慢下降，从而为提前步入衰退期的欧洲经济创造迥然不同的环境，为痛苦挣扎的消费者提供一丝安慰。

European Economic Recession Ahead

European economies are seeing slower growth in world trade, a possibly overvalued euro, and other challenges. Results for the first quarter of this year could have made us believe that Europe would remain relatively immune from the U.S. slowdown and the disruptions in financial markets. Since then, however, a flurry of data from across the region consistently suggests that such views were overly optimistic, and a major slowdown is about to occur in the second half of this year. Gross domestic product (GDP) in the Eurozone contracted at a 0.8% annual rate in the second quarter. Additionally, the survey of purchasing managers in manufacturing and services dropped to its lowest level in history. Meanwhile, consumer price inflation in the Eurozone accelerated to 4.1% in the 12 months, its highest level since the introduction of the single currency. Inflation also accelerated in the United Kingdom to 4.4% year-on-year. We consider the outlook for inflation in the next 12 months to be the most critical variable for Europe's economies. Indeed, we think a deceleration on the back of lower oil prices would create a very different environment for monetary policies and provide a relief for hard-squeezed consumers. Until then, however, Europe should brace itself for a period of stagflation.

Economic storm gains strength. Economic reports published recently

欧洲经济提前步入衰退期

就全球贸易来看，欧洲经济似乎增长较缓，被高估的欧元和其他的挑战有可能是罪魁祸首。 今年第一季度的经济成就让我们认为，相对而言，欧洲能在美国不景气的经济和动荡的金融市场中独善其身。 然而，从那时以来，一系列引起恐慌的跨地区数据不断表明，这种观点实在是过于乐观，在今年下半年经济很可能出现大规模放缓的趋势。 欧元区的国内生产总值（GDP）在第二季度以年率0.8%的速度萎缩。 此外，对制造业和服务业采购经理的调查显示，购买力已经降至历史最低水平。 与此同时，欧元区的消费物价连续12个月加速上涨，膨胀指数达4.1%，这是自欧元区实行单一货币以来的最高水平。 与上年同期数字相比，英国的年通货膨胀率也加速上升至4.4%。 我们认为，未来12个月内的通货膨胀走向对欧洲经济是最为关键的变量。 我们甚至认为，减缓较低原油价格的回落将会为货币政策创造迥然不同的环境，为痛苦挣扎的消费者提供一丝安慰。 但在此之前，欧洲可能要经历一段滞涨期。

经济风暴表现出强悍的力量。 近期公布的经济报道描绘了黯淡的经济前景。 有数据表明，欧洲经济目前正处于风暴的中心。 这场风暴包括：美国经济疲软导致世界贸易低迷，坚挺的欧元汇率加

painted a bleak picture. The data are indicative that European economies are currently in the middle of a storm. Its components include: A downturn in world trade induced by the weakening U.S. economy and whose effects are compounded by the strong euro exchange rate; the unwinding of the housing bubbles in key economies such as the United Kingdom, Spain, and Ireland, now extending to other countries such as France, Denmark, and Portugal; and accelerating retail price inflation on the back of surging commodity prices. This curtails consumers' purchasing power and prevents central banks from adopting more supportive policies, while lenders clamp down on credit growth as wholesale funding dried up.

In the face of this slew of negative data, business and consumer sentiment is heading south. The Eurozone purchasing managers index (PMI) tumbled to its lowest level in the 10-year history of the series. The PMI decline was mirrored in the national business surveys. The IFO business confidence survey for Germany showed a marked decline in business leaders' expectations of future conditions, comparable to what was seen when the German economy began to slow. The ZEW indicator of economic sentiment, which focuses more on investors' expectations in that same country, showed a similar deterioration.

Consumer surveys are similarly bleak, reporting a sharp deterioration on the back of worsening conditions in labor markets, as weak domestic demand and margin compression lead companies to curtail hiring. The biggest drop in confidence took place in Spain, which is hardly surprising given the fast deceleration in economic growth taking place at the moment in that country, although French sentiment also plummeted① to levels not

---

① plummet['plʌmit] vi.垂直落下

剧了这种影响；英国、西班牙和爱尔兰等主要经济体的房地产泡沫逐渐破裂，现在已波及法国、丹麦和葡萄牙等其他国家；飞涨的商品价格背景促使零售价格加速通胀。 这就降低了消费者的购买力，阻止中央银行采取更多的扶持政策，而由于大规模的融资枯竭，贷款方还要进一步压缩信贷规模。

面对如此众多的负面数据，企业和消费者的情绪正变得越来越糟糕。 欧元区的采购经理人指数（PMI）跌至 10 年来的最低点。采购经理人指数的下降是国家经济状况的反映，德国慕尼黑经济研究所对德国的企业信心指数调查表明，与德国经济刚开始减速时相比，商界领袖对未来经济前景的期望值有明显的下降。 欧洲经济研究中心对经济信心指数的研究更多地聚焦于德国投资者的期望值，其结果显示了类似的环境恶化。

对消费者的调查同样令人沮丧，报告称，由于国内需求疲软和保证金压缩导致公司裁员，局势日益糟糕的劳动力市场急剧恶化。西班牙的信心指数降幅最大，考虑到目前该国经济增速彻底放缓的窘境，出现这种情况也就不足为怪，但欧洲作为一个整体正在经历增长乏力之际，法国的经济形势也骤然下跌，难以预测。 在英国，领取失业救济金的人数上升到 15 500 人，这足以显示就业市场是多么的不景气。 根据欧洲汽车制造商协会（ACEA）的调查，6 月份欧洲汽车的单月签售率在 7.9% 。 然而，欧洲汽车制造商协会各成员国的分项数据显示，经济衰退在地区之间分布不均：就签约率而言，法国增加了 1.5% ，德国增加了 1.0% ，相比之下，英国市场签约率减少了 6.1% ，意大利减少了 19.5% ，西班牙则减少了 30.8% 之多。

seen when Europe as a whole was experiencing anemic① growth. In the United Kingdom, the number of benefit claimants rose by 15,500 in June, highlighting a weakening labor market. European car sales contracted by 7.9% in the month, according to ACEA, the European Association of Car Manufacturers. The breakdown of the ACEA numbers shows, however, that the economic slowdown is uneven across the region: In France (+1.5%) and Germany (+1.0%), the number of registrations increased, while the markets in the United Kingdom (-6.1%), Italy (-19.5%), and Spain (-30.8%) deteriorated.

All these negative signals point to the same question: Is the European economy about to enter into a period of recession, with several consecutive② quarters of negative growth? The strong euro is weighing on the performance of Eurozone exports. On a trade-weighted basis, the exchange rate of the euro against the zone's major trading partners strengthened since the beginning to reach its highest level. At a time when foreign demand for Eurozone products, particularly from the United States but also from the weakening United Kingdom economy, is sliding, a strong currency is an obvious impediment③.

That said, more positive factors should also be considered. One is that Eurozone exporters have benefited significantly from the rising import demand from oil-exporting countries. Export revenues of major oil-exporting countries rose to $1.3 trillion from about $412 billion, on the back of the sustained rise in oil prices. A study issue of the European Central Bank's (ECB) monthly bulletin showed that despite the growing

---

① anemic[ə'niːmik] *adj.*贫血的
② consecutive[kən'sekjutive] *adj.*连续的
③ impediment[im'pedimənt] *n.*阻碍某事物发展的人或物

　　所有的这些负面的信号都指向了相同的问题：在经历了连续几个季度的经济负增长之后，欧洲经济是否已经进入了衰退期？ 坚挺的欧元正影响着欧元区的出口表现。 以贸易份额为参考基准的欧元汇率，自创建以来一直对主要贸易伙伴的货币处于升值状态，以期达到价值的最高点。 现在，国外市场对欧元区产品的需求正处于下滑状态，特别是来自美国和经济疲软的英国的需求一落千丈，强势货币是一个明显的障碍。

　　即便如此，我们也应注意到更多的积极因素。 其中之一便是欧元区的出口商极大地受益于来自石油输出国不断上升的进口需求。在原油价格持续上涨的背景之下，主要石油输出国的出口税收从4 120亿美元上升至1.3万亿美元。 欧洲中央银行（ECB）发布的一份月度研究报告表明，尽管亚洲出口在这些市场持续增长，欧元区的出口商近几年也一直能占据庞大和稳定的份额，平均可达25%。然而，这其中也有些许细微之处需要推敲，因为俄罗斯一直在其中起着主要的作用，而欧元区出口商在其他石油输出国（主要是石油输出国组织）的出口份额由25%略微下降至21%。 但在同期，美国对石油输出国（包括俄罗斯）的进口份额由12%下降至7.5%。也就是说，尽管强势货币制造了障碍，欧元区出口商仍然能够在俄罗斯保持或平衡促进市场份额的增长。 欧元区对石油输出国组织和俄罗斯出口额年增长率分别为7%和17%，这大大高于非欧元区年出口增长5%的平均水平。 这些经济体的强劲需求会持续刺激欧元区的出口。

　　另一个缓解因素来自于欧元汇率本身的未来走势。 我们的基本预测是期待欧元对美元的汇率会达到顶点，接近1：1.6。随后，由于

share of Asian exports in these markets, Eurozone exporters have been able to maintain a high and stable market share in recent years, averaging 25%. This positive outcome must be nuanced①, however, as it has been driven mainly by Russia, as Eurozone exports' market share in other oil-exporting countries (mainly OPEC) declined slightly to 21% from 25%. But over that same period, the U.S. market share in total imports of oil-exporting countries (Russia included) decreased to 7. 5% from 12. 0%. In other words, Eurozone exporters were able to maintain or even increase in Russia their market share despite the handicap of a strong currency. The annual growth in export volumes of goods to OPEC and Russia was on average 7% and 17%, respectively, significantly above the average growth in extra-Eurozone exports of around 5%. Strong demand from those economies will continue to boost Eurozone exports.

The second mitigating factor comes from the outlook for the euro exchange rate itself. Our baseline forecast expects the euro exchange rate to peak against the U. S. dollar near 1. 60. Then, the rate should slowly decline, as the fundamentals begin to turn in favor of the U.S. currency, with weaker growth prospects in the Eurozone and an increased probability of an interest rate hike in the United States. Overall, Eurozone export growth should drop to 4%. German exports are likely to follow a similar trend. French exports, after an upbeat performance in the first quarter of this year, should experience a very modest rise in the second half of the year, leading to an average increase of 3.9%.

(996 words)

---

① nuance [njuːˈɑːns] *n.*细微差别

人们对于欧元区增长预期的下降等基本因素的变化可能会支持美元走势，而且美国很有可能加息，所以欧元对美元的汇率会缓慢下降。就整体而言，欧元区的出口增长会降至 4%。德国的出口也呈现出类似的走势。法国的出口在经历了上半年的不佳表现之后，下半年可能会有温和的增长，从而使全年增长率达到 3.9%。

知识链接

IFO 德国慕尼黑经济研究所。IFO 是德国经济信息研究所注册协会的英文缩写，它于 1949 年成立于慕尼黑，是一家公益性的、独立的经济研究所，被称为德国政府智库之一。德国经济信息研究所编制的 IFO 经济景气指数（IFO Business Climate Index），是对包括制造业、建筑业及零售业等各产业部门每个月均进行调查，每次调查所涵盖的企业家数在 7 000 家以上，依企业评估目前的处境状况，以及短期内企业的计划及对未来半年的看法，为观察德国经济状况的重要领先指标。

heading south 情况变得越来越糟糕。go south 这一词组与南部地区（the south）没有什么关系，它不过是根据地图"上北下南"的规定，才用来代表任何下降趋势、走势。如果是某些人 go south，这意味着他们某种程度上让你失望了；如果是股票市场 go south，你将很可能会被套牢；如果运动员 go south，这意味着他已经过了巅峰时期；如果是电脑的软硬件 go south，那意味着这些软硬件坏了。所以，go south 是一个非常有表现力的习语，可以非常灵活地运用于表述各种带有贬义的情形。

题　记

　　历史是一面镜子。世界在"一战"中付出了生命和财产的惨重代价，但它在很长一段时间内无法恢复商品购买力，以适应战后十几年间由于工业革命而导致的产能的急剧增长。20世纪30年代的全球化，使世界经济恢复了活力，但美国却在大萧条期间选择了闭关自守，半个世纪以前整合的全球经济只留下一片残缺的记忆。历史是一部教科书。在当今恐怖主义、战争和一系列毁灭性的金融危机猖獗肆虐之际，全球经济终究还是幸免于难，这场危机牵动了世界最先进的经济体系和金融系统全球化的神经：它会降低自由化金融市场的意愿，它会破坏自由市场资本主义的可信性，它会恶化世界经济的表现。以史为鉴可以明得失。全球化的新时代既是银行危机的新时代，更是金融危机考验全球化耐力的新时代。

Financial crisis tests durability of globalization

Globalization has been the great economic and political theme of the past three decades. It has brought the labor supplies of Asia into the world economy. It has transformed the operations of companies and financial markets. But will it survive the financial crisis? One precedent — that of the 1930s — is disturbing enough to give even the optimistic pause.

The first world war damaged, but did not destroy, the globalization of late 19th and early 20th century. The world economy recovered its vitality in the 1920s. Then came the US stock market crash of 1929 and the financial melt-down of the 1930s. During the great depression, the world chose autarky①. By the late 1930s, the integrated global economy of half a century before was little more than a memory. Will today's prove more robust? The good news is that it has already survived terrorism, war and a series of devastating② financial crises. As Carmen Reinhart of the University of Maryland and Kenneth Rogoff of Harvard have shown in a

---

① autarky [ˈɔːtɑːki] n.闭关自守
② devastating [ˈdevəsteitiŋ] adj.破坏性的

金融危机对全球化耐力的考验

　　全球化已经成为过去 30 年来伟大的经济和政治主题。 它把亚洲的劳动力供给带入到世界经济之中。 它转变了公司和金融市场的运行。 但是它会幸免于金融危机吗？ 20 世纪 30 年代的一个先例足以令人不安地让乐观主义者望而却步。

　　第一次世界大战损害了、但尚未摧毁 19 世纪后期和 20 世纪早期的全球化。 世界经济在 20 世纪 20 年代恢复了它的活力。 接下来的 1929 年，美国股市行情暴跌，20 世纪 30 年代迎来了金融大崩盘。 在大萧条期间，世界选择了闭关自守。 到 20 世纪 30 年代后期，半个世纪以前整合的全球经济只不过是一个记忆。 当今的经济会更具稳健性吗？ 好消息是，尽管恐怖主义、战争和一系列毁灭性的金融危机猖獗肆虐，全球经济终究还是幸免于难。 正如马里兰大学的卡门·雷哈特和哈佛大学的肯尼思·罗格夫在一篇有重大影响的论文中阐述的那样，全球化的新时代一直是银行危机的新时代。在 20 世纪 90 年代早期，当大多数这些危机发生在新兴经济体中时，它们也会使日本和斯堪的纳维亚的经济跌入低谷。 就日本来说，金融危机阻碍了超过 10 年的经济发展。

　　留心的读者会注意到，以国家受影响的比例来衡量，危机的发

seminal① paper, the epoch of globalization has been an epoch of banking crises. While most of these crises occurred in emerging economies, they also brought Japan and the Scandinavian economies low in the early 1990s. In the case of Japan, the financial crisis afflicted the economy for more than a decade.

Attentive readers will notice that the incidence of crises, measured by the proportion of countries affected, reached its apogee② in the late 1990s, whereupon it collapsed. This looked encouraging: Maybe, some hoped, the era of crises was coming to an end, as people learned how open financial systems should work. The bad news is that this view now seems extremely naive. The current financial crisis affects the US and Europe, which account for more than half of world output, measured at market exchange rates. Judged by the share of the world economy affected, this is the most significant financial crisis since the 1930s. This crisis also affects the world's most advanced economies and financial systems. This is no crisis of backwardness, but one of sophistication.

The lessons of history, though, are clear. The economic isolationism of the 1930s, epitomized by America's Smoot-Hawley tariff, cruelly intensified the Depression. To be sure, the World Trade Organization (WTO) and its multilateral trading rules are a bulwark against protection on that scale. But today's globalised economy, with far-flung supply chains and just-in-time delivery, could be disrupted by policies much less dramatic than the Smoot-Hawley act. A modest shift away from openness — well within the WTO's rules — would be enough to turn the

---

① seminal [ˈsiːminl] *adj.*有创意的
② apogee [ˈæpədʒiː] *n.*最高点

生率在 20 世纪 90 年代后期达到顶峰，然后轰然倒塌。 这看上去是鼓舞人心的：也许有人希望，危机时代即将结束，因为人们了解了公开的金融系统应该如何运行。 坏消息是，这种观点现在似乎极端幼稚。 目前的金融危机影响着美国和欧洲，以市场汇率来测量，它们占据世界产出的一半以上。 根据世界经济受影响的比重判断，这是自 20 世纪 30 年代以来最严重的金融危机。 这场危机也影响着世界最先进的经济体系和金融系统。 这不是一个滞后性的危机，而是一个具有成熟度的危机。

然而，历史的教训历历在目。 20 世纪 30 年代，以美国斯姆特-霍利关税法为典型代表的经济孤立主义残忍地加剧了大萧条。 诚然，世界贸易组织（WTO）及其多边贸易规则在一定程度上是对抗保护主义的壁垒。 但是在经济全球化的今天，供应链遍布世界各地，货物能够即时送达，危害程序比斯姆特-霍利关税法小得多的法案就可以破坏全球经济。 只需要在不违背世界贸易组织规则的范围内适度闭关，就足以让经济衰退更加严重。

全球经济衰退的消息本身就够糟糕了，但它还给全球化时代的自由市场带来了最大的威胁。 这是三十多年来全球经济的两大引擎——贸易和资本流动——首次同时反其道而行之。 世界银行表示，流入新兴市场国家的净私人资本可能只有去年的一半，当年的记录是 1 万亿美元；与此同时，全球贸易量也将首次出现萎缩。

这样一个危机对全球化会有怎样的影响呢？ 这取决于延续宽泛的全球自由经济政策。 尽管技术——特别是信息与通信成本的减少——发挥着很大的作用，但它本身并不能驱动全球化。 此外，金融系统走向开放，接收进港的直接投资和贸易自由化等决策也同样

recession much nastier.

This news is bad enough in itself; but it also poses the biggest threat to open markets in the modern era of globalization. For the first time in more than a generation, two of the engines of global integration-trade and capital flows-are simultaneously shifting into reverse. The World Bank says that net private capital flows to emerging economies are likely to be only half the record $ 1 trillion, while global trade volumes will shrink for the first time.

What then might such a crisis do to globalization, which depends on the continuation of broadly liberal economic policies across the globe? While technology — particularly the reduction in the costs of information and communications — has played a big part, it does not drive globalization on its own. Also important have been decisions to move towards open financial systems, accept inward direct investment and liberalize trade. Trade seems to be the engine of globalization. In each successive business cycle, trade has grown faster than world output. Between recent five years, for example, world exports of manufactures grew at a trend rate of 7. 7 per cent a year, in real terms, while output of manufactures grew at 4 per cent. As the growth of trade accelerated, it seems to have pulled the world economy into faster growth, as well.

The financial crisis of today threatens globalization in three ways. First, it will reduce willingness to liberalize financial markets. If even the US and Europe cannot manage liberalized financial markets, can emerging economies hope to do so? Second, it will undermine the credibility of free-market capitalism. This will affect not just finance, but, quite possibly, trade and direct investment as well. The more intrusive governments become in the high-income countries, the more

重要。 贸易似乎是全球化的引擎。 在每一连续的商业周期中，贸易比世界产出发展得更快。 例如，在最近的 5 年间，全球制造业的出口以每年 7.7% 的速度增长，然而按实值计算，制造业产出的增长率只有 4%。 当交易增长加速时，它好像也在拉动世界经济更快地增长。

当代的金融危机在三方面威胁着全球化。 首先，它会降低自由化金融市场的意愿。 如果连美国和欧洲都不能管理自由化的金融市场，新兴经济体能期望做到吗？ 其次，它会破坏自由市场资本主义的可信性。 这不仅会影响金融，而且很可能也会影响贸易和直接投资。 在高收入国家，政府的干预越多，世界其他国家越是不愿意听从他们关于自由市场优点的见解。 最后，它会恶化世界经济的表现。 目前的状况貌似合情合理，但如果美国和欧洲进入严重的经济衰退期，就有望出现经济民族主义，这是令人感到忧虑的。

多哈多边贸易协商的失败无疑加大了这种危险。 在中国和印度的大力推动下，21 世纪已经见证了新兴经济体非同寻常的蓬勃发展。 虽然这些国家即使在困难时期也应该继续快速发展，但他们的节奏很可能会放慢。 那么，这潜在地成为一个转折点，它不仅涉及金融界，而且关系到金融全球化、甚至是全球一体化的进程。 这在很大程度上取决于如何迅速和有效地处理危机。 同样，相关的经济衰退持续多久也起着关键的作用。

世界能在多大程度上远离自由化尤为重要。 幸运的是，金融界的过度行为不会过多地污染市场经济。 但是，在这个危机仍然处于顶峰的时刻，这只不过是一丝希望。 要确保这点希望变成现实，还取决于政策制定者。 人们必须吸取经验教训。 但是，从这些经验

unwilling the rest of the world will be to listen to their lectures on the virtues of free markets. Finally, it will worsen the performance of the world economy. If, as now seems plausible, the US and Europe go into a significant recession, a rise in economic nationalism is to be expected — and feared.

The failure of the Doha round of multilateral trade negotiations must increase this danger. The 2000s have seen extraordinarily dynamic growth in emerging economies, driven largely by China and India. While these countries should continue to grow fast even in difficult times, their pace would probably slow. This then is, potentially, a turning point not just for the financial sector, but for financial globalization and even globalization as a whole. Much depends on how swiftly and effectively this crisis is dealt with. Much depends, too, on how long the associated recession lasts.

Much depends, not least, on how far the world turns away from liberalization. With luck the excesses of the financial sector will not taint[1] the market economy too much. But, at this moment, when the crisis is at its peak, this is but a hope. It is up to policy makers to ensure that it turns out to be a fact. Lessons must indeed be learned. But among those lessons is not a need for self-sufficiency. That would add economic disaster to financial calamity.

(947 words)

---

① taint [teint] *vt.* 污染

教训中我们可以借鉴的是，不再需要维系闭关自守的策略。 闭关自守只会给金融灾难增加经济浩劫。

知识链接

The Smoot-Hawley Tariff Act 斯姆特-霍利关税法。斯姆特-霍利关税法于1930 年经签署成为法律，该法案将2 000多种的进口商品关税提升到历史最高水平。当时在美国，有1 028名经济学家签署了一项请愿书抵制该法案。而在该法案通过之后，许多国家对美国采取了报复性关税措施，使美国的进口额和出口额都骤降50％以上。一些经济学家认为，斯姆特-霍利法案是导致美欧之间贸易规模从1929 年的历史高位急剧衰退到1932 年历史低位的催化剂——伴随着这次衰退的是大萧条的开始。

Doha Development Agenda 多哈回合（DDA）。2001 年 11 月，在卡塔尔首都多哈举行的世贸组织第四次部长级会议启动了新一轮多边贸易谈判，又称"多哈发展议程"，或简称"多哈回合"。谈判内容包括农业、非农产品市场准入，与贸易有关的知识产权，争端解决，贸易与发展等议题。

题　记

　　精彩纷呈的商标设计在五花八门的商品市场中给企业或者产品提供了独特的识别元素。商标是一种商业工具，展示着企业的专业水准和竞争能力，如麦当劳的"M"是个圆润的棱角，代表着美味、干净和舒适；而摩托罗拉的"M"棱角分明、双峰突出，以充分表达品牌的高科技属性。创建商标要使用矢量图形绘制软件，以调整大小，保持设计的完整性、透明度和清晰度，如百事可乐的圆球中间是一根似乎一直在流动着的白色飘带。商标设计要避免错综复杂和结构精细，如苹果公司那"被咬了一口的苹果"标识非常简单，却让人过目不忘。商标的颜色应该限制在三种以内，如耐克品牌的红色一勾，尽管是最简单的商标，但它却无处不在，给人以丰富的联想。其实，每个产品的商标都有着属于自己的精彩的故事，并深深地影响着普通人的日常生活。

Wonderful Performance
in Logo Design

Logos① can be described as visual icons that provide a unique identification element to a business or product. Logos provide quick visual recognition of a Company which in-turn builds branding. Business owners and overly enthusiastic artists can often go astray in their efforts to design the perfect logo. There are too many examples of logo designs that look uninspired, overtly abstract or seem to be nothing more than whimsical art. Many of these logos are designed without forethought into usage, application or even cost impact upon a business. So how do you create a logo that makes Business sense? Consider following a few simple guidelines:

Remember that your logo is a Business tool. Your design concept should begin with a commitment to portray your business as professional and competent. A logo is not an art piece! Avoid using elements that may give a "dated" look such as those 1970's flowers that were on so many Volkswagen Beetle cars. A logo design should take into consideration how, when and where the logo will be used. A logo has a cost impact

---

① logo [ˈlɔgɔ] n.商标

精彩纷呈的商标设计

商标可以被描述为视觉图标，它给企业或者产品提供了独特的识别元素。 商标提供了快捷的公司视觉标识，并随之构建了品牌。公司老总和过度狂热的艺术家往往在不遗余力地设计商标时误入歧途。 有太多这样的例子，有些商标图案看上去缺乏灵感，过分抽象，或者看起来只不过是异想天开的艺术。 这类商标的设计缺乏深谋远虑，许多都没有考虑实际效果、应用价值甚至对企业的成本影响。 那么，如何创建具有商业意义的标识呢？ 请考虑以下几条简单的建议：

请记住，商标是一种商业工具。 你的设计概念首先应该恪守承诺，展示企业的专业水准和竞争能力。 商标不是一件艺术作品！要避免使用可能带有"过时"外观的元素，例如太多的大众甲壳虫汽车上还标有 20 世纪 70 年代的花商标。 商标设计应该考虑如何、何时和在哪里使用商标。 商标被推出的当天，就会影响企业的经营成本。 设计商标远不仅仅是聘请艺术家或在线艺术商店，堆砌形状和颜色——它是一个商业决策。

使用矢量图形绘制软件创建商标。 简言之，使用矢量制图法创建的图像可以调整大小，并保持设计的完整性。 透明度、清晰度或

upon your business from the day that it is introduced. There is more to designing a logo than simply hiring an artist or online art shop to assemble shapes and colors — it is a Business decision.

Create your logo using vector graphics software. Simply put, images done in vector graphics can be resized and maintain design integrity. There is no loss in clarity, sharpness or definition and the file size remains constant. A common program for creating vector graphics is Adobe Illustrator. Software like Photoshop, which works in pixels, is better suite to working with photos and texture style areas. You can create your original image in any software but have it redone in a vector graphics format before you print or reproduce① your logo. After all, a logo is all about sharp image.

Avoid complicated and intricate designs. A logo that is too intricate hinders rapid visual identification. The viewer is required to "study" the image in order to mentally process the image and relate its identification to a given company. Note the simplicity and high visual impact of the Nike "Swish", an excellent image. Another reason to avoid complicated designs is that they do not reduce well. A busy, intricate logo on the side of a company truck may look wonderful but when the same logo is reduced in size for use on a Business card it may become a meaningless blob of ink. Keep it simple and clean.

Limit color selection to a maximum of three colors. Ideally use one or two colors but never more than three. There are three main reasons for this guideline. One, your printing costs for printing Business cards, letterhead, envelops, labels, etc. are increased for every additional color

---

① reproduce [riːprəˈdjuːs] vt. 复制

分辨力不仅不会受损，而且文件的大小会保持不变。 创建矢量制图法的通用程序是绘图软件。 Photoshop 等软件以像素为单位进行组合，是处理照片和纹理风格区域的更好的套件。 你可以使用任何软件来创建原始图像，但是在打印或复制商标之前必须用矢量图形格式重新处理。 毕竟，商标应该是完全清晰的图像。

避免错综复杂和结构精细的设计。 设计得太复杂的商标会妨碍快捷的视觉识别。 观察者需要"研究"图像，以便在大脑中处理图像，将它的标识与给定的公司联系起来。 例如，耐克"嗖地快速移动"的商标既简单又给人高度的视觉冲击力，是一个优秀的图像。 另外一个避免复杂设计的原因是，当商标缩小时就会变得模糊。 一个五花八门、设计复杂的商标印在公司卡车的侧面可能看起来很精彩，但是同样的缩小体积、印在名片上时，就变成了一坨毫无意义的墨水。 商标应该保持简洁和干净。

商标的颜色最多应该限制在三种以内。 理想的状态是使用一种或两种颜色，但绝不要超过三种。 提出这种设计方案主要有三种理由。 首先，每增加一种你需要的颜色，印刷商业名片及印有抬头的信笺、信封、标签等的成本就会增加。 你的"廉价"商标设计最终可能花费你很多钱。 第二条理由是，在某些媒介中，你的视觉冲击力甚至识别能力都将会减少或完全消失。 想想看，一个由不同色彩叠加的商标看上去挺不错的，对不对？ 但当你传真你的提议或信件的时候，商标此时呈黑白状态，情况会是如何呢？ 这种黑白版本（灰度图像）仍然会提供区别吗？ 例如用来提升色彩感的孔雀图案，经由传真后看上去像一只火鸡，这就是商标色彩转换丧失的例子。 最后需要注意的是，选择色彩时需要考虑文化和市场标准。

that you require. Your "cheap" logo design could end up costing you a lot of money. Reason number two, your visual impact or even identification could be diminished or completely lost in some mediums. Consider a logo that has overlaid images of different colors — looks nice, right? What about when you fax your proposal or letter and your logo is now in a black and white realm? Does the black and white (grayscale) version still provide distinction? An example of lost-in-translation logo is a peacock used to promote color and via fax it ends up looking like a turkey. A final note on color selection is to carefully consider cultural and marketplace standards. For example, red may be lesser choice for a medical company due to the negative association of red to blood/danger whereas green might infer safety or a positive status.

Consistency and control in font usage. Do not use over two font styles, as it may be distracting and confusing. Try to use a standard font such as Times New Roman, Arial, etc. as it makes commercial reproduction of your image easier. Any font style should be sans serif and typically non-script to improve clarity in small format reproduction. An exception is a logo/name where the logo is the script font such as the trade name of a popular soft drink in a uniquely shaped bottle.

Check Trademark and Registration Rights. While a new logo runs a low statistical chance of violating any trademark or registration rights of any existing logo it is not a bad idea to make some effort to confirm this before you publish your new logo. And after you have settled on a final logo design you should take the effort to register or trademark your own logo. If you need an example of why then consider the yellow pages "Walking Fingers" logo. The design was never trademarked or registered and has no copyrights protection — it could have been, but wasn't — a

举例来说，医药公司较少选用红色的标识，因为红色容易让人产生血液或危险的负面联想，而绿色则可以暗示安全或积极的状态。

字体使用的一致性和控制度。不要使用两种以上的字体，因为它可能分散注意力并造成混乱。尝试使用新罗马体、Arial等标准字体，因为这会使商业图像的复制更容易。任何字体样式都要用无衬线字体，通常用非书写字体，以提高小型版式复制的清晰度。商标或名字采用书写体的标识是个例外，例如流行软饮料形状独特的瓶子上标注的商品名。

检查商标和注册权。从统计学的角度看，虽然新商标侵犯任何现有商标标识和注册权的几率很低，但是在公布你的新商标以前，做些努力来证实这一点并不是坏事。确定了最终商标设计之后，应该尽力注册或认证你自己的商标。如果你需要了解为什么必须这么做，不妨想一想电话号码簿中"步行手指"标识这个例子。这个设计从来没有注册商标或登记，没有申请版权保护——其实它本来可以这么做，但它没有这么做，从而导致标识的原创者损失惨重。

每个产品的商标都有着属于自己的精彩故事。在史蒂夫·乔布斯、史蒂夫·沃兹尼亚克和罗纳德·韦恩三人决定成立公司时，乔布斯正好从一个苹果园旅行回来，他向沃兹建议把公司命名为"苹果电脑"，苹果公司的名称就此诞生。况且，史蒂夫·乔布斯本人就是一个果食主义者，他认为这个名字"有趣、生机勃勃且温文尔雅"。最初的商标由三位创始人之一的罗纳德·韦恩设计，只在生产 Apple-I 时使用，为牛顿坐在苹果树下看书的钢笔绘画。但它几乎立即就被广告设计商罗伯·让诺夫的"彩虹苹果"标识代替，并配合 Apple-II 的发布使用，即人们现在熟悉的有一个缺口的彩虹色苹

huge loss of value for the original creators.

All products of trademarks have their own wonderful stories. Apple was so named because Jobs was coming back from an apple farm when Steve Jobs, Steve Wozniak and Ronald Wayne decided to set up a company, so he suggested warding the company named "apple computer". Steve Jobs, who was on a fruitarian diet, thought the name was "fun, spirited and not intimidating". Apple's first logo, designed by Ron Wayne of the three and only used in Apple-I, depicts Sir Isaac Newton sitting under an apple tree. It was almost immediately replaced by Advertising designer Rob Janoff's "rainbow Apple", used in the publication of Apple-II, the now-familiar rainbow-colored silhouette of an apple with a bite taken out of it. When Janoff presented Jobs with several different monochromatic① themes for the "bitten" logo, Jobs immediately took a liking to it. While Jobs liked the logo, he insisted it be in color to humanize the company. "The logo was designed with a bite so that it would not be confused with a cherry", as Steve Jobs once said. The colored stripes were conceived to make the logo more accessible, and to represent the fact the Apple II could generate graphics in color. With the roll-out of the new iMac later on, Apple discontinued the rainbow theme and began to use monochromatic themes, nearly identical in shape to its previous rainbow incarnation, on various products, packaging and advertising. A silver metal with shadow version of the monochrome logo has been used up until now.

(1,053 words)

---

① monochromatic [ˌmɔnəkrəˈmætik] *adj.*单色的

精彩纷呈的商标设计

果图像。 当让诺夫把"咬掉一口"的标识配上几个不同的单色调主题送给乔布斯审查时，乔布斯立刻喜欢上了这个商标。 虽然乔布斯喜欢这个商标，但他坚持要用彩色，以使公司显得人性化。 乔布斯曾说："被咬掉一口的设计只是为了让它看起来不像樱桃。"设计彩色的条纹使商标更加平易近人，也代表了这样一个事实，即 Apple-II 可以生成彩色的图像。 随着新 iMac 苹果电脑的推出，苹果公司停止使用彩虹主题，开始在各种各样的产品、包装和广告中使用单色布景主题的商标，其形状几乎与先前的彩虹标识完全相同。 带有银灰色金属阴影的单色苹果标识一直使用至今。

知识链接

Yellow pages （电话簿中刊载公司、厂商电话的）黄页。

题　记

　　这可不是危言耸听，全球技术服务公司的高管们正在窃窃私语：聪明如印孚瑟斯和威普罗公司，他们正在占领西方公司的办公室。威普罗公司充满活力的二重唱——两位高管共同担任公司总裁的新体制，无疑为公司的迅猛发展注入了新鲜血液。这场二重唱的主角是韦斯瓦尼和帕冉奇佩。他们两人都在精英机构受过教育，性格互补，且良好的共事成效令一众高管惊羡不已，俯首称臣。韦斯瓦尼精力充沛，严肃中透露出友善；而帕冉奇佩擅长插科打诨和讲述诙谐的逸闻趣事。韦斯瓦尼擅长合作，而帕冉奇佩却更擅长策略和计划。韦斯瓦尼负责处理企业解决方案、基础设施服务和其他领域的信息技术外包，而帕冉奇佩负责金融服务、电信和媒体。威普罗公司充满活力的二重唱即将拉开序幕，他们有机会证明两个人的力量是否确实优于一个人的力量。

Dynamic Duo

The first time Suresh Vaswani and Girish Paranjpe met as young ambitious executives at Wipro in the early 1990s, they had no idea that one day the two of them would be running the company. India's third largest outsourcing company was then firmly in the hands of controlling shareholder Azim Premji, one of the founding figures of India's multibillion-dollar computer services outsourcing business. So they were surprised when Mr. Premji announced his retirement as chief executive and appointed them joint chief executives of Wipro. In sharing the post, the duos were being asked to embark① on a management first for India. Mr. Premji would, however, continue as chairman.

"Mr. Premji was in Electronics City," says Mr. Paranjpe, referring to the group's campus in Bangalore, India's Silicon Valley. "He said let's go to your office and talk about something he had in mind. That's when I thought: 'Wow, is this really happening?' " Six months on from their appointment, is "the power of two", as they call it, proving to be

---

① embark [im'bɑːk] *vi.* 从事,着手

充满活力的二重唱

当年轻气盛的高管苏里士·韦斯瓦尼和吉瑞希·帕冉奇佩在 20世纪 90 年代早期第一次在威普罗公司见面时，他们怎么也没有想到两人有一天会共同执掌公司。控股股东阿齐姆·普莱姆基当时牢牢地掌控着这家印度的第三大外包公司。阿齐姆·普莱姆基是印度数十亿美元的电脑服务外包业务的创始人之一。所以当普莱姆基先生宣布从首席执行官的位置上退休、并任命他们联合执掌威普罗公司时，他们感到异常惊讶。分担职位的两人组合被要求首先在印度着手管理工作。而普莱姆基先生则继续担任董事长。

帕冉奇佩先生说："普莱姆基先生在电子城。他说，我们到你办公室去，讨论一些他考虑好的想法，当时我在想：'哇，这是真的吗？'"电子城指的是集团在素有印度硅谷之称的班加罗尔园区。他们上任至今已经有 6 个月了，他们称之为的"两个人的力量"是否证明优于一个人的力量呢？或者如同怀疑者所声称的那样，像威普罗公司这样久经考验和快速增长的集团，这样做只是处理混乱的一种方法？考虑到大部分收入依赖于美国金融部门和美国经济的其他部分，面对一个行业的不确定性，这是一个特别紧迫的问题。威

235

better than one? Or are the skeptics right that at a group as sophisticated and fast-growing as Wipro it is just a recipe for chaos? This is a particularly pressing question given the uncertainty facing an industry that depends for a large part of its earnings on the US financial sector and other parts of the American economy. Outsourcing firms like Wipro take care of everything from maintaining the software and hardware of overseas clients, to advising them on new technology, to handling billing of their customers or processing their mortgage applications. The Indian IT outsourcing industry has become a pillar of the economy, generating export earnings of more than $ 40bn a year.

The pair discuss their roles in the boardroom of Wipro's open-plan corporate headquarters in Sarjapur, Bangalore. Mr. Vaswani works here while Mr. Paranjpe still has his office at the group's modern IT campus in Electronics City. Both appear relaxed in open-necked shirts. Mr. Vaswani is ebullient①, with a no-nonsense friendliness, while Mr. Paranjpe is adept at the soundbite② and the humorous anecdote. It is a mix they use to good effect. "Since we have different personalities, we find people and clients interact differently with us. So that becomes a good tactic. Some clients respond better to me and others to Suresh," Mr. Paranjpe says. The two do not socialize much together outside corporate functions and admit they have different interests. Mr. Vaswani enjoys new Bollywood films and going

---

① ebullient [i'bʌljənt] *adj.*感情等奔放的
② soundbite ['saund̩bait] *n.*一小段话(或一句名言)

普罗这样的外包公司管理着各种事务，包括维护海外客户的软件和硬件、建议他们使用新技术、处理他们客户的账单，或者处理其抵押贷款申请等，事无巨细，一应俱全。 印度的信息技术外包产业已成为经济的一大支柱，每年创造的出口收入超过 400 亿美元。

两人在威普罗设在班加罗尔·萨迦佩的开敞式公司总部的会议室中讨论了他们的任务。 韦斯瓦尼先生就在此工作，而帕冉奇佩的办公室依然设在集团在电子城中的现代信息技术园区。 两人都穿着敞领衬衫，显得很轻松。 韦斯瓦尼先生精力充沛，严肃中透露出友善；而帕冉奇佩先生擅长插科打诨和讲述诙谐的逸闻趣事。 他们的性格互补，往往会产生很好的效果。 帕冉奇佩先生认为，"因为我们的性格不同，所以我们发现人们和客户对我俩的反应不一样。 因此，这反而成为了一个很好的策略。 有些客户更愿意与我接触，有些则更喜欢与韦斯瓦尼打交道。"两人在公司的合作之外共同参加社会活动的机会并不多，并承认他们有不同的兴趣。 韦斯瓦尼先生喜欢新宝莱坞的电影，散步时用他的苹果平板电脑收听 20 世纪 70 年代和 80 年代的摇滚音乐，他表示，"我认为这是迄今为止最杰出的音乐"。 而帕冉奇佩先生认为，如今工作妨碍了他的业余爱好。"我曾经是一个狂热的读者，每周至少读一本书，但现在已经大幅减少。"

他们两人都在精英机构受过教育。 韦斯瓦尼先生在 1985 年进入威普罗公司，就职集团的信息技术部前在印度克勒格布尔理工学院攻读工程学，并在印度艾哈迈达巴德管理学院攻读了管理学。 当

for walks while listening to 1970s and 1980s rock music on his iPad, "I don't think any outstanding music is being produced these days", he says, while Mr. Paranjpe says work gets in the way of hobbies now. "I used to be an avid reader, at least one book a week, but that has come down drastically."

Both were educated at elite institutions. Mr. Vaswani studied engineering at the Indian Institute of Technology Kharagpur and management at the Indian Institute of Management Ahmedabad before joining Wipro in 1985 to work in the group's information technology business. At that point, IT was marginal to the business, accounting for only $ 2m- $ 3m of Wipro's revenue — the vast bulk of sales came from its consumer goods business. Last fiscal year, the IT business generated about $ 4. 3bn against about $ 300m for consumer goods. "In those days, our consumer products division used to think they were funding our IT business. Now it's a different story, " he says.

Mr. Paranjpe studied commerce at Bombay University and worked at Swedish Match, a tobacco company, and a management consulting firm before joining Wipro 18 years ago as the chief financial officer for one of its business units in the consumer division. The pair first met in the early 1990s. They spoke frequently as Mr. Vaswani, working with Mr. Premji on business development, tried to build up his knowledge of the consumer products division. Since then, they have often occupied posts alongside each other in various units of the group and have come to know each other's strengths and weaknesses. Mr. Paranjpe says that while his

时，信息技术只是公司的边缘业务，仅占威普罗总收益的 200 万～300 万美元，大部分的销售来自其日用消费品业务。 在上一财政年度，信息技术业务产出了 43 亿美元的收益，而日用消费品业务仅获利 3 亿美元。"当时，我们的消费品部门认为他们赞助了我们的信息技术业务。 现在是另一回事了。"他如是说。

帕冉奇佩先生在孟买大学攻读过商科，随后就职于瑞典火柴公司，并在一家烟草公司和一家管理咨询公司工作过。 18 年前，他进入威普罗公司，在消费者部中的一个事业部担任首席财政官。 两人首次见面是 20 世纪 90 年代初期。 韦斯瓦尼先生与帕冉奇佩先生一起工作时，两人经常就业务拓展交换意见，韦斯瓦尼先生试图构建自己对消费产品部门的知识。 从那以后，他们经常共同担任集团内各个部门的职位，而且渐渐了解了彼此的优缺点。 帕冉奇佩先生表示，他的同事擅长合作，而他却更擅长策略和计划，或者用他的话说就是"试图看清拐角处"。 帕冉奇佩先生认为，"苏雷什极度强势，他有一种顽强的能力，追求大多数人认为不可能做到的事。"他讲述了几年前的一个外包合同，当时他俩都认为已经和印度的一家大型银行谈妥，应该是板上钉钉的事了。 但客户端的首席执行官却突然告诉他们，他另外选择了一家跨国公司。 帕冉奇佩先生说道："苏雷什说：'这还不够，再给我们一次机会吧。'他让普莱姆基先生打电话给那位客户，我们最终使他们改变了主意。 这是在门口阻止竞争，这种行为大大鼓舞了团队的士气。"

但是，在不同的职位一起工作是一码事，共同承担高层工作是

colleague is good at operations, he is better on strategy and planning, or "trying to see around corners", as he puts it. "Suresh is intense and he has an ability to doggedly① pursue what most people think impossible to do," Mr. Paranjpe says. He recounts one outsourcing contract a few years ago that the pair thought they had sewn up with a large Indian bank. Instead the client's chief executive suddenly told them he was instead opting for a multinational. "Suresh said: 'That's not OK, give us another shot.'" Mr. Paranjpe says. "He got Mr. Premji to call the client and finally we were able to get them to change their mind. It was stopping competition at the gate — it was a huge morale booster for the team."

But while working together in different positions is one thing, sharing the top job is another. The pair say they manage the firm by taking joint responsibility for over-arching issues — such as strategy and the financial performance of the company, human resources and major acquisitions — while dividing the different business lines between them. Mr. Paranjpe is in charge of financial services, telecoms and media, while Mr. Vaswani handles enterprise solutions, infrastructure services and other areas of IT outsourcing. Mr. Paranjpe says joint-CEO structures have acquired a bad reputation because most are forced marriages, the awkward products of mergers or acquisitions. In Wipro's case, the shared responsibility is part of a carefully thought-out plan. "The good thing is you're not lonely if you have to take a very tough decision. You've got your

---

① doggedly ['dɔgidli] *adv.*顽强地

另一码事。　两人说他们以这样的方式管理公司：他们对最重要的问题共同承担责任，如公司的策略和财政业绩，人力资源和重大收购等；而两人之间又有不同的业务分工。　帕冉奇佩先生负责金融服务、电信和媒体，而韦斯瓦尼先生处理企业解决方案、基础设施服务和其他领域的信息技术外包。　帕冉奇佩表示，联合首席执行官的构架已经声名狼藉，因为大多数这样的构架都是被迫联姻，是兼并或收购中的棘手产物。　根据威普罗的情况，共同承担责任是深思熟虑计划的一部分。　韦斯瓦尼先生开玩笑地说："好处是你在必须做出一个艰难的决策时不再是孤身一人。　你有你的合作伙伴，可以断定什么是最好的行动方案——我不想说'大错特错'。"

但是他们承认，与惯常的情况相比，这种安排需要更多的沟通，以确保员工获得的信息不至于鱼龙混杂。　虽然他们的日程安排不允许他们每周正式见面，但他们会用电子邮件联系或电话不断。当客户需要快速答复时，双重领导也是个难题。　帕冉奇佩先生说："有时候你会不假思索地拿起电话。　你不能说：'等一下，我要先和苏雷什商量下。'这就需要很多信任，但这是唯一可行的方法。"

但到目前为止，从数字上看，共同管理的作用非常有效。　在 6月收尾的第二季度的收益是 13.9 亿美元，比上年增长 43%，而净盈利增加 15%，达到 1.9 亿美元。　然而，随着美国金融业中的其他主要客户的深层问题，印度的外包行业正面临自 8 年前高科技泡沫破灭后的最不确定期。　威普罗公司充满活力的二重唱即将拉开序幕，他们有机会证明两个人的力量是否确实优于一个人的力量。

partner — I don't want to say 'in crime' — to figure out what is the best course of action, " jokes Mr. Vaswani.

But they admit the arrangement requires more communication than usual to ensure staff do not get mixed messages. While their schedules do not allow them formally to meet every week, they e-mail and call endlessly. Dual leadership can also be difficult when a client needs answers quickly. "Sometimes you've got to take a call on the spur of the moment. You can't say: 'Hold on, I need to talk to Suresh first.' It requires a lot of trust but that's the only way to make it work, " says Mr. Paranjpe. And he says that, for newcomers to the organization, the joint-CEO arrangement can look very confusing. "Optically it sometimes is not very attractive, " Mr. Paranjpe says.

But so far, the joint role has been good for the numbers. Revenue for the quarter ending in June was $ 1. 39bn, up 43 per cent on the year before, while net profits increased 15 per cent to $ 190m. However, with the deepening problems of other major clients in the US financial sector, India's outsourcing industry is facing its most uncertain period since the tech bubble burst eight years ago. Wipro's dynamic duo are about to get the chance to prove whether the power of two is really better than one.

(1,167 words)

知识链接 🔍

Wipro 威普罗信息科技公司（Wipro Infotech Ltd.）。威普罗信息科技公司是一家印度信息科技服务综合供应商，提供信息技术基础设施产品，产品支持，系统整合，信息技术管理，全外包服务，应用开发，组合实施解决方案和咨询服务。该公司凭借近半个世纪的信息技术领域经验，深入的区域知识，强大而高质量的流程，以及最为优秀的同业联盟的支持，成为全球领先的系统整合服务供应商。

题　记

　　"驿马快信"利用快马接力在加利福尼亚州和密苏里州间传递邮件，在美国西部的开拓史上留下了一段传奇。当横跨北美大陆的电报系统完工后，"驿马快信"便销声匿迹，马放南山。150年后的今天，美国邮政管理局又卷入了另一场与科技的赛跑——一场不可能赢的竞赛。曾经令人称奇的美国邮政可以用骡子来保证位于大峡谷底部哈瓦苏帕印第安保留区的通邮，还会使用机动雪爬犁为阿拉斯加边远地区提供服务，但现今的手写信件逐渐被电子邮件、短信以及社会媒体等交流方式所取代，更多的人在网上收发账单、进行商业活动，美国人世代相传的邮政业正在走向"崩溃的边缘"。"驿马快信"以识时务者为俊杰的高姿态，轻而易举地退出了行业的竞争；但尽管美国邮政存在的理由正在迅速从我们眼前消失，衰败的态势可能难以逆转，接收它破产的命运却仍然让人百倍煎熬……

The Postal Service on Brink of Default

The Pony Express① was famous for moving mail at astounding speed. Missouri to California in only 10 days! A triumph.

It was also short-lived. Three people, Russell, Majors and Waddell, started a company called the Pony Express. The Pony Express carried mail and news throughout the West. The Pony Express was much faster than the stagecoach. Established in 1860, it lasted only as long as the territory it covered lacked the telegraph. Humans and horses could not match the speed of electrical signals. So when the transcontinental telegraph was completed in 1861, the company's three investors reacted swiftly. It was shut down after only 18 months.

Now, 150 years later, the United States Postal Service is engaged in another race with technology, one it can't possibly win. But because the service is a quasi-independent government agency, it continues to maintain the huge human and mechanical infrastructure that was assembled for a pre-Internet age.

The Postal Service proudly proclaims just how big it is. It has 574,000 employees, making it the nation's second-largest civilian employer, after

---

① Pony Express 快马邮递

濒临崩溃的邮政业

"驿马快信"公司因其惊人的邮件运输速度而闻名遐迩。从密苏里州到加利福尼亚州只需 10 天！一个惊人的胜利。

但这个公司却只不过是昙花一现。拉塞尔、梅吉斯和华德尔三人当时组建了一个名叫"驿马快信"的公司，负责在美国西部运送邮件和新闻。"驿马快信"要比当时的公共马车快多了。当电报覆盖了那些尚未完善电讯系统的区域之后，创立于 1860 年的"驿马快信"便寿终正寝。人和马与电波信号的速度无法相提并论。所以在 1861 年，当横跨北美大陆的电报系统建设完成时，快马邮递公司的三位投资者迅速作出反应，在运营了仅 18 个月后宣告关闭公司。

150 年后的今天，美国邮政管理局又卷入了另一场与科技的赛跑，这是一场不可能赢的竞赛。但因为美国邮政管理局是一个半独立的政府机构，它继续维持着庞大的人员资质和机械基础设施，他们是前互联网时代的组合。

美国邮政管理局自豪地宣告，它是多么庞大。它有 57.4 万名员工，这使它成为国家继沃尔玛之后的第二大平民雇主。美国邮政管理局拥有 215 625 台运营车辆，是世界上最大的民用车队。这些车辆每年横越 1.25 亿英里的路程，消耗 3.99 亿加仑的燃料。它为

Wal-Mart. The service runs 215,625 vehicles, the world's largest civilian fleet. Those vehicles traverse 1. 25 billion miles annually and consume 399 million gallons of fuel. Its carriers serve 151 million homes, businesses and post office boxes.

And the Postal Service can't resist a tacit① little boast at the end of that long list of big numbers: It receives zero tax dollars for its efforts.

Bravo②! But one could point out that this is the same Postal Service that posted multibillion-dollar deficits for the past five consecutive fiscal years; another is expected to be reported for this fiscal year, which ended Friday. The mail service Americans have known for generations is on "Brink of Default", as handwritten communication has all but disappeared — replaced by emails, text messages, and social-media — and billing and other commercial transactions are increasingly conducted over the Internet. It is curious that last year, the year before this dismal run of losses, happened to be the very year when total mail volume peaked. In the last year, some 213. 1 billion pieces were processed. And the total was just 171 billion this year.

Stamped mail is the category that has declined most steeply in the last decade — 47 percent since 2001. "Standard" mail, the official euphemism for junk mail that until 1996 was called third class, dropped only 8 percent over the same period.

The decline in mail volume has been accompanied by widening losses: $ 8. 5 billion for last year, and a projection of nearly $ 10 billion for this year. More important, first-class mail, the Postal Service's biggest moneymaker, has fallen 25 percent during the past decade. That's a huge

---

① tacit ['tæsit] *adj.*缄默的,不言而喻的
② bravo [ˌbrɑ'vɔ] *int.*好极了

1.51 亿个家庭、企业和邮政信箱提供邮政服务。

在这一长串庞大数字的终端，美国邮政管理局多少有点无法掩饰的心照不宣的自吹自擂：它通过自身的努力换取了零税率收益。

太棒了！ 但是人们也难免会指出，同样是这个美国邮政管理局，曾在过去连续 5 年的财政年度出现过数 10 亿美元的赤字，而且在周五结束的本财政年度有望再次报告亏损数字。 由于手写信件逐渐被电子邮件、短信以及社会媒体等交流方式所取代，更多的人在网上收发账单、进行商业活动，美国人世代相传的邮政业正在走向"崩溃的边缘"。 令人好奇的是，在本年度连续亏损、惨淡经营之前的去年，竟然是邮件总量达到顶峰的一年。 去年递送的邮件量约达2 131亿件。 今年的邮件总数只有1 710亿件。

在过去 10 年中，邮戳邮件是总量下降最快的一种邮件——自 2001 年以来下降了 47% 。"标准"邮件被官方委婉地称呼为垃圾邮件，1996 年时还被认为是第三类邮件，在同期仅仅下降了 8% 。

邮件数量的下降一直与亏损的扩大如影相随：去年的亏损达 85 亿美元，据估计，今年的亏损近 100 亿美元。 更重要的是，美国邮政管理局最大的收入来源第一类邮件的数量在过去的 10 年里下降了 25% ，这是触及底线的严峻问题。 2020 年的情况会更糟，第一类邮件数量预计将减少一半。

值得赞扬的是，美国邮政管理局承认，它面临着一个新的现实问题。 这是邮政总局局长帕特里克·多纳霍提出的见解。 在公布本季度业绩时，美国邮政管理局描述了"电子分流如何持续导致第一类邮件减少"的问题。 第一类邮件的税收较去年同期下降了 8.7% 。 在过去 10 年的前五个年头，不断增加的企业垃圾邮件抵消

problem for its bottom line. And it gets worse. By 2020, first-class mail volume is expected to drop by half.

The Postal Service, to its credit, acknowledges that it faces what Patrick R. Donahoe, the postmaster general, calls a new reality. In releasing results for the quarter, the service described how "electronic diversion continues to cause reductions in first-class mail." Revenue from first-class mail declined 8.7 percent from the period a year earlier. As is known to all, during the first half of the last decade, the slow decline of first-class mail was balanced by rising stacks of corporate junk. When the economy tanked, both went into a free fall.

The postal unions avert[①] their eyes. They say that the service ran into trouble solely because Congress has required huge payments for future retirees' health care costs. Silly me: I thought funding benefits fully was a good thing.

On its Web site, the American Postal Workers Union disputes the notion that "hard-copy mail is destined to be replaced by electronic messages." Mail volume was down, it says, because its principal component — advertising — had fallen in the recession. "As the nation and the world emerge from economic stagnation, hard-copy mail volume will expand," it asserts. But that, of course, ignores the rise of the Internet, and its ever-growing use for checking bills or sending payments — with no need for that army of 500,000.

The Internet can't be used to tele-transport packages, of course, and our use of package delivery services, including the Postal Service's, has grown with e-commerce. But the Postal Service is running large deficits, bumping up against the $15 billion limit it is permitted to borrow, and

---

① avert [ə'vəːt] vt. 避免，防止，转移

了第一类邮件数量的减少，但经济衰落后两种邮件均出现下滑趋势。 这是美国人家喻户晓的实情。

邮政工会转移了他们的视野。 他们表示，就是因为国会需要为未来的退休人员支付巨额的医疗保健费用，美国邮政管理局才遇到了麻烦。 依我之愚见：我认为全额福利基金是一件好事。

在美国邮政管理局的网站上，美国邮政工人工会驳斥了"电子讯息注定要取代纸质邮件"的观念。 工会声称，邮件的数量下降是因为它的主要组成部分——广告——在经济衰退期有所减少。 它断言，"随着国家和世界从经济停滞中恢复元气，纸质邮件的数量将会扩大"。 当然，这种推论忽略了互联网的发展，以及网上越来越盛行的支票付账和转账支付等手段。 美国邮政业不再需要 50 万人的大军了。

当然，互联网不能用于远距离的运输包装，我们使用的包裹投递服务，包括美国邮政管理局的包裹投递服务，正在与电子商务同期增长。 但是，美国邮政管理局正处于巨额财政赤字亏空状态，即将达到法定负债 150 亿美元的上限，如果国会不出手相助，美国邮政将濒于破产的边缘。

作为几个包裹投递服务供应商中的一员，这是美国邮政管理局想要达到的预定目标吗？ 有谁真正关心过美国邮政管理局或美国邮政总署是否在门口的台阶上投递过包裹呢？

邮政监督管理委员会的前主席、现任乔治梅森大学公共政策学教授的李·弗利茨奇勒认为，我们的邮政服务应该被视为一种传播媒介，以"标准"邮件的形式向四面八方传播完全相同的信息，它不应该被看做是一种通信媒介。 如果国会要使美国邮政摆脱困境，

is on the brink of default unless Congress comes to the rescue.

Is this where the Postal Service wants to make its stand, as a package delivery service, one among several providers? Does anyone really care whether the Postal Service or U.P.S. drops the package at the doorstep?

A. Lee Fritschler, a professor of public policy at George Mason University and a former chairman of the Postal Regulatory Commission, says our Postal Service should be viewed not as a communications medium but as a broadcasting medium, spraying identical messages, in the form of "standard" mail, far and wide. If Congress had to bail out the Postal Service, it would effectively be subsidizing the private interests that use the service to distribute advertising cheaply. "Why on earth should our government be subsidizing a broadcast medium?" Professor Fritschler asks.

Some say subsidies are perfectly defensible if the service fulfills a noble civic function. Richard R. John, a historian at the Columbia University Graduate School of Journalism, points out that the post office ran a deficit during most years between the 1830s and the 1960s. But today, when junk mail is predominant, "postal management is unable to articulate a compelling vision of the public good, " he says.

In 1861, it was easy to decommission the Pony Express, a technologically obsolete, privately owned delivery service. A century and a half later, we have a delivery service whose raison d'être is rapidly vanishing before our eyes. This one is owned by all of us, however, and we are paralyzed, unable to decide what to do.

(988 words)

它就应该有效地资助私有利益，允许美国邮政低价经销广告。 弗利茨奇勒教授质疑道："我们的政府究竟为什么要资助广播媒介呢？"

一些人认为，如果服务满足了公民的高品质需求，补贴是完全站得住脚的。 哥伦比亚大学新闻研究生院的历史学家理查德·约翰指出，在 19 世纪 30 年代和 20 世纪 60 年代之间，邮局的运营经常遭遇财政赤字困境。 但是他认为，在垃圾邮件占主导地位的今天，"邮政管理无法为公众利益表达引人注目的愿景"。

在 1861 年，"驿马快信"公司轻而易举地退出了行业的竞争，它本是一个拥有过时的技术、私人邮递服务公司。 一个半世纪以后，我们有了递送服务，但它存在的理由正在迅速从我们眼前消失。 然而，虽然这是一家属于我们所有人的公司，但我们还是无能为力，无法决定该做些什么。

知识链接 🔍

Pony Express 驿马快信公司。驿马快信公司创立于 1860 年 4 月，在 1861 年 10 月横跨北美大陆的电报系统完工后就告停用，总共存在了一年半的时间。尽管存世不长，它却在美国西部历史上留下了一段传奇。驿马快信制是美国近代一项利用快马接力、在加利福尼亚州和密苏里州间传递邮件的系统。驿马快信东起密苏里州的圣约瑟夫市，西至加利福尼亚州的沙加缅市，全长约 2 900 公里，共设 157 个驿站，每个骑手一般骑行 120 至 160 公里，每隔 16 至 24 公里便换马一次。

题　记

　　当罗马帝国的辉煌终成声遏行云的绝响之时，谁能料到它对当代的英国经济竟起着苟延残喘的护犊之功？英国在摆脱罗马帝国的统治之后的经济衰退使后来的所有危机都黯然失色。在罗马统治下的英国，金、银、铜三种金属货币通过担保和丰富的交换媒介促进了经济的发展；制造业成为经济的核心，罗马墓地中发现的许多柳钉靴子和棺材用铁钉表明，当时在罗马统治下的英国拥有大量的简单铁制品；密集的城镇网络从较大的定居点一直延伸到沿陆路和水路分布的小型商业中心。5世纪的经济崩溃使罗马时代的鼎盛繁荣如过眼烟云，它的突发性与规模使当时的英国人很难有信心期待经济最终恢复到克劳迪亚斯大帝入侵前已经达到的水平。罗马统治下的英国经济竟然如此戏剧化地崩溃，可见英国这匹马的行动桀骜不驯，即使让它纵辔而行，它也不会顺着某个方向狂奔而去。

On Thinking of Britain Economy
under the Roman Empire Way

As we face an uncertain and worrying New Year, we can at least console ourselves with the fact that we are not living 1,600 years ago, and about to begin the year 410. In this year Rome was sacked, and the empire gave up trying to defend Britain. While this marks the glorious beginnings of "English history", as Anglo-Saxon barbarians began their inexorable conquest of lowland Britain, it was also the start of a recession that puts all recent crises in the shade.

The economic indicators for fifth-century Britain are scanty, and derive exclusively from archaeology, but they are consistent and extremely bleak. Under the Roman empire, the province had benefited from the use of a sophisticated coinage in three metals — gold, silver and copper — lubricating the economy with a guaranteed and abundant medium of exchange. In the first decade of the fifth century new coins ceased to reach Britain from the imperial mints on the continent, and while some attempts were made to produce local substitutes, these efforts were soon abandoned. For about 300 years, from around AD 420, Britain's economy functioned without coin.

Core manufacturing declined in a similar way. There was some

英国经济的罗马帝国式思考

当我们面对一个既不可预测又令人担忧的新年时，我们至少可以用这样一个事实来安慰自己，那就是我们并不是生活在 1600 年前、410 年即将开始的时候。 就在这一年，罗马遭到洗劫，于是这个帝国放弃了保卫不列颠的尝试。 当盎格鲁撒克逊的野蛮人开始对不列颠洼地无情征服之时，"英国历史"便开启了辉煌的篇章，但它也是经济衰退的开始，这场衰退使近期的所有危机都黯然失色。

仅从考古学的角度追根寻源，英国在 5 世纪的经济表现真是难觅踪迹，充其量也是既能协调一致又极其惨淡凄凉。 在罗马帝国的统治下，各领地从复杂的货币使用中受益匪浅，这种货币包括金、银、铜三种金属，通过担保和丰富的交换媒介促进了经济的发展。在五世纪的第一个十年，欧洲大陆的帝国铸币厂停止向英国输送新的硬币，虽然有人尝试生产本地的替代品，但是这些努力很快就被放弃。 大概从公元 420 年起，在近 300 年的时间里，英国的经济在没有硬币的情况下运行。

核心制造业以同样的方式衰落。 武士贵族阶层需要持续不断地生产一些一流的金属武器，以显示其财富和地位，但是在纯实用性产品的制造方面，却发生了令人吃惊的变化，而且都是朝着坏的方

continuity of production of the high-class metalwork needed by a warrior aristocracy to mark its wealth and status; but at the level of purely functional products there was startling change, all of it for the worse. Roman Britain had enjoyed an abundance of simple iron goods, documented by the many hob-nail boots and coffin-nails found in Roman cemeteries. These, like the coinage, disappeared early in the fifth century, as too did the industries that had produced abundant attractive and functional wheel-turned pottery. From the early fifth century, and for about 250 years, the potter's wheel — that most basic tool, which enables thin-walled and smoothly finished vessels to be made in bulk — disappeared altogether from Britain. The only pots remaining were shaped by hand, and fired, not in kilns① as in Roman times, but in open "clamps②".

We do not know for certain what all this meant for population numbers in the countryside, because from the fifth to the eighth century people had so few goods that they are remarkably difficult to find in the archaeological record; but we do know its effect on urban populations. Roman Britain had a dense network of towns, ranging from larger settlements, like London and Cirencester, which also served an administrative function, to small commercial centres that had grown up along the roads and waterways. By 450 all of these had disappeared, or were well on the way to extinction. Canterbury, the only town in Britain that has established a good claim to continuous settlement from Roman

① kiln [kiln] n.(砖,石灰等的)窑,炉
② clamp [klæmp] n.夹钳,螺丝钳

258

面转化。 罗马墓地中发现的许多柳钉靴子和棺材用铁钉表明，当时在罗马统治下的英国拥有大量的简单铁制品。 就像硬币一样，这些都在五世纪的早期销声匿迹，生产了富有魅力和实用的转盘陶器的制造业也难逃厄运。 从五世纪早期起，在近 250 年间，制陶工人的轮子全部从英国消失殆尽，这种最基本的工具曾使大量薄壁和外形光滑的器皿制造成为可能。 唯一保留下来的是用手工捏造、采取"夹钳"敞开式的铸造方式烧制的罐，而不是古罗马时代在窑中烧制的产品。

我们不一定知道所有这一切对生活在乡村的普通人来说意味着什么，因为从五世纪到八世纪，人们的商品是如此之少，肯定非常难找到相应的考古资料。 但我们知道它对城市居民的影响。 罗马统治下的英国有密集的城镇网络，他们从较大的定居点一直延伸到沿陆路和水路分布的小型商业中心。 伦敦和赛伦塞斯特等较大的定居点还起着行政职能的作用。 到 450 年的时候，这一切已经无影无踪，或者即将遭遇灭顶之灾。 坎特伯雷是英国唯一的小镇，这个定居点从罗马时期一直延续到现在，具备良好的底蕴。 相比他们真实的城市特征，小镇五世纪至七世纪的小棚屋虽然如过眼云烟，但他们却给人们留下了更为深刻的印象。 此外，正是在伦敦和撒克逊南安普敦等贸易城镇再度崛起的八世纪，城市生活才又回到英国。

从 5 世纪初开始的两三百年间，英国的经济恢复到公元 43 年罗马入侵很久前都没有达到的水平。 5 世纪经济崩溃的最令人吃惊的特征是其突发性与规模。 摆脱罗马帝国的统治之时，如果英国直接恢复到其曾经享有的前罗马铁器时代，我们可能不会感到惊奇。 但是，就在罗马入侵之前，与 5 世纪和 6 世纪的英国相比，英国南部

times to the present, impresses us much more for the ephemeral① nature of its fifth to seventh-century huts than for their truly urban character. Again it was only in the eighth century, with the reemergence of trading towns such as London and Saxon Southampton, that urban life returned to Britain.

For two or three hundred years, beginning at the start of the fifth century, the economy of Britain reverted to levels not experienced since well before the Roman invasion of AD 43. The most startling features of the fifth-century crash are its suddenness and its scale. We might not be surprised if, on leaving the empire, Britain had reverted to an economy similar to that which it had enjoyed in the immediately pre-Roman Iron Age. But southern Britain just before the Roman invasion was a considerably more sophisticated place economically than Britain in the fifth and sixth centuries: it had a native silver coinage; pottery industries that produced wheel-turned vessels and sold them widely; and even the beginnings of settlements recognisable as towns. Nothing of the kind existed in the fifth and sixth centuries; and it was only really in the eighth century that the British economy crawled back to the levels it had already reached before Emperor Claudius's invasion. It is impossible to say with any confidence when Britain finally returned to levels of economic complexity comparable to those of the highest point of Roman times, but it might be as late as around the year 1000 or 1100. If so, the post-Roman recession lasted for 600-700 years.

We can take some cheer from this sad story — so far our own

---

① ephemeral [ə'femərəl] adj.短暂的,朝生暮死的

的经济在相当程度上更为复杂：它有一个本地的银币制度；生产和广泛销售转盘器皿的陶瓷产业；定居点也开始具备城镇的雏形。 五世纪和六世纪时，这种繁荣的景象根本就不复存在。 真正进入 8 世纪后，英国经济才缓慢地恢复到克劳迪亚斯大帝入侵前已经达到的水平。 与那些罗马时代的鼎盛期相比，很难说有没有信心期待英国最终恢复到经济繁荣期，但它可能在迟至 1 000 年或者 1 100 年左右才重现旧貌。 如果是这样，那么后罗马时代的衰退就可能持续600—700 年。

听完这个悲惨的故事我们可以欢呼雀跃，迄今为止，我们自己的问题显得完全无足轻重。 但是，幸灾乐祸绝不是非常令人满意的情绪，在这种情况下，显然不应该出现思维错位。 罗马统治下的英国经济竟然如此戏剧化地崩溃，我们应该停下来思考一下个中的原因。 几乎可以肯定的是，古罗马时代的经济达到了精细化和专业化的水平，它导致了经济崩溃的突发性和灾难性的规模。 罗马统治下的英国人口已经增长，他们习惯于从专业生产商那里购买他们的陶器、钉子和其他的基本商品，这些生产商散居各处，相距甚远，他们反过来又依赖于分布广泛的市场，以维持他们的专业生产。 5 世纪的不安全感到来之时，这种给人印象深刻的空中楼阁轰然倒塌，只留下这样一群人：他们没有想要的商品、也没有他们就地生产时需要的技能和基础设施。 与罗马时期的那些人相比，他们需要几个世纪才能重建专业化和交易的城镇网。

一种经济的结构越复杂，它的表现就会越脆弱，它的解体也可能越来越支离破碎。 当然，我们的经济与罗马统治下的英国经济属于不同的复杂范畴。 我们很可能不是在很多英里之外，而是在地球

problems pale into insignificance. But schadenfreude① is never a very satisfying emotion, and in this case it would be decidedly misplaced. The reason the Romano-British economy collapsed so dramatically should give us pause for thought. Almost certainly the suddenness and the catastrophic scale of the crash were caused by the levels of sophistication and specialisation reached by the economy in Roman times. The Romano-British population had grown used to buying their pottery, nails, and other basic goods from specialist producers, based often many miles away, and these producers in their turn relied on widespread markets to sustain their specialised production. When insecurity came in the fifth century, this impressive house of cards collapsed, leaving a population without the goods they wanted and without the skills and infrastructure needed to produce them locally. It took centuries to reconstruct networks of specialisation and exchange comparable to those of the Roman period.

The more complex an economy is, the more fragile it is, and the more cataclysmic② its disintegration can be. Our economy is, of course, in a different league of complexity to that of Roman Britain. Our pottery and metal goods are likely to have been made, not many miles away, but on the other side of the globe, while our main medium of exchange is electronic, and sometimes based on smoke and mirrors. If our economy ever truly collapses, the consequences will make fifth-century Britain seem like a picnic.

(968 words)

---

① schadenfreude [ˈʃɑːdənˌfrɔidə] *n.* 幸灾乐祸
② cataclysmic [ˌkætəˈklizmik] *adj.* 大变动的

262

的另一边制造陶器和金属制品，而我们的主要交换媒介是电子，有时候还不怎么靠谱。 如果我们的经济出现真正的崩溃，其后果将使五世纪的英国看上去像一顿郊外的野餐。

知识链接 🔍

Emperor Claudius 克劳迪亚斯大帝。克劳迪亚斯大帝出生在公元前 10 年 8 月 1 日高卢的古罗马帝国世家。他的父亲是奥古斯都，即罗马帝国第一代皇帝恺撒的甥孙、养子、继承人；母亲是东罗马帝国的统治者马克·安东尼的女儿。他的叔父是古罗马皇帝提比略。克劳迪亚斯天生体质虚弱，喜欢思考和阅读，所以隐居幕后，过着相对安全的生活。46 岁时出任他的侄子、罗马帝国第三位皇帝卡里古拉的执政官。于公元 41 年 1 月 24 日在侄子卡里古拉被卫士刺杀后称帝，公元 50 年，他收养他的第四位妻子的儿子尼禄作为养子，并许诺尼禄在他死后继位。然而不久之后，当克劳迪亚斯大帝决定让其亲生子继位之后，第四位妻子阿格利皮纳痛下决心毒死了克劳迪亚斯大帝，修改了遗嘱。克劳迪亚斯大帝死于公元 54 年 10 月 13 日。

题　记

　　对现代商务旅行者来说，公司卡是与你的笔记本电脑或手机同样价值连城的工具。它可以帮助你赢得客户和完成交易。你无论到哪里都可以随身携带公司卡，但你是否知道，公司卡正在帮助你的公司监视你的一举一动，你并不是在任何场合都可以使用公司卡。你每个月要填写一份公司派送的清单，报告公司卡上的支出费用；由于新开发的报告软件的应用，企业可以通过更加密切地监控员工开支和处理支付的成本这两种方式加强开支监管；公司的管理人员现在可以使用基于网络的工具，逐条查看公司卡上的各项开支，从机票到酒店迷你酒吧的小吃。应该说腐败是人类社会最为古老的犯罪，存在于几乎任何社会形态。尽管人类已经来到 21 世纪，腐败仍然是割之不去的毒瘤。而公司卡作为一种支付方式，却最大化地提升了普通公司内部的监管能力。

Your Corporate Card
Is Watching You

Increasingly, companies use corporate cards not only to win business and save money, but also to keep tabs① on employees.

For modern business travelers, it's as valuable a tool as your laptop or cell phone. It can help you win clients and close deals. You take it everywhere you go but you can't always use it. And if you use it the wrong way, it could get you fired — or worse. What is it? It's the corporate card sitting in your wallet, and it's helping your company keep tabs on you.

The corporate card began as a way to ensure that employees could pay for what they needed — whether last-minute airfare to Chicago or a steak dinner for 12 clients — to win business. Corporate cards, in theory, work just like any credit card, except that the company picks up the tab. Every month the issuer would send out a statement and the executive — or more often his assistant — would submit his expenses.

Usually in the form of illegible and half-crumpled receipts stapled

---

① tab [tæb] *n.*标签

公司卡正在监督你的一举一动

公司越来越频繁地采用公司卡的管理方式，这种做法不仅赢利和省钱，而且还对员工起着监管作用。

对现代商务旅行者来说，公司卡是与你的笔记本电脑或手机同样价值连城的工具。它可以帮助你赢得客户和完成交易。你无论到哪里都可以随身携带公司卡，但你并不是在任何场合都可以使用公司卡。如果你使用公司卡的方式不太恰当，可能会被解雇，或许还更糟。公司卡是什么？它是公司放在你钱包里的卡，它正在帮助你的公司监视你。

公司卡作为一种支付方式，本意是要确保员工在需要时可以付款，以抢占商业先机，如在紧急关头购买到芝加哥的机票，或为12位客户准备牛排晚餐。从理论上讲，公司卡的作用似乎等同任何信用卡，只不过是公司在买单。发行者每个月会派送一份清单，经理——更多的时候是他的助手——则会提交他的费用。

报账单通常字迹模糊，半皱巴巴地用纸装订在一起，这可苦了会计部门的工作人员，他们还得费力地辨认这些字迹。可以推测，造假的机会相当大。两人晚宴是招待客户还是你的女朋友，谁会知道呢？区分合理费用与非合理费用常常是如此之难，而开张支票也

onto paper that the poor folks in the accounting department would have to decipher①. As one can imagine, the opportunities for padding were considerable. Who's to know if that dinner for two was for clients or your girlfriend? And the difficulty of separating the legitimate expenses from the non was such that it was often easier to just write the check.

This is an Orwellian twist. But today, thanks to new reporting software, businesses can tighten up their expenses and stop the wastage by both more closely monitoring employee spending and reducing the costs of processing the payments. It is progress with an Orwellian twist, however. Big Brother might not know what you're thinking, but he sure knows how you spend your time — and the company's money.

Corporate cards allow companies access to detailed information on employee spending. Travel managers can now use Web-based tools to view itemized② purchases of everything from airline tickets to snacks from the hotel minibar. This information helps companies negotiate discounts and "preferred vendor" deals with the hotels, airlines, and car rental services that employees use most often. The Boston business research firm Aberdeen Group found that companies save 1. 3% to 3% of their total travel spending by negotiating contracts with preferred vendors, and the cost of processing an expense report is $ 26 less. "Travel is often thought of as a cost of doing business, " said Andrew Bartolini, a commercial card analyst for Aberdeen. "But today's business climate demands that

---

① decipher [di'saifə] vt.破译
② itemize ['aitəmaiz] vt.列出清单

不过是举手之劳。

这是一种扭曲的奥威尔现象。 在当今社会，由于新开发的报告软件的应用，企业可以通过更加密切地监控员工开支和处理支付的成本这两种方式加强开支监管，并杜绝浪费。 然而，这又是一个扭曲的奥威尔现象的进步。 公司老总可能不知道你究竟在想什么，但他肯定知道，你在怎样消费你的时间和公司的钱。

公司卡让公司了解员工开支的详细信息。 旅行社的管理人员现在可以使用基于网络的工具，逐条查看各项开支，从机票到酒店迷你酒吧的小吃。 这种信息帮助公司与员工最常使用的酒店、航空公司和汽车租赁公司商谈折扣和"首选供应商"。 波士顿商业研究公司的阿伯丁集团发现，与首选供应商洽谈合同节省了 1.3% 至 3% 的旅行总支出，处理成本报告的开支在 26 美元以下。 阿伯丁集团的商业卡分析师安德鲁·巴托里尼表示，"旅游往往被认为是经营商业的成本。 但是，今天的商业环境要求，普通公司内部必须严格监管最大的可控费用。"

摩根大通公司商务卡解决方案的总经理弗兰克·杜姆布拉斯基认为，"现金有利于歹徒作案，现在，买任何东西它都已不再是首选的支付方法。 从公司的角度来看，它是信息管理。 旅行卡允许人们按供应商、城市和类别等单点查阅所有的交易数据。

快速偿还是关键。 雇主也可以有所选择，限制人们自动套用公司卡，商务旅客可以支付航班、汽车出租和旅馆住宿，但不可以在零售商店使用公司卡。 万事达信用卡目前正在开发一个称为持续控制的功能，让雇主实时监控员工的开支，信用卡每使用一次，都会发送一封电子邮件更新信息。

strict attention is paid to the largest controllable expense within the average company."

"Cash is good for gangsters, but these days it's not the preferred method for paying for anything," said Frank Dombroski, managing director of commercial card solutions at JPMorgan Chase. "From the company standpoint, it's about information management. Travel cards allow a single point of access to all of their transactional data, by vendor, by city, and by type."

Rapid reimbursement is the key. Employers can also choose to restrict the use of corporate cards automatically by enabling business travelers to pay for flights, car rentals①, and hotel accommodations, but blocking card use at retail stores. MasterCard is currently developing a feature called inControl that will allow employers to monitor employee spending in real time by sending e-mail updates each time a card is used.

Business travelers who use their corporate cards might have to forgo② some perks of traveling on the company dime. Unauthorized long-distance calls and $ 20 martinis at the hotel bar might be harder to sneak by travel managers, but corporate cards have the advantage of convenience.

On average, corporate card users are usually reimbursed within five to six days as opposed to 10 to 12 for employees that use personal cards, says American Express' Vergara, who added that reimbursement③ was the

---

① rental ['rentl] *n.*租金额

② forgo [fɔː'gəu] *vt.*放弃

③ reimbursement [ˌriːim'bəːsment] *n.*付还

使用公司卡的商务旅行人士可能不得不放弃一些由公司出钱的额外津贴。 差旅经理们较难偷偷摸摸地享用未经批准的长途电话费和旅馆酒吧 20 美元的马丁尼酒，但公司卡的优点是方便。

平均而言，公司卡的用户通常在 5 至 6 天内偿还费用，而员工个人卡则可延长至 10~12 日，美国运通公司的维加拉补充说，对于频繁的商业旅行者来说，付还是最重要的问题。 有些发卡单位也有行政法人卡程序，为挑选出来的员工提供额外的好处。 行政信用卡的特点包括进入机场的候机大厅、礼宾服务和旅游升级等。

公司卡有潜力扩大到中型公司。 对于有公司卡项目的企业来说，最大的挑战是确保信用卡按时付款。 根据一项研究，一家签有个人责任协议的公司，每月大约有 4.8% 的员工拖欠债务，提交给公司、并签有公司责任协议的旅行卡报表中，14% 的报表没有收据证明。

今年的旅游预算可能会缩小，金融分析家和发卡公司认为，信用卡市场即使在经济疲软情况下也将继续盈利。 在过去 5 年中的每一年，公司卡的开支已经增长了 12% ~14%，阿巴丁集团的巴托里尼补充说，公司卡项目仍然有着巨大的潜力，可以拓展到中、小型公司的低端市场。 巴托里尼认为："规模中等的公司并不知道，他们也可以和首选的供应商谈判并成功交易。 对非常小的公司而言，好处之一是预先协商好储蓄计划，例如，与航空公司共同承办的联名卡。"

most important issue for a frequent business traveler. Some card issuers also have executive corporate card programs that provide additional benefits for select employees. Features of an executive card can include access to an airport lounge, concierge services, and travel upgrades.

The corporate card has the potential to expand to midsize companies. The greatest challenge for businesses with corporate card programs is ensuring that a card is paid on time. Each month, around 4. 8% of employee payments at a company with an individual liability agreement are delinquent and 14% of the travel card statements submitted to companies with corporate liability agreements are unsupported by receipts, according to a research.

Travel budgets may be shrinking this year, but financial analysts and card issuers say the corporate card market will continue to be profitable even in the softening economy. Spending on corporate cards has increased by about 12% to 14% in each of the last five years, according to Aberdeen Group's Bartolini, who added that there is still tremendous potential for card programs to expand down-market into midsize and small companies. "Midlevel companies don't know they can also be successful in negotiating first-supplier deals, " Bartolini said. " For very small companies, one of the benefits is a prenegotiated saving program — for example, co-branded cards with airlines."

(853 words)

知识链接 🔍

Orwellian 奥威尔现象。在 20 世纪世界经典作家中，乔治·奥威尔（George Orwell，1903-1950）可谓声名显赫。在西方世界，奥威尔的名字几乎家喻户晓。他的作品至今已发行千万册，被翻译成多种文字，畅销全球。作为高等文学的典范，奥威尔的政治小说及随笔评论一直是英美大学的重要修读书目。在世界各地，几乎每年都会有一些大型的奥威尔学术研讨会，或奥威尔电影纪念周之类的学术活动。他的一些作品甚至被改编成儿童读物和动画片。奥威尔作品中的独特话语已经成为当今的国际语言。他的作品《动物庄园》（Animal Farm）历久不衰，被学者称为"动物庄园的美丽神话"（The Myth of Animal Farm）。现代英语中甚至还出现了诸如"奥威尔现象"（Orwellism，Orwellian）之类的专门词汇，指受严格统治而失去人性的社会现象。

题　记

　　当世界经济衰退的言论风生水起之际，光怪陆离的资本市场却上演了一场新兴经济体与发达经济体"争宠"的好戏。金融危机让西方发达国家的经济陷入泥潭，其产生的"余震"影响依然令人心悸，而一度前途未卜的欧债危机又为世界经济的前路蒙上阴影。在这一背景下，投资者就像躲避瘟疫一样竞相对发达经济体避而远之。而作为新兴经济体的典型代表——俄罗斯、印度、巴西和中国却用经济增长的强劲表现推动着世界经济走出阴霾。他们在塑造责任感的同时，引导新兴市场经济从封闭市场转向开放市场；他们的一个关键特征就是本国和外国投资两者都在增加；因为市场转型而存在的不稳定性，新兴市场给那些敢于增加投资组合风险的投资者提供了机会。风水轮流转，好戏当连台。人们期待新兴经济体权衡好本国的政治和社会因素，努力实现经济社会全面协调可持续发展。

An Emerging Market Economy

A term coined in 1981 by Antoine W. Van Agtmael of the International Finance Corporation of the World Bank, an emerging, or developing, market economy（EME）is defined as an economy with low-to-middle per capita income. Such countries constitute approximately 80% of the global population, representing about 20% of the world's economies. Although a loose definition, countries whose economies fall into this category, varying from very big to very small, are usually considered emerging because of their developments and reforms. Hence, even though China is deemed one of the world's economic powerhouses, it is lumped into the category alongside much smaller economies with a great deal less resources, like Tunisia. Both China and Tunisia belong to this category because both have embarked on economic development and reform programs, and have begun to open up their markets and "emerge" onto the global scene. EMEs are considered to be fast growing economies.

EMEs are characterized as transitional, meaning they are in the process of moving from a closed to an open market economy while building accountability① within the system. Examples include Eastern bloc

---

①　accountability [əˌkauntəˈbiliti] *n.*责任

新兴市场经济

1981 年，世界银行国际金融公司的安东尼·W·阿格塔米尔创造了一个新的术语：新兴市场经济（EME），或发展中的市场经济。根据定义，新兴市场经济是指人均收入处于中、低等水平的经济。这些国家约占全球人口的 80%，世界经济的 20%。虽然这是一个宽松的定义，属于这个经济类别的国家无论是很大还是很小，由于他们的发展和改革，通常都被定义为新兴经济国家。因此，尽管中国被视为世界经济强国之一，还是被划归到资源少得可怜的突尼斯这类较小的经济体之列。之所以把中国和突尼斯归为一类，是因为它们都在进行经济发展与改革项目，并且已经开始开放它们的市场，"出现"在全球舞台上。新兴市场经济被认为是快速发展的经济。

新兴市场经济的特征是过渡，意思是他们在塑造责任感的同时，正处于从封闭市场转向开放市场的过程中。东方集团国家就是这样的例子。一旦作为新兴市场的国家着手经济改革项目，就必将具备更加强大和更负责任的经济表现水平，以及在资本市场的透明度和有效率。新兴市场经济的国家也会对其汇率体制进行改革，因为稳定的本国货币可以为一种经济建立信心，尤其是当外国人打算

countries. As an emerging market, a country is embarking on an economic reform program that will lead it to stronger and more responsible economic performance levels, as well as transparency and efficiency in the capital market. An EME will also reform its exchange rate system because a stable local currency builds confidence in an economy, especially when foreigners are considering investing. Exchange rate reforms also reduce the desire for local investors to send their capital abroad (capital flight). Besides implementing reforms, an EME is also most likely receiving aid and guidance from large donor countries and/or world organizations such as the World Bank and International Monetary Fund.

One key characteristic of the EME is an increase in both local and foreign investment (portfolio and direct). A growth in investment in a country often indicates that the country has been able to build confidence in the local economy. Moreover, foreign investment is a signal that the world has begun to take notice of the emerging market, and when international capital flows are directed toward an EME, the injection of foreign currency into the local economy adds volume to the country's stock market and long-term investment to the infrastructure. For foreign investors or developed-economy businesses, an EME provides an outlet for expansion by serving, for example, as a new place for a new factory or for new sources of revenue. For the recipient country, employment levels rise, labor and managerial skills become more refined, and a sharing and transfer of technology occurs. In the long-run, the EME's overall production levels should rise, increasing its gross domestic product and eventually lessening the gap between the emerged and emerging worlds.

Because their markets are in transition and hence not stable, emerging markets offer an opportunity to investors who are looking to add

投资的时候。 汇率改革还可以降低本国投资者将资本转移海外（资本外逃）的欲望。 除了推行改革，新兴市场经济也最容易接收主要援助国和/或世界组织的帮助和指导，如世界银行和国际货币基金组织。

新兴市场经济的一个关键特征就是本国和外国投资（投资组合和直接投资）两者都在增加。 一个国家投资的增长往往说明，该国具备了建立本国经济的信心。 此外，外国投资是一个信号，它说明世界已经开始关注新兴市场，当国际资本直接流入新兴市场经济时，外国资本的注入增加了本国市场的资本存量和基础建设的长期投资。 对外国投资者或发达经济的企业来说，新兴市场经济为它们的扩张提供了一个渠道，比如，为一家新工厂提供服务或者为财政收入开辟新资源。 对受援国来说，本国国内的就业水平上升，劳动和管理技术更加优化，科技分享和转让也在发生。 从长期来看，新兴市场经济总体生产力水平应该会提高，从而使国内生产总值增加，最终缩小新兴国家和发达国家之间的差距。

因为市场转型而存在的不稳定性，新兴市场给那些敢于增加投资组合风险的投资者提供了机会。 有些经济体可能倒退回一场没有完全解决的内斗，或者政府的改变引爆的一场革命，这些都有可能导致国有化的回归、财产征用以及资本市场的瘫痪。 微妙的汇率波动可能转变为全面贬值，致使投资者要么在可能的政治混乱中投机取巧，要么对银行系统失去信心。 因为在新兴市场投资的风险比在发达市场投资的风险要高，恐慌、投机和下意识的反应也会更普遍，如在 1997 年的亚洲金融危机中，当时流入这些国家的国际投资组合实际上已经开始回流，这就是一个很好的例子，说明了新兴市

some risk to their portfolios. The possibility for some economies to fall back into a not-completely-resolved civil war or a revolution sparking a change in government could result in a return to nationalization, expropriation①, and the collapse of the capital market. Delicate exchange rate fluctuations could transform into an all-out devaluation resulting merely from investors speculating in the possibility of political disorder or losing faith in the banking system. Because the risk of an EME investment is higher than one of a developed market, panic, speculation and knee-jerk reactions are also more common — the 1997 Asian crisis, during which international portfolio flows into these countries actually began to reverse themselves, is a good example of how EMEs can be high-risk investment opportunities. However, the bigger the risk, the bigger the reward, so emerging market investments have become a standard practice among investors aiming to diversify while adding risk.

An emerging market economy must have to weigh local political and social factors as it attempts to open up its economy to the world. The people of an emerging market, who before were protected from the outside world, can often be distrustful of foreign investment. Emerging economies may also often have to deal with issues of national pride because citizens may be opposed to having foreigners owning parts of the local economy. Moreover, opening up an emerging economy means that it will also be exposed to not only new work ethics and standards but also cultures as well: indeed the introduction and impact of, say, fast food and music videos to some local markets has been a by-product of foreign investment. Over the generations, this can change the very fabric of a

---

① expropriation [ˌekspɹəupriˈeiʃən] n.没收

场经济在如何创造高风险的投资机会。然而，风险越大，收益也高，所以新兴市场投资已经成为投资者的一种标准实践，尽管追求多样化增加了风险。

当一个新兴市场经济体试图向世界开放它的经济时，必须先权衡一下本国的政治和社会因素。由于处于新兴市场经济体的民众以前都处于被保护状态，不受外部世界的影响，因此常常对外国投资持怀疑的态度。此外，新兴市场经济往往还需要处理好民族自尊心的问题，因为民众可能会反对外国人占有本国的部分经济市场。而且，开放新兴的市场经济意味着它不仅要面临新的职业道德和标准，还要面临多元的文化：例如，快餐和音乐电视的引进和影响，对一些本国市场来说，就是外国投资的副产品。经过几代人，就可以改变这个社会的结构，而人们如果不完全信任这种变化的话，就可以绝地反击，阻止它的发展。

虽然新兴市场国家可以期待更好的机会，并给外国和发达经济体提供新的投资区域，但是，新兴市场国家的政府当局也需要考虑开放市场对本国人民的影响。此外，当投资者考虑对新兴市场经济体进行投资的时候，需要判断其中的风险。新兴市场经济体兴起的过程可能有困难、缓慢，有时常常停滞不前。即使新兴市场经济过去在全球和本国的竞争中生存了下来，但是它们还要越过一些巨大的障碍才能达到目标。

知识链接

International Finance Corporation　国际金融公司(IFC)。国际金融公司

society and if a population is not fully trusting of change, it may fight back hard to stop it.

Although emerging economies may be able to look forward to brighter opportunities and offer new areas of investment for foreign and developed economies, local officials of EMEs need to consider the effects of an open economy on its citizens. Furthermore, investors need to determine the risks when considering investing into an EME. The process of emergence may be difficult, slow and often stagnant at times. And even though emerging markets have survived global and local challenges in the past, they had to overcome some large obstacles to do so.

(867 words)

是世界银行下属机构之一。1956 年 7 月正式成立，总部设于华盛顿。它虽是世界银行的附属机构，但它本身具有独立的法人地位。国际金融公司的宗旨主要是：配合世界银行的业务活动，向成员国特别是其中的发展中国家的重点私人企业提供无须政府担保的贷款或投资，鼓励国际私人资本流向发展中国家，以推动这些国家的私人企业的成长，促进其经济发展。

题　记

　　爱琴海文明造就了西方近代的战略文化，它以"生存竞争"、"弱肉强食"作为人之本性和认知世界的基本范式，把社会达尔文主义演绎的竞争和冲突作为生存的基本法则。而当今新一轮爱琴海金融风暴中的"狼群行为"又将爱琴海文明中的战争、侵略、扩张和掠夺的合法性淋漓尽致地呈现给世界。葡萄牙（Portugal）、爱尔兰（Ireland）、希腊（Greece）和西班牙（Spain）这四个首字母合起来，恰好是英文"PIGS"的"欧猪五国"（当然还包括意大利），过度举债，入不敷出。他们一方面为刺激经济而不惜血本，另一方面又由于经济下滑而税收骤降，似乎要活活把自己"绞死"在债务的十字架上。病急乱投医。人们把肆虐的财政紊乱归咎为债券的投机者、愚蠢的评级机构、不负责任的债务人和不讲道理的债权人的"狼群行为"，但到目前为止，还没有得出诊断结果。欧盟的问题不仅仅是抗议这种病入膏肓的财政危机。

Wolf-pack Behavior

Europe is trying to fix its own raging fiscal disorder. So far it hasn't even nailed the diagnosis.

European leaders still don't understand what caused the Aegean Contagion that swept through the eurozone. Swedish Finance Minister Anders Borg blamed "wolf-pack behavior" by speculators. Others have railed against clueless rating agencies, feckless debtors, and unreasonable creditors. Then there are those who ask if there's an inherent flaw in the bond markets that made them cascade, turning vague worries into scary, self-fulfilling prophecies.

You can't defeat an enemy you don't understand, and unless Europe gets a better grasp on what went wrong, it will be vulnerable to more turmoil, even with the nearly $ 1 trillion backstop lending authority that calmed markets. "I still think it's a very fragile situation, " says Gary Gorton, a Yale University economist.

The reality isn't all that complicated. Europe was vulnerable to contagion, and remains so, because its governance and its financial system are weak. It was lax① fiscal oversight that allowed nations such as Greece to violate European Union rules on the size of their budget deficits

---

① lax [læks] *adj.*疏忽的

狼群行为

欧洲正在试图解决自己肆虐的财政紊乱。到目前为止，还没有得出诊断结果。

欧洲的领导人还没有明白，是什么席卷了欧元区、引起了这场爱琴海的风波。瑞典财政大臣安德斯·伯格指责投机者是"狼群行为"。其他人则严词谴责愚蠢的评级机构、不负责任的债务人和不讲道理的债权人。那么，还有些人在质疑，债券市场是否存在固有的缺陷，垃圾债券泛滥成灾，从而使含糊其辞的焦虑转变为提心吊胆、自我应验的预言。

你不可能打败任何一个你不理解的敌人，除非欧洲能够更好地理解到底什么出错了，它还会很容易陷入更多的动荡，即使有近1万亿美元的贷款担保权来稳定市场。耶鲁大学的经济学家加里·戈顿说："我仍然认为，脆弱的经济可能会无可挽救地被摧垮。"

现实并不都是那样复杂。欧洲易受伤害，歪风蔓延，当前依然如此，因为它的治理和财政系统弱不禁风。这是宽松的财政监督的过失，它允许希腊这样一些国家违反欧盟的规则，首次超出了其预算赤字的规模。过度杠杆化的投资者使事情变得更糟糕：当他们的希腊债务价值下降时，他们被迫卖掉其他资产，以减少投资组合的

in the first place. Overleveraged investors made matters worse: When the value of their Greek debt fell, they were forced to reduce the size and risk of their portfolio by selling other assets — the debt of Portugal and Spain, for example.

In retrospect, Europe's crisis was a done deal last year, when a new Greek government announced that its deficit-to-gross domestic product ratio would be 12. 7 percent, more than double what the previous government had projected and four times what the European Union allows. Interest rates on Greek debt, which had been nearly as low as rates on German bonds, inched upward. In a vicious circle, the higher rates themselves increased Greece's debt burden. That made default more likely and pushed rates even higher. Standard & Poor's lowered Greece's credit rating to junk. The yield on two-year Greek government bonds hit 18 percent. Yields on Portuguese bonds reached 6 percent that day, double their level of three weeks earlier. Spanish and Italian credit was beginning to be affected as well.

Eventually the Europeans had no choice but to agree to a backstop lending arrangement for seriously threatened governments. That brought two-year Greek bond yields back down to a bit below 7 percent — about what an American might pay for a car loan but far higher than any other eurozone nation pays to service its debt.

Now that it has some breathing room, Europe needs to think hard about what just happened. The best place to start is with another contagion, the 2007-09 financial crisis that began with shoddy① subprime mortgage lending in the U.S. In his new book, Slapped by the Invisible Hand, Yale's Gorton describes the dangerous tipping point that

---

① shoddy [ˈʃɑdi] *adj.* 劣质的

规模和风险——例如，葡萄牙和西班牙的债务。

回首往事，欧洲危机在去年已成定局，当时新一届希腊政府宣称，赤字对国内生产总值比例已达 12.7%，是前任政府计划的两倍多，并且是欧盟可接受数值的四倍。希腊债务的利率与德国的债券收益一样低，在缓慢上升。这是一个恶性循环，它们本身的较高利率增加了希腊的债务负担。这就更有可能不履行法律义务，甚至推高利率。标准普尔下调了希腊的信用评级，将其降至垃圾级。两年期的希腊政府债券收益下降 18%。葡萄牙的债券收益在同一天达到 6%，是他们前三个星期水平的三倍。西班牙和意大利的信用度也开始受到影响。

欧洲人终于别无选择，不得不与受到严重威胁的政府保持一致，支持担保贷款安排。这使两年期的希腊债券收益再次跌落，略低于 7%——大约相当于美国人所要支付的汽车贷款，但远远高出其他欧元区国家支付的债务费用。

既然欧洲还有些喘息的空间，就需要深入思考究竟发生了什么事。最好的方式是从另一场恶劣影响开始，即 2007—2009 年始于美国的劣质次级抵押贷款金融危机。耶鲁大学的戈顿在其新作《被无形的手掴耳光》中描述了危险的临界点，当投资者对他们看来理所当然的复杂的金融工具失去信念的时候，这个转折点就会来临。

按揭证券与国债一样受到威胁，投资者考虑的是收益和信誉评级，不会质疑它的内涵究竟是什么。当次级抵押贷款开始拖欠的时候，投资者突然想知道，他们投资组合中的有价证券是否包含一些这种坏账，同时又发现他们无法抽出这些资产。他们产生了恐惧感，期待获得帮助，以摆脱困境。根据戈顿定义的术语，有价证券

comes when investors lose faith in complicated financial instruments they once took for granted.

Mortgage-backed securities had been treated like Treasuries — investors looked at the yield and the credit rating and didn't bother asking what was inside. When subprime mortgages started going into default, investors suddenly wanted to know if the securities in their portfolio contained any of those bad loans — and discovered they couldn't disentangle the assets. They got scared and bailed out. In Gorton's terminology, the securities went from being "information-insensitive" (a good thing for market liquidity) to "information-sensitive" (bad). Gorton says the same fate befell Greek bonds when players in the credit default swap market began digging up information pointing to a risk of default that bond investors hadn't bothered to ferret out in advance.

As with a physical disease, financial contagion spreads faster in a weakened population. Europe's problem is that many of Greece's creditors are themselves debtors on a massive scale. If the value of their assets declines, the only way they can stay solvent is by reducing their debt, and the only way they can pay down the debt is by selling assets, which pushes their price down even further, exacerbating[1] the problem and spreading it to other securities.

It's revealing that the ultimate beneficiaries of Europe's rescue are the big banks, not the Greeks, who will barely touch any rescue money before it goes out the window to their lenders.

To prevent a spreading financial contagion, then, it's not just the debtors that need to develop a stronger immune system. It's the creditors, too. As Princeton University economist Markus Brunnermeier pointed

---

① exacerbate [igˈzæsəbeit] vt.使加剧,使恶化

从"信息非敏感"（这对市场流动性是好事）转向"信息敏感"（这对市场流动性是不祥的征兆）。戈顿认为，当信贷违约掉期市场上的投资者开始挖掘事先没有费力搜寻的违约风险之时，同样的厄运就会降临希腊债券。

正如身体上的疾病一样，金融危机传染在弱势群体中传播更快。欧洲的问题是，希腊的许多债权人本身也是大规模的债务人。假如他们的资产价值下降，他们具备偿付能力的唯一方式是减少债务，而他们可以偿还债务的唯一方式是卖掉财产，这样做会使其价格进一步大幅度下降，从而加剧问题的恶化，并使它蔓延到其他的债券。

不言而喻，欧洲获救后的最终受益人是大银行，而不是希腊人。债权人从银行的窗口猎获救援资金之后，希腊人才有可能得到一丁点的施舍。

那么，为了阻止金融危机的蔓延，债权人需要建立更强大的免疫系统。不仅仅只是债权人的责任，债务人也需要如此。普林斯顿大学的经济学家马库斯·布鲁那米尔在"解读流动性和信贷紧缩"中指出，大型跨国投资银行在2007—2008年度严重依赖所谓的回购资金。他们使用债券、资产担保证券以及抵押物之类的方式借钱。回购贷款人提供了最好的隔夜贷款条款，因为抵押物失去的价值风险不大。但是，假如债务人不能偿还债务，他们必须减价出售资产，继而停止给他们的客户发放贷款。

人们可以想象，这些大型投资银行在这场危机中吸取了教训，自己放弃了隔夜回购贷款，毕竟，这迫使他们每天都在骗取新的贷款，否则就会破产。事情并不完全如此。《彭博商业周刊》运用美

out, "Deciphering the Liquidity and Credit Crunch," the big global investment banks became heavily dependent in 2007-08 on so-called repo financing. They borrowed money using bonds, asset-backed securities, and the like for collateral. Repo lenders give the best terms on overnight loans because there's less risk the collateral will lose value. But if borrowers can't roll over their debt, they must sell assets at fire-sale prices — and, in turn, stop extending loans to their clients.

One might suppose that these large investment banks learned their lesson in the crisis and weaned themselves off overnight repo loans — which, after all, force them to scrounge① up fresh loans every single day or go bust. Not quite. Bloomberg Businessweek updated Brunnermeier's calculation using publicly available data from the Federal Reserve Board and the Federal Reserve Bank of New York. As of the end of 2009, overnight and continuing repo loans were down more than 40 percent from their peak, but still funded 15 percent of the big banks' assets. Even after the pullback, overnight repo grew 155 percent. Bottom line: A big chunk of their financing remains precarious.

Many Europeans would prefer to blame the crisis on outsiders, the favorite scapegoats being speculators and ratings agencies. German Foreign Minister Guido Westerwelle called for the creation of a European credit rating agency. Complaining about the U. S. rating agencies, Pierre Lellouche, the French minister for European affairs, told The New York Times: "I'd be interested to know what these 30-year-old boys know about the disaster they are causing to people in Spain or Portugal or anywhere else." In reality, the rating agencies were no more than the bearers of bad tidings. Greeks are tired of having ancient ancestors quoted

---

① scrounge [skraʊndʒ] *vi.* 骗取

国联邦储备委员会和纽约联邦储备银行公开的数据，更新了布鲁那米尔的计算。 2009 年年底，隔夜和持续回购贷款从峰顶回落了40%，但仍然给大银行提供了 15% 的资产资助。 即使是在回落之后，隔夜回购仍然增长了 155%。 盈亏底线显示，大笔的融资仍然岌岌可危。

许多欧洲人更喜欢将他们的危机归结于局外人，他们最喜欢的替罪羊是投机商和评级机构。 德国外长圭多·韦俗斯勒呼吁创建欧洲信用评级机构。 法国驻欧洲事务部长在《纽约时报》上抱怨美国的评级机构说："我有兴趣了解 30 岁的男人对西班牙、葡萄牙以及其他任何对人们造成灾难的地方的看法。"事实上，评级机构不再是乱摊子的忍受者。 希腊人厌倦了他们对其祖先的引证，但他们却将古希腊悲剧诗人索福克勒斯的话视若珍宝："没有人喜欢带来坏消息的信使。"

对于最高赤字的国家，现在的挑战是切断政府的开支，并且在缓慢增长或完全衰退时增加税收。 尤其是希腊，尚不清楚它是否需要凝聚社会的力量来这样做。 同样难以预测的是，如果德国不能兑现它的承诺，它如何继续推进给希腊的担保贷款。 墨西哥自治技术学院研究新兴市场债务危机的经济学家桑德拉·瓦伦蒂娜说："这个交易是必要的。 我不知道这是否充足。"

欧盟的问题与 1781—1788 年年轻而脆弱的美国面临的问题类似，当时美国的宪法尚未获得通过。 根据"十三州邦联宪法"，联邦政府无权征税，资金依赖于各州的出资。 后来成为美国第一任财政部部长的亚历山大·密尔顿在 1780 年警告说："没有税收，一个政府就没有权力。 必须要制定这种绝对财政拥有权的规则。"所

at them, but it's hard to resist citing Sophocles: "No one loves the messenger who brings bad news."

For countries with the highest deficits, the challenge now is to cut government spending and increase revenue in a time of slow growth or outright recession. It's not clear whether Greece in particular will be able to muster the social solidarity necessary to do so. It's equally difficult to see how Germany will go ahead with backstop loans to Greece if the country doesn't meet its commitments. "This deal is necessary. I don't know if it's sufficient, " says Sandra Valentina Lizarazo, an economist at the Mexico Autonomous Institute of Technology who has studied emerging-market debt crises.

The EU's problems resemble those of the young and weak United States of America from 1781 until 1788, before the Constitution was ratified. Under the Articles of Confederation, the federal government had no power to tax. It relied on contributions from the states. Alexander Hamilton, who later became the nation's first Treasury secretary, warned in 1780 that "without revenues, a government can have no power. That power which holds the purse-strings absolutely, must rule." So Europe is discovering nearly 230 years later. For Europe, the strongest defense against another bout of Aegean Contagion would be a unified Continental government with authority over taxation and spending — a United States of Europe. A unified Europe would have the power to prohibit, not just remonstrate① against, the fiscal frivolity② that brought on this virus.

(1,264 words)

---

① remonstrate [ri'mɒnstret] vi.抗议
② frivolity [fri'vɒliti] n.轻浮

以，欧洲在将近 230 年后发现了这些规则。 对欧洲来说，抵御新一轮爱琴海金融风暴蔓延最强大的方式就是建立欧洲大陆联合政府，启用权力手段控制税收和开支，形成欧洲联合国。 一个统一的欧洲有权禁止、而不仅仅是抗议这种病入膏肓的财政危机。

知识链接 🔍

Sophocles 索福克勒斯。索福克勒斯是古希腊悲剧诗人（约公元前 496—406 年），他既相信神和命运的无上威力，又要求人们具有独立自主的精神，并对自己的行为负责，这是雅典民主政治繁荣时期思想意识的特征。他根据他的理想来塑造人物形象，即使处在命运的掌握之中，也不丧失其独立自主的坚强性格。他认为命运不再是具体的神，而是一种抽象的概念。

题 记

    在股市下挫的行情中作为中小投资者的我们，面对充满着很多不确定因素的情况，应该怎样作出自己的投资决定，是频繁地换手，减仓持有现金；还是重视中长期的收益，长期持有？让我们来看看被非理性繁荣俘虏了的恐慌先生的"智慧投资"。上周，他开车在华尔街到处乱逛，诚惶诚恐地担心自己的投资组合一蹶不起。周一，恐慌先生兴高采烈地投资 10 万美元，购买了先锋 500 指数基金；周二，先锋 500 基金适度复苏，恐慌先生对于他的销售决策感觉良好；周三，市场再次暴跌的迹象表明信贷市场正在紧缩，恐慌先生觉得他的投资具有敏锐的眼光；周四，尽管人们对货币市场基金的安全性忧心忡忡，但股市却开始一路走高；周五，股市继续反弹，但恐慌先生却错失当天以及星期四的收益。恐慌先生被牢牢套住，损失了 4 700 美元，错过了 300 美元的收益。

Mr. Panicked's "Smart Investing"

引 题

Allow me to introduce you to Mr. Panicked.

He went on a wild Wall Street ride last week, worrying himself sick over his portfolio. He heard those smarty pants financial advisers on television and radio urge small investors to avoid rash investment decisions. They talked about the dangers of selling low and buying high and locking in losses. But what did they know? If they're so smart, they'd have jumped out of the market last year, never mind last week. They all said the same thing.

And Mr. Panicked was right about that last statement. Last week, I sounded like everyone else. I joined the chorus of financial writers and advisers warning small investors to resist panic and the urge to liquidate① their portfolios in favor of all cash. Unoriginal as my advice was, I stand by it. I stood by it when the Dow Jones industrial average dropped 504 points last Monday and then rose 141 on Tuesday, fell 449 on Wednesday and regained 778 on Thursday and Friday.

---

① liquidate ['likwideit] *vt.*清算

恐慌先生的"智慧投资"

请允许我向您介绍恐慌先生。

他上周开车在华尔街到处乱逛，担心自己的投资组合一蹶不起。 他收听了那些自作聪明的金融投资顾问在电视和电台的演讲，他们呼吁小型投资者应该避免作出草率的投资决策。 他们谈论了抛低买高以及投资被套牢而带来损失的危险性。 但是他们怎么知道这些呢？ 如果他们真的这样聪明的话，他们去年就应该逃离市场，根本不用待到上周再做决定了。 他们都在唠叨着同样的事情。

投资顾问最后的陈述还是征服了恐慌先生。 上周，我像其他人一样陈述了自己的观点。 我加入了财经作家、投资顾问者的大合唱，警告小型投资者抵制恐慌，并敦促他们不要将自己的证券投资组合全部清算成现金。 尽管我的建议缺乏独创性，但我却赞成这种建议。 上周一，道琼斯工业平均指数下跌504点，然后在周二上升141点，周三下跌449点，星期四和星期五又上升778点。 这就是我赞成这种观点的原因。

下次股市出现自由下滑时，我将提出相同的、非独创性的建议。 这并不是说，你从不需要改变你的投资组合，而是最好在平心静气的反思下作出投资决定。 我认为像我一样的财经类作家和投资

And I will offer the same, unoriginal advice the next time the stock market appears to be in a free fall. That's not to say you should never makes changes to your portfolio, but rather that investment decisions are best made amid calm reflection. Where I think financial writers and advisers like me fall short is explaining why it's unwise to panic when your portfolio has fallen tens of thousands of dollars in a short spell and appears almost certain to fall even more.

I'll use my friend Mr. Panicked and last week's events as an example of what might happen when you panic during market turmoil. I'll assume my imaginary investor, Mr. Panicked, started last week with an even $ 100,000 in the Vanguard 500 Index fund, the widely held, low-cost fund that tracks the performance of the Standard & Poor's 500 Index. He awoke that Monday morning to the news Lehman Brothers had collapsed and Bank of America had taken over the iconic bull of Wall Street, Merrill Lynch.

Mr. Panicked decided to avoid panic in the stock market crisis. Certain his entire life savings was at risk, Mr. Panicked logged on to his online account at midday and placed an order to sell his entire stake in the Vanguard 500. On the previous, the fund's closing share price was $ 115. 79. At the time of Mr. Panicked's sell order, the Standard & Poor's Index was down less than 2 percent. But because mutual funds can be bought and sold only at the closing price for a day, Mr. Panicked had to withstand further declines in the S&P 500 Index as the market went into a late-day tailspin. His sale went through at the 4 p.m. price of $ 110. 36 a

顾问的不足之处在于：只有当你的投资组合已经在很短的时间内下跌了数以万计的美元，并且看来几乎肯定还要下降更多的时候，你才能解释恐慌为什么是不明智的。

我将用我的朋友恐慌先生和上周发生的事件作为例子，来说明市场动荡时期你的恐慌会导致什么事情发生。 我将假设，我想象的投资者恐慌先生，上周开始投资 10 万美元，购买了先锋 500 指数基金，这是一种追随标准普尔 500 指数绩效、广泛持有的、低成本的基金。 他周一早上醒来时听到了雷曼兄弟破产以及美国银行收购华尔街金牛的形象——美林的新闻。

恐慌先生决定在股市危机中避免恐慌。 毫无疑问，恐慌先生毕生的储蓄处于风险之中，他在中午时分登录自己的网上账户，敲入指令出售其全部的先锋 500 股份。 在这之前，该基金的收盘价是115. 79 美元。 就在恐慌先生敲入出售指令时，标准普尔指数骤然下跌，还不到先前的百分之二。 但是，由于共同基金一天内只能以收盘价进行买卖，恐慌先生不得不承受市场进入第二天混乱时标准普尔 500 指数的进一步下跌。 他在下午 4 时以每股 110. 36 美元的价格卖出，他获得95 300美元，损失了4 700美元，或 4.7% 。

周二，市场稍有回暖，先锋 500 基金适度复苏，增长了 1.7% 。当整个市场关注的焦点集中在保险业巨头美国国际集团是否是下一个破产的公司时，恐慌先生对于他的销售决策感觉依然良好。

到了周三，市场再次暴跌的迹象表明信贷市场正在紧缩，恐慌先生更觉得他的某些投资具有敏锐的眼光。 先锋 500 基金的跌幅当天超过百分之四，基金的份额价格现在是 106.98 美元，一周内跌了近百分之八。

share and he garnered $ 95,300 from the sale, down $ 4,700, or 4. 7 percent.

On Tuesday, the market recovered slightly and the Vanguard 500 fund made a modest recovery, rising 1. 7 percent. But Mr. Panicked still felt good about his sell decision as all the market talk centered on whether the insurance giant AIG would fall next.

By Wednesday, Mr. Panicked felt even more certain about his investing acumen① as the market took another nose dive amid signs the credit market was tightening. The Vanguard 500 fund fell more than 4 percent that day with the fund's share price now at $ 106.98, nearly 8 percent less than where it started the week.

Starting Thursday, funny things began to happen in the stock market. It began to rise even as worries arose about the safety of money market funds and talk surfaced about a government agency to take over bad assets from banks. On Thursday, the Vanguard 500 share price climbed 4. 4 percent. Then on Friday, the stock market rally continued as big investors welcomed Treasury Secretary Henry Paulson's proposed bailout for banks.

By midday Friday, Mr. Panicked was overtaken by irrational exuberance②. He decided it was time to jump back in the market by plowing his $ 95,300 in cash from his sale earlier in the week back into

---

① acumen [əˈkjuːmen] n.敏锐
② exuberance [igˈzjuːbərəns] n.繁茂

恐慌先生的"智慧投资"

从周四开始，股票市场开始发生令人啼笑皆非的事情。 尽管人们对货币市场基金的安全性忧心忡忡，表面上对政府机构接管银行不良资产闲言碎语，但股市却开始一路走高。 周四，先锋 500 股票价格上涨 4.4%。 紧接着，财政部长亨利·保尔森提出的救助银行的建议受到了大投资者们的欢迎，股市在周五继续反弹。

周五中午，非理性繁荣俘虏了恐慌先生。 他决定，是时候重回股票市场了，他用本周早些时候出售先锋 500 基金得到的 95 300 美元重新买入先锋 500 基金。 但是，他又不得不购买当天的收盘价 116.14 美元，较之前一天上涨了百分之四。 他不能购买他最初想买的那么多股票，他遗憾地错失当天以及星期四的收益。

这对投资者来说，无非是老调重弹。 本周，恐慌先生开始时有 10 万美元，结束时只有 95 300 美元。 如果他正襟危坐，并听取了相同的、乏味的建议，他本周结束时就会有 100 300 美元，因为先锋 500 指数基金在这一周有 0.3% 的收益。 相反，恐慌先生被套住了，损失了 4 700 美元，错过了 300 美元的收益。

下一次你听厌了重弹的老调时请牢记在心：停下来，深呼吸，学习怎样保存你的现金。

知识链接 🔍

Dow Jones Industrial Average 道琼斯工业平均指数。它由 30 种有代表性的大工商业公司的股票组成，且随经济发展而变大，大致可以反映美国整个工商业股票的价格水平。

Standard & Poor's 500 Index 标准普尔 500 指数（S&P 500 Index）。这个

the Vanguard 500 fund. But again, he had to buy at the day's closing price of $ 116.14, up 4 percent from the previous day. He could not buy as many fund shares as he first thought and he missed out on that day's gains as well as Thursdays.

This is the same old advice for investors. For the week, Mr. Panicked started with $ 100,000 and ended with $ 95,300. Had he sat tight and listened to the same, boring advice he would have ended the week with $ 100,300 as the Vanguard 500 Index fund posted a.3 percent gain for the week. Instead, Mr. Panicked locked in a $ 4,700 loss and missed out on a $ 300 gain.

Keep that in mind the next time you get tired of hearing the same old advice: Stop, Breathe in and Learn What to Do to Keep Your Cash

(821 words)

股票指数由标准普尔公司创建并维护，它是记录美国 500 家上市公司的一个股票指数，因此风险更为分散，能够反映更广泛的市场变化。标准普尔 500 指数覆盖的所有公司，都是在美国主要交易所，如纽约证券交易所、Nasdaq 交易的上市公司等。

题 记

人们普遍认为，信用证是 19 世纪发生的一次国际贸易支付方式上的革命，这种支付方式首次使不在交货现场的买卖双方在履行合同时处于同等地位，在一定程度上使他们重新找回了"一手交钱，一手交货"的现场交易所具有的安全感。实际上，信用证的起源可以追溯到公元前 3000 年的古埃及和巴比伦通行的黏土本票；12 世纪和 13 世纪意大利的热那亚、威尼斯、佛罗伦萨和其他欧洲城市使用的汇票和信用证；马可·波罗 13 世纪发现的中国货币的使用手段和其他的可流通单据；17 世纪信用证在欧洲大陆和英国已经成为了普通的金融工具；19 世纪的跟单信用证就是现代信用证的雏形；20 世纪 50 年代，信用证在美国的国内商业中已赢得了主导地位；在当今的世界贸易中，信用证的使用呈稳定的趋势。信用证上雕刻的是永恒的历史神韵，世界文明的遗产。

The Heritage of Civilization: Letter of Credit

Understanding the nature of letters of credit as an international financial device and the reason why they have become widely used by merchants all over the world requires us to find out its historical origins. Some scholars believe that the origins of letters of credit go back to ancient Egypt and Babylon, which had an adequate system of banking. Rufus Trimble mentions a clay promissory note of Babylon dating from 3000 B. C., exhibited in the University Museum of Philadelphia, USA, which provided for repayment of an amount and the interest on a specific date. Wigmore refers to an evidence of an obligation made in 248 B.C. in Egypt "for the repayment, in wheat, or upon default double its value, of a loan of money from one Zenon, which ends with: and the right of execution shall rest with Zenon and the person bearing the note on behalf of Zenon". It is also verified① that banks of ancient Greece prepared letters of credit "on correspondents with the view to obviating② the actual transport of specie in payment of accounts".

---

① verify ['verifai] *vt.*已证实的
② obviate ['ɔbvieit] *vt.*消除

文明的遗产:信用证

　　理解信用证作为国际金融工具的性质和世界各地的商人广泛使用信用证的原因需要我们找出它的历史起源。 一些学者认为,信用证的起源可以追溯到拥有完备的银行系统的古埃及和巴比伦。 鲁弗·特林布尔提到了美国费城大学博物馆展出的黏土本票,据此可以追溯到公元前 3000 年的巴比伦,这种本票规定了还款数额和具体日期的利息。 威格莫尔引用了埃及公元前 248 年制定的一项义务作为证据:"从泽农处贷款得到的钱用小麦偿还,否则,违约时支付两倍于它的价值。 最后指出,泽农拥有行刑的权利,计息票据人代表泽农。"这条义务还证实,古希腊的银行为来往客户准备了信用证,"意在用预付金的形式取消实际交易中的硬币"。

　　随着罗马帝国的崩溃,银行的作用以及贸易国之间的商业交易大大降低。 热那亚、威尼斯、佛罗伦萨和其他欧洲城市直到 12 世纪和 13 世纪早期才又重建银行。 此时,商家们不得不面临两个主要的问题:一是带着黄金旅行异常危险;二是商业产生的货币不足以满足贸易商的需求。 商人们试图解决这些问题,他们最早使用的工具是汇票和信用证。 在其早期的历史中,这些支付手段以一种非常相似的方式运作,信用证被用来补充汇票。

With the collapse of the Roman Empire the role of the banks as well as the great extent of commerce between trading nations diminished. It was not until the 12th and early 13th century that banks in Genoa, Venice, Florence and other European cities were re-established. At this time merchants had to face two major problems: (a) travelling with gold was very dangerous; and (b) commerce generated currency that was not sufficient to satisfy the needs of traders. The earliest devices with which merchants tried to solve these problems were with the bills of exchange and letters of credit. In their early history these payment instruments operated in a very similar way, and letters of credit were used to supplement the bills of exchange.

There are commentators who believe that their development in Europe was inspired by the discoveries made by Marco Polo in the 13th century who reported the use of currency and other negotiable documents in China, concluding that such a measure was one of the reasons for "the ways and means by which the Great Chan can have and indeed does have more treasures than all the kings in the world". In any case, it was impossible to conduct commerce via caravan without some sorts of documentary letters. To explain their early operation Professor Dolan gives the following example: "a Florentine merchant who bought wool from an Amsterdam merchant could issue a bill of exchange to the Dutch merchant's agent in Florence directing a third party (the drawee①) to pay the sum due for the wool. The agent, having taken the bill in payment for the wool, could travel across Europe or by sea to a commercial center, where he would meet the drawee and ask the drawee for payment.

---

① drawee [drɔːiː] *n.*受票人

　　有评论家认为，马可·波罗在 13 世纪的发现开启了信用证在欧洲的发展之路。 马可·波罗报告了中国的货币使用和其他的可流通单据，由此得出结论："伟大的中国通过这些方法和手段可以拥有、并确实拥有比世界上所有的国王多得多的财富"，这一流通手段就是原因之一。 在任何情况下，没有某种形式的跟单证书而仅凭大篷车来进行商业交易是不可能的。 为了解释信用证早期的交易程序，杜兰教授给出了下面的例子："一名佛罗伦萨商人从一名阿姆斯特丹商人那里购买了羊毛，佛罗伦萨商人可以向在佛罗伦萨代表第三方（受票人）的荷兰商家的代理人出具汇票，支付羊毛应得的金额。受理了羊毛支付款的代理人，可以穿越欧洲或乘船到达一个商业中心，他将在那里会见付款人，并要求付款人付款。"

　　他这么做是因为他充分地认识到，这种"货币"对商人是无价之宝，对拦路抢劫的土匪和横行海上的海盗来说并无价值可言。 对那些有胆量的商人来说，他们的单据很快就受到了怀疑，所以，商品的价格要么大打折扣，要么在交易时被断然拒绝。 为了证明票据的分量，他需要得到付款人的声明，表明付款人将支付或接受该票据。 这份声明就是信用证。 德·鲁弗还提到了 1385 年到 1401 年间在布鲁日和意大利的梅第奇银行使用的信用证。 当时信用证上的各项条款与现代信用证的规定惊人的相似。

　　17 世纪时，信用证在欧洲大陆和英国已经成为了普通的金融工具。 在这个时候，它们的功能更像一张旅行支票。 到 19 世纪，英国银行事实上已经垄断了信用证的签发业务。 之所以如此，是因为这样一个事实：即在世界贸易中，英镑是人们最认可的货币，而且伦敦的银行家在国际金融领域取得了卓越的立场。 在美国，信用证

He could do so armed with the knowledge that such "currency", while valuable to merchants, was of little value to the brigands who stalked the highways and the pirates who sailed the seas. It did not take long for some enterprising merchant, whose paper was suspect, and, therefore, subject to heavy discount or to outright rejection in the trade, to strengthen his bills by obtaining the drawee's announcement that he, the drawee, would pay or accept the bills. The announcement was a letter of credit. De Roover also refers to letters of credit used by the Medici Bank in Bruges and in Italy between 1385 and 1401. The various provisions of the letters are strikingly similar to those of the modern letters of credit.

By the 17th century letters of credits were common financial instruments both in the European continent and in England. At this time they functioned more like a traveller's cheque. By the 19th century British banks had a virtual monopoly on the issuance of letters of credits. This was due to the fact that in world trade the Pound Sterling was the most accepted currency and the bankers of London gained a pre-eminent position in the field of international finance. In the United States letters of credit emerged from the "competition of houses for business, which led to the issuance of promises to accept drafts against shipments". The growing number of manufacturers and their relationships with foreign traders, the specialization of banking activities and the technological development such as the more frequent use of telegraph for communicating the terms of the contracts facilitated the increasing use of letters of credit.

On the other hand, letters of credit were not used exclusively by merchants. Thomas Jefferson, third president of the US, wrote the following letter to Captain Meriwether Lewis in 1803 on the occasion of

从"商业住宅竞争"中脱颖而出，从而导致了承诺签发，以接受出货时的汇票。 越来越多的制造商与外国商人打交道，银行业务活动的专业化与技术的发展相互融合，如交流合同条款时电报的频繁使用，这些都促使人们越来越多地使用信用证。

另一方面，信用证并不仅限于商人使用。 美国第三任总统托马斯·杰斐逊，在 1803 年给即将率队远征、探索西部荒野地区的梅里韦瑟·刘易斯上尉写了下面的信："亲爱的先生，你即将踏上征程，探索密西西比河的流程和发源地，我们只能利用美国信贷给你财政支持，为此，我在此授权，你可以找美国国务卿、财政部长、战争与海军部长支取经费，为了获得资金以及你和你手下的必需品，你可能会发现，这些汇票会准时到期支付。"

第一次世界大战的爆发打破了已经确立并获得信任的贸易链，这种贸易链本来已经存在于世界各地的商人之间。 为了维持交易，商人们被迫与不知名的或不受信任的企业建立新的联系。 这些情况有利于信用证的广泛使用，它邀请了一位值得信赖的发薪人员、一家银行，参与到商家的活动之中。 到 20 世纪 50 年代，信用证在美国的国内商业中已赢得了主导地位，同时被广泛地应用到国际交易中。

自第二次世界大战以来，世界贸易中信用证的使用呈稳定的趋势。 虽然偶尔出现的贸易融资替代手段使信用证的使用黯然失色，但它已"被证明是一种灵活的工具，它可以轻而易举地适应国际贸易中不断变化的条件需求"。 正如科佐采科指出的，"在距离不断缩小、贸易不断增加的世界里，这样一个高度可靠、灵活的支付和融资手段将是持续的需求"。

leading an expedition to explore the wild western territory: "Dear Sir, In the journey which you are about to undertake for the discovery of the course and source of the Mississippi, your resource can only be in the credit of the US, for which purpose I hereby authorize you to draw on the Secretaries of State, of the Treasury, of War and of the Navy of the US, as you may find your drafts will be most negotiable for the purpose of obtaining money or necessaries for yourself and your men. I solemnly pledge the faith of the United States that these drafts shall be paid punctually at the date they are made payable."

The outbreak of World War I broke the well-established and trusted trading links that had existed between the merchants worldwide. In order to keep on trading merchants were forced to create new links with firms often unknown or not trusted. These circumstances were favorable for the extensive use of letters of credit which invited a trustworthy paymaster, a bank, into the merchant's relationship. By the 1950s letters of credit had earned a predominant position in domestic commerce of the United States and were also widely used in international transactions.

Since World War II the use of letters of credit in world trade remains steadfast. Although from time to time the emergence of alternative means of trade finance overshadows the use of the letter of credit, it has "proven to be a flexible instrument, which can be readily attempted to the needs of changing conditions in international trade". As Kozolchyk points out "in a world of shrinking distances and increasing trade there will be a continuing need for such a highly reliable, and flexible means of payment and financing".

(1,071 words)

文明的遗产:信用证

知识链接

Letter of Credit 信用证。是银行根据进口商的要求，向出口商所签发的在有效期限内，凭规定的货运单据，支付一定金额的、有条件的付款承诺书。

题　记

　　经济在衰退过后踏上崎岖坎坷的复苏之路，曾经在经济危机最严峻时刻形成的全球经济合作精神正在消逝。种种迹象表明，一场没有硝烟的货币战争正在悄悄上演：日元的单边降息刺激了其他的经济体；巴西打响了汇率阻击战；韩国升级了外汇管制；澳大利亚联储停止加息；人民币兑美元汇率中间价再创新高；一度挑战过美元霸主地位的欧元已经落入美国的圈套，伤痕累累。这场一触即发的货币战争令全球的老百姓谈虎色变，要保护自己免受货币贬值可能性的影响，很多人都不知道该做些什么。有人青睐最佳生活成本增加福利选择权，有人投资房地产，还有人投资公用事业和其他收益的股票。人们既不期待经济重蹈 20 世纪 30 年代大萧条的覆辙，也不愿意到最近的街角卖苹果谋生，更不愿意到装满纸币的手推车上买早上的咖啡。只要守住底线，"就可以把狼关在门外。"

The World on the Brink
of a Currency War

The latest hot topic among economic talking heads is the coming currency war. According to conventional wisdom, there's a risk that major countries will — simultaneously — try to revive their sluggish economies by pushing down the value of their currencies. That strategy could backfire, according to this line of thought, stifling international trade, tipping economies back into recession, and possibly causing Depression-style hyperinflation① to boot. Get ready to sell apples on the nearest street corner and buy your morning coffee with a wheelbarrow② full of paper money. It all sounds very unpleasant.

But the dogs of war are unlikely to slip their leash. In a classic currency war, a country prints money, holds interest rates down, or intervenes in foreign exchange markets in order to depress the value of its own currency. That makes the country's exports cheaper and more attractive for foreign buyers. In theory, this can enable an economy to

---

① hyperinflation [ˌhaipərinˈfleʃən] n.恶性通货膨胀
② wheelbarrow [ˈwilbærəʊ] n.独轮手推车

全球货币战争一触即发

经济名嘴们最近讨论的热门话题是即将到来的货币战争。 根据传统观点,一些经济大国同时通过货币贬值复苏低迷的经济是有风险的。 根据这个思路,这种策略也许事与愿违,它会抑制国际贸易,重新推动经济的倒退,除此之外,还有可能导致大萧条式的恶性通货膨胀。 做好准备,到最近的街角卖苹果、到装满纸币的手推车上买早上的咖啡吧。 这一切听起来让人很不舒服。

但是战争浩劫不太可能失控。 在一个经典的货币战中,国家大量印制纸币,保持低利率,或者干预外汇市场,以期达到抑制本国货币的价值。 这将使这个国家的出口更加便宜,并且对国外的消费者更有吸引力。 在理论上,与完全依赖拉动内需的可能性相比,这种举措会使经济增长得更快。 唯一的麻烦是,如果每一个国家都追求相似的策略,他们全都同时降低货币的价值,那么没有一个国家能获得比他们的贸易伙伴更多的好处。

这可能看起来仿佛就是现在发生的事,因为最大经济体中的许多大国都在采取这种抑制本国货币价值的政策。 但是它们这么做还有从根本上不同的理由:即为了处理国内的经济问题,而不是推动

grow faster than would be possible on the basis of domestic demand alone. Only trouble is, if every country pursues a similar strategy, they all devalue their currencies at the same time and no country gains an advantage over its trading partners.

It may look as though that's what's happening now, since many of the largest economies are following policies that could depress the value of their currencies. But they're doing so for fundamentally different reasons — to address domestic economic problems rather than to boost exports. And while this creates some real risks, they aren't the ones that the term "currency war" implies.

Currency wars — and trade wars generally — have their origins in a 17th and 18th century economic theory known as mercantilism①. The idea was that a country's wealth comes from selling more than it buys. A colonial empire could achieve this positive balance of trade by acquiring cheap raw materials from its colonies and then ensuring that it exported more finished goods than it imported. This was usually accomplished with tariffs that made imports very expensive.

Such an approach couldn't work in the modern world. Countries don't get cheap raw materials from colonies anymore. They have to buy them — especially oil — on the open market. So while currency devaluation makes exports cheaper for foreign buyers, it also makes essential imports more expensive. For Europe in particular, which imports so much of its energy, devaluation isn't necessarily a plus.

---

① mercantilism [məˈkæntilizəm] n.重商主义

出口的增长。 虽然这么做会产生一些实际的风险，它们也不是"货币战争"这一术语暗示的那些国家。

货币战（通常称之为贸易战）起源于 17 世纪和 18 世纪的经济理论，被称为重商主义。 这个理念是：销售额超过购买率是国家财富积累的一种方式。 殖民帝国利用殖民地获取廉价原料，然后确保销售的制成品多于进口，从而达到这种贸易正平衡。 使进口产品非常昂贵的关税通常是完成货币战争的手段。

这样一种方法在当今世界丝毫不起作用。 各国再也不能从殖民地获取廉价的原材料了。 它们不得不在开放的市场上买进原材料——特别是石油。 所以，对国外消费者来说，虽然货币贬值使出口产品更加便宜，但也使生活必需品的进口更加昂贵。 对欧洲来说更是如此，欧洲进口了这么多的能源，货币贬值不一定是好事。

为了促进出口，经济尚未全面发展的国家可能仍然会采取抑制货币价值的手段，因为它们缺乏足够的内需来维持经济的发展。 例如，拉丁美洲在某种程度上出现了这种情况。 但是在最大经济体中，只有中国还处于通过控股降低汇率而获得贸易优势的阶段，中国在这个阶段受益匪浅。

自从 9 月份以来，日本的货币贬值了 17%，逆转了日元在过去三年的升值。 就像许多欧洲国家一样，美国提倡的政策似乎也在针对他们的货币贬值，但它们没有率先动手，以免挑起一场贸易战。 美联储采取了购买债券扩充货币供应的量化宽松政策，主要目的是刺激内需。 同时，欧洲人呼吁实施比较便宜的欧元货币，它们希望

Countries with economies that are not fully developed may still depress their currencies to promote exports because they don't have sufficient domestic demand to sustain their growth. That occurs to some degree in Latin America, for instance. But among the largest economies, only China is still at a stage where it can benefit significantly by holding its currency down to gain a trade advantage.

Japan has pushed its currency down 17% since September, reversing the yen's appreciation over the previous three years. And the U.S., as well as many European countries, advocate policies that appear to be aimed at devaluing their currencies, but they're not doing it chiefly to foment a trade war. The Federal Reserve's quantitative easing — buying bonds to swell the money supply — is aimed principally at stimulating domestic demand. European advocates of a cheaper euro currency, meanwhile, are hoping to make national debt easier to finance, not trying to pump up exports. In fact, the continent's greatest exporter, Germany, is the country least amenable to currency devaluation.

The actual point of current policies is to lower the real cost of money — that is, the effective interest rate that borrowers pay after inflation is taken into account — in order to spur consumer spending and business investment. That reduction can be achieved by pushing down interest rates and by allowing inflation. So rather than seeing what's going on today as the beginning of a global trade war, we should think about it as a side effect of economic stimulus. And in theory, as economies recover, the policies could be reversed before chronic inflation becomes entrenched. But as I said, there are risks to all this — and in practice,

使国家债务融资更容易，而不是极力扩大出口。 事实上，欧洲最大的出口国——德国，是最少实行货币贬值政策的国家。

为了刺激消费性开支和商业投资，目前政策的现实之处在于降低实际的借款利息，也就是说，要考虑借款人在通货膨胀之后支付的有效利率。 通过下推投资利率和允许通货膨胀，可以达到这种下降。 所以，我们与其将目前正在发生的事看做是贸易战争的开始，倒不如将其视为经济刺激的副作用。 并且在理论上，随着经济的复苏，在慢性通胀根深蒂固之前，这种政策还有逆转的可能。 但正如我所说，这一切都充满了风险，实际上，通胀很容易失控。

要保护自己免受货币贬值可能性的影响，很多人都不知道该做些什么。 即将退休的人应该青睐最佳生活成本增加福利选择权。房地产可能是一个明智的投资，因为价格是如此的低廉，尤其是当买房的费用与租房的费用竞争力相当的时候。 在金融投资中，避免长期债券是很有道理的，因为它们的支出固定不变。 最好选择公用事业和其他收益的股票，因为它们的股息会随着时间的流逝提高。原材料生产企业是一个防守型的选择，特别是一些收益率超过 3% 或更多的国际石油股票。

所以，忘掉有关货币战争的所有讨论。 目前正在发生的事与贸易毫不相干，所有的一切与债务、增长和通货膨胀息息相关。 即使全球经济危险地复活过去，它也不会重蹈 20 世纪 30 年代大萧条的覆辙。 相反，它将回到 20 世纪 70 年代，当时美联储扩大了货币供应量，意在抵消因石油危机引起的经济衰退，但却以鼓励两位数的

inflation can easily get out of hand.

There isn't a lot individuals can do to protect themselves against such a possibility. People about to retire should favor benefit options with the best cost-of-living increases. Real estate can be a smart buy now that prices are down so much, especially buying a home if it's financially competitive with renting. Among financial investments, it makes sense to avoid long-term bonds because their payouts are fixed. Utilities and other high-yield stocks are preferable because they raise their dividends over time. And raw materials producers can be a defensive choice, especially some of the international oil stocks with yields of 3% or more.

So forget all the talk of a currency war. What's going on has nothing to do with trade and everything to do with debt and growth and inflation. If the global economy is in danger of reliving the past, it will not be a repeat of the 1930s. Rather, it will be a repeat of the 1970s, when the Federal Reserve expanded the money supply to offset the economic slowdown caused by the oil crisis — and ended up encouraging double-digit inflation.

Current easy money policies may well create some inflation, although perhaps not as much as 40 years ago. But in any event, revived growth with some inflation is preferable to stable prices accompanied by depression. The problems of the 1970s can all be overcome — except perhaps the hairstyles.

(909 words)

通货膨胀而告终。

知识链接 🔍

Quantitative Easing 量化宽松（QE）。主要是指中央银行在实行零利率或近似零利率政策后，通过购买国债等中长期债券，增加基础货币供给，向市场注入大量流动性资金的干预方式，以鼓励开支和借贷，也被简化地形容为间接增印钞票。